Praise for *The Buried Book*

"Damrosch creates vivid portraits of archaeologists, Assyriologists and ancient kings, lending his history an almost novelistic sense of character. . . . [He] has done a superb job of bringing what was buried to life."

—*The New York Times Book Review*

"Lively and accessible . . . In his telling, *The Epic of Gilgamesh* is nothing less than the drama of a newly urban and self-domesticated humankind coming to terms with its loss of wildness. The ancient epic comes to life in Damrosch's reading."

—*Boston Sunday Globe*

"In crisp, undusty prose, literature prof Damrosch excavates the entire adventure story."

—*Entertainment Weekly* (A-)

"Useful, entertaining and informative."

—*The Washington Post*

"Artful, engrossing . . . Damrosch has a good eye for the details."

—Salon.com

"In the tradition of Edmund Wilson, Columbia literature professor Damrosch unearths the first great masterpiece of world literature. . . . Damrosch's fascinating literary sleuthing will appeal to scholars and lay readers alike."

—*Publishers Weekly* (starred review)

"A graceful example of how rigorous scholarship and erudition can inform and animate popular history."

—*Kirkus* (starred review)

"David Damrosch's *The Buried Book* is a remarkably original, narrative analysis of the loss, rediscovery, and literary-spiritual values of the ancient epic *Gilgamesh*. There is somber wisdom and wit in Damrosch's comprehensive story, which finds room for Philip Roth's *The Great American Novel* and the murderous fictions of Saddam Hussein. It is salutary to be reminded by Damrosch that ultimately we and Islam share a common literary culture that commenced with *Gilgamesh*."

—Harold Bloom, author of *Where Shall Wisdom Be Found?*

"*The Buried Book* is a thrilling intellectual adventure: a brilliant study of Gilgamesh, it is also a rich and complex narrative of colonialist adventurers, obsessed scholars, anxious theologians, and contemporary writers all caught up in the ancient epic's amazingly wide net."

—Stephen Greenblatt, author of *Will in the World: How Shakespeare Became Shakespeare*

"An altogether compelling narrative of a crucial episode in cultural history. This is a book that vividly demonstrates why humanism matters and how it is enhanced by exercising an unconventionally broad reach."

—Robert Alter, author of *The Five Books of Moses: A Translation with Commentary*

THE BURIED BOOK

THE BURIED BOOK

THE LOSS AND REDISCOVERY
OF THE GREAT EPIC OF GILGAMESH

DAVID DAMROSCH

A HOLT PAPERBACK

Henry Holt and Company

New York

Holt Paperbacks
Henry Holt and Company, LLC
Publishers since 1866
175 Fifth Avenue
New York, New York 10010
www.henryholt.com

A Holt Paperback® and ® are registered trademarks of Henry Holt
and Company, LLC.

Distributed in Canada by H. B. Fenn and Company Ltd.

Library of Congress Cataloging-in-Publication Data

Damrosch, David.
    The buried book : the loss and rediscovery of the great Epic of Gilgamesh /
David Damrosch.—1st ed.
        p. cm.
    Includes index.
    Contents: The broken tablets—Early fame and sudden death—The lost
library—The fortress and the museum—After Ashurbanipal, the deluge—
At the limits of culture—The vanishing point.
    ISBN-13: 978-0-8050-8725-3
    ISBN-10: 0-8050-8725-7
    1. Gilgamesh. 2. Assyriology—History. I. Title.

PJ3771.G6D36 2007
809'.93353—dc22   2006049523

Henry Holt books are available for special promotions and premiums.
For details contact: Director, Special Markets.

Originally published in hardcover in 2007 by Henry Holt and Company

First Holt Paperbacks Edition 2008

Designed by Meryl Sussman Levavi

Printed in the United States of America

P1

For Diana, Eva, and Peter—
a book about exploration,
as you go out into the world

Gilgamesh is stupendous! ... I consider it to be the greatest
thing that can happen to a person.

—RAINER MARIA RILKE (1916)

———◆———

Hopes, long cherished, were now to be realized, or were to end
in disappointment. Visions of palaces underground, of gigantic monsters, of sculptured figures, and endless inscriptions,
floated before me. After forming plan after plan for removing the earth, and extricating these treasures, I fancied myself wandering in a maze of chambers from which I could find
no outlet.

—AUSTEN HENRY LAYARD,
Nineveh and Its Remains (1849)

———◆———

He came a far road, was weary, found peace,
    and set all his labors on a tablet of stone. . . .
See the cedar tablet-box,
    release its clasp of bronze!
Lift the lid of its secret,
    take out the tablet of lapis lazuli, and read
the struggles of Gilgamesh and all he endured.

—*The Epic of Gilgamesh*

CONTENTS

THE BURIED BOOK

Black Sea

Istanbul

Troy

LYDIA

HITTITES

ANATOLIA

Aleppo

Ugarit

CYPRUS

Mediterranean Sea

Tyre

Jerusalem

ARABIA

EGYPT   Cairo

Miles
0   150
0   150
Kms.

R. Nile

Red Sea

© 2006 A. Karl/J. Kemp

URARTU

Lake Van

Caspian
Sea

The
ANCIENT
NEAR EAST

MEDIA

Nineveh
Mosul
ASSYRIA

Tehran

MESOPOTAMIA

Tikrit

Behistun

Baghdad

Susa

BABYLONIA

Babylon

R. Euphrates

Uruk

R. Tigris

ELAM

Ur

PERSIA

Persepolis

Borders of modern Iraq

• *Baghdad*
Modern city names

Persian Gulf

INTRODUCTION

WHEN HISTORIES COLLIDE

The Great Mound of Kouyunjik, opposite Mosul.

EARLY in April of 1840, a young British traveler arrived in the dusty provincial capital of Mosul in what is now northern Iraq. Restless, ambitious, and completely unsure of what he should do with his life, Austen Henry Layard had just spent several months wandering around Greece, Turkey, and the Levant, admiring the monumental ruins left by the Greeks and Romans throughout the eastern Mediterranean. Now he was venturing into unsettled regions rarely visited by European travelers, for it was said that uncharted sites around Mosul held imposing remains of Nineveh and other ancient

Assyrian cities. The reports Layard had heard were both true and false: the sites were there, yet when Layard went out to them, he was astonished to discover that there was *nothing to see*. All that remained of the great Mesopotamian civilizations were formless mounds of earth, forty or fifty feet high and up to a mile wide, with not one temple, not one pillar, not one sculpture in sight.

Far from disappointing him, the desolation of the Assyrian sites only fired Layard's imagination. As he later wrote, a traveler crossing the Euphrates would seek in vain for "the graceful column rising above the thick foliage of the myrtle" or the elegant curves of an amphitheater above a sparkling bay. "He is now at a loss to give any form to the rude heaps upon which he is gazing," Layard continued. "The more he conjectures, the more vague the results appear. The scene around is worthy of the ruin he is contemplating; desolation meets desolation; a feeling of awe succeeds to wonder; for there is nothing to relieve the mind, to lead to hope, or to tell of what has gone by." Then and there, Layard resolved that he would be the one to uncover the history buried in the bleak mounds before him.

Layard and a handful of other archaeological explorers soon embarked on one of the most dramatic intellectual adventures of modern times: the opening up of three thousand years of history in the cradle of civilization. Layard led the way with spectacular discoveries at two different sites. At a site south of Mosul, he uncovered beautifully carved reliefs and a set of magnificent, human-headed winged bulls that became centerpieces of the British Museum's collection; across the Tigris from Mosul he found the long-buried ruins of Nineveh. There he discovered the vast palace built by the Assyrian king Sennacherib, its endless corridors and seventy rooms

lined with two full miles' worth of carved reliefs; not for
nothing had Sennacherib named it "Palace Without Rival."

As spectacular as the carvings were, Layard's most important find was literary: he and his Iraqi friend and assistant
Hormuzd Rassam uncovered the major library assembled by
Sennacherib's grandson, Ashurbanipal. Layard and Rassam
shipped a hundred thousand clay tablets and fragments back
to the British Museum, and these proved to be keys to uncovering the region's ancient history and its rich literature. The
greatest of the thousands of texts that Layard and Rassam
brought to light is *The Epic of Gilgamesh*, the first great masterpiece of world literature.

This book tells the story of that long-buried book, a history
of imperial conflict and of cross-cultural cooperation. During
the epic's varied life, it has cut across many of the divides
that arose during the long history of the intertwined civilizations that flourished in Mesopotamia and the eastern
Mediterranean. *Gilgamesh* links East and West, antiquity and
modernity, poetry and history, and its echoes can be found in
the Bible, in Homer, and in *The Thousand and One Nights*. At
the same time the epic illuminates the profound conflicts that
persist within each culture, and within the human heart itself.
"Why," Gilgamesh's divine mother Ninsun asks the sun god,
"did you afflict my son Gilgamesh with so restless a spirit?"

As it unfolds, *The Epic of Gilgamesh* becomes a searching
meditation on the nature of culture. After ill-advised adventures lead to the sudden death of his beloved friend Enkidu,
Gilgamesh is overwhelmed with despair and a deep fear of
death. He abandons his city and goes in search of immortality,
whose secret he believes he can learn from his ancestor Uta-
napishtim, miraculous survivor of the Flood that swept over
the earth centuries before. After a long and perilous journey

Gilgamesh finally meets Uta-napishtim, only to find that he
cannot transcend the human condition after all. Gilgamesh's
quest may have failed, but along the way he learns lessons about
just and unjust rule, political seductions and sexual politics,
and the vexed relations among humanity, the gods, and the
world of nature.

Though it is one of the earliest explorations of these perennial themes, this haunting poem isn't a timeless classic, in the
sense in which Ben Jonson spoke of Shakespeare's works as
"not of an age, but for all time." Instead, *Gilgamesh* has lived
in two very different ages, the ancient and the modern, and
only in these. A story of the fragile triumph of culture in the
face of death, the epic strangely came to illustrate its own
theme through its turbulent history. It was widely read in the
Near East for a thousand years, until it vanished amid the
eclipse of the region's ancient cultures, buried under succes-
sive waves of empire, from the Persians to the Romans and
their successors. The epic was buried in ruin mounds along
with Mesopotamia's entire written production, as people
stopped speaking the region's older languages and lost even
the ability to read the cuneiform script in which the works
were written. Unexpectedly, the epic reemerged in the nineteenth century into a scene of renewed imperial conflict,
involving Arabs, Turks, Persians, Kurds, Chechens, Jews,
Englishmen, Russians, and others in the waning years of the
Ottoman Empire. The choices these rivals made in the nineteenth century set the stage for the conflicts being played out
in Iraq today.

Layard and Rassam uncovered Ashurbanipal's great library, but they had no way to know what it contained, for no
one in the world could read the intricate cuneiform characters inscribed on the clay tablets. A group of gifted linguists

worked during the next two decades to unlock the secrets of cuneiform writing and to decode the ancient language of Akkadian, in which most of the tablets were written. Finally, in 1872, a young assistant curator named George Smith came upon the Gilgamesh epic as he worked his way through the myriad of tablets and fragments in the British Museum's collection. The epic aroused intense interest and controversy from the moment Smith began to translate it, as his readers realized that this distant text had much to tell them about a work at the heart of Western culture: the Bible. Smith found that Gilgamesh's ancestor Uta-napishtim was an early version of Noah, and his tale of the Flood broadly agreed with the biblical account but differed in some significant details.

Within days of this discovery, sermons and newspaper editorials began to engage in sharp debate: What did the Babylonian version prove, the truth of biblical history or its falsity? As the *New York Times* noted in a front-page article, "For the present the orthodox people are in great delight, and are very much prepossessed by the corroboration which it affords to Biblical history. It is possible, however, as has been pointed out, that the Chaldean inscription, if genuine, may be regarded as a confirmation of the statement that there are various traditions of the deluge apart from the Biblical one, which is perhaps legendary like the rest." Smith's scholarly detective work brought the ancient epic squarely into the middle of the heated Victorian controversy over creation and evolution, religion and science, a debate that continues today.

Some further detective work is required today, though, to get the full benefit of the epic's rich history. Layard, Rassam, and Smith wrote voluminous books about their adventures, but they rarely told the whole story in print: as proper Victorians, they could be irritatingly discreet just when they approached the heart of the conflicts in which they were involved, and like all memoirists they shaped their tale for public ends. To get a three-dimensional picture, it is necessary to supplement their books with other sources. Fortunately, the British Museum and the British Library have preserved many of their private letters and journals, which are fresh, lively, and often surprisingly candid. Most of these papers have been buried for a century in these archives, never published or even discussed. These materials give a vivid picture of what was going on behind the scenes, and at important points they correct received ideas that are flat-out wrong.

Archival research sometimes becomes almost its own branch of urban archaeology. Whereas the British Library's holdings have been comprehensively catalogued and cross-indexed, the British Museum's departments have much more informal archives, consisting of yellowing file folders, masses of correspondence going back two hundred years, and stacks of old account books. The museum's curators have the most precise knowledge of every artistic artifact in their care, but departmental records can be stored in rather haphazard ways. In a small field like Assyriology, everyone knows their discipline's history in a general way, but it is rarely studied in depth. Documents concerning the early days of archaeology are scattered, and finding key sources can be a chancy affair, following an uncertain trail from one informant to another.

I had this experience in talking with two curators in the British Museum's Department of Near Eastern Antiquities, Susan Collins and Irving Finkel. They generously took time away from their curatorial work on several occasions to supply me with cuneiform tablets, old letters, and Victorian newspaper clippings, yet I drew a blank when I asked for sources on a crucial episode involving Hormuzd Rassam. He had gone on to a distinguished career after discovering Ashurbanipal's palace but late in life had become embroiled in disputes with the museum's rising young Egyptologist, E. A. Wallis Budge. The conflict had culminated in a disastrous lawsuit that Rassam filed against Budge in 1893, and I was sure that the museum must have records of this suit. Dr. Collins was able to find some newspaper reports and a few unrelated letters from Budge, but nothing more. Dr. Finkel, too, was at a loss, but just as I was about to leave, some stray remark prompted him to pause, thoughtfully stroking his bushy white beard. There was, he suggested, another archivist I could talk to, at the museum's little-visited Central Archive, and perhaps I might find something there.

So I made my way to the Central Archive, which is reached, oddly, through an unmarked door at the back of the British Museum gift shop. Once through that door, I walked through a series of darkened, echoing rooms filled with empty bookshelves (the books having been transferred to the recently constructed British Library), then came to a warren of small offices, among which is the Central Archive. Of the seven days of the week, it is open to the public for five hours on Tuesdays. In the archive I found a trove of information: an entire folio scrapbook labeled "Rassam v. Budge, 1893." It contained extensive records of the pivotal lawsuit, including the pleadings and the actual transcript of the judge's detailed summation to the jury. Turning the musty pages of this volume, I experienced the archaeologist's sense of discovery as a long-lost drama unfolded, day by day, in the summer of 1893.

Archaeologists work their way down through time, from the present-day surface back through layer after layer of the

ever more distant past. This book proceeds in the same way
into "the dark backward and abysm of time," in Prospero's
phrase. The following chapters will go from what is known to
what is unknown, from what is near in space and time to what
is far away. The account begins with the lives of the two people who played decisive roles in the epic's modern recovery:
George Smith, who found the epic in the British Museum only
to lose his life in Syria a few years later; and Hormuzd Rassam, discoverer of Ashurbanipal's palace, whose major contributions to archaeology were long suppressed by his English
rivals. Starting in the Victorian period, we will then work
down in time to explore the ancient era of the tablets' burial
in the burning ruins of Ashurbanipal's palaces in Nineveh; to
examine the mature epic and the early cycle of songs from
which it grew; and, finally, to reach Gilgamesh himself at the
threshold of history nearly five thousand years ago, architect
of Uruk's independence and builder of its magnificent wall.

    This journey into antiquity has parallels in the ancient
text itself, when Gilgamesh leaves his city in search of the secret of eternal life, making the dangerous journey to find his
ancestor, "Uta-napishtim the Faraway." Journeys ideally end
with a return home—in this case, back to the present—and the
epilogue of this book will look at *Gilgamesh*'s renewed life in
the present. It has come to figure in the literary work and the
political musings of figures as disparate as Philip Roth and
Saddam Hussein, and even as a point of reference in the first
and second Gulf Wars. The most ancient masterpiece of world
literature has become bound up with the most current of events
today.

CHAPTER 1

THE BROKEN TABLETS

Arabs and Nestorians moving a slab at Kouyunjik.

FORGOTTEN for more than two thousand years, *The Epic of Gilgamesh* reentered history on a brisk November day in 1872. Its twelve broken tablets had been mixed in among the hundred thousand fragments that Henry Layard and Hormuzd Rassam had shipped back to London from Nineveh a quarter century before. For years the epic lay cradled in the crates and drawers of the British Museum's massive collection while scholars gradually deciphered the tablets' cuneiform script and began to read them. Slowly, an entire world was coming to light as the researchers worked through the huge jumble of materials before them: receipts for oxen, slaves, and casks of wine, petitions to the Assyrian kings, contracts, treaties, prayers, and reports of omens the gods had planted in sheep's livers. Much of this material was of interest to only a handful of specialists, but then an assistant curator named George Smith came upon an electrifying passage.

Smith was working at a long table piled with tablets, in a second-floor room overlooking the bare branches of the plane trees in Russell Square. He could read the tiny cuneiform markings only when enough light came through the tall windows. Fearful of fire, the museum's trustees had refused to allow gas lighting in the museum, and in 1872 Edison's incandescent bulb was still just a gleam in its inventor's eye. The museum did supply covered lanterns for a select number of senior staff, but Smith was too junior to enjoy the use of one. On days of dense London fog—frequent in the fall and winter— the museum would close and the entire staff would be sent home. So it must have been a fairly clear day when George Smith came upon a piece of tablet whose lines referred to a flood storm, a ship caught on a mountain, and a bird sent out in search of dry land.

Like many of his contemporaries, George Smith was obsessed with biblical history. How much of the Bible was true? Textual critics had begun dissecting the Bible's layers of composition, casting doubt on the accuracy of its historical accounts; the more advanced German scholars were even claiming that such major figures as Abraham and Moses had never really existed. And if the parting of the Red Sea was merely a legend, what of the Resurrection of Jesus? Advances in geology, meanwhile, were undercutting the foundational stories of Creation, Eden, and the Flood—had any of it really happened? Was earthly life truly God's sacred creation or was it just the product of blind chance, as Darwin's radical new theories implied? Contemplating a cliff studded with fossils of extinct species, the eminent poet Tennyson had a grim vision of Nature, "red in tooth and claw," proclaiming: "A thousand types are gone; / I care for nothing, all shall go."

While he worked on his tablets, George Smith was on the lookout for passages that might confirm information from the Bible; within his Assyrian sources he had already established solid dates for a couple of minor events in Israelite history. But now he was on to something truly sensational: the first independent confirmation of a vast flood in ancient Mesopotamia, complete with a Noah figure and an ark. Yet he could read only a few lines of the tablet, much of which was encrusted with a thick, lime-like deposit. He desperately needed to know what was written beneath this crust.

The British Museum had an expert restorer on contract, a former tobacconist named Robert Ready. Ready was hired by the hour on the days the museum was open to the public, but he had to supplement his income with outside work. He developed many innovative methods of restoration but treated them as trade secrets, revealing them only to his four sons. Ready alone could clean the tablet, but he was away on private business when Smith found the crucial fragment. As Smith's colleague E. A. Wallis Budge later recalled, "Smith was constitutionally a highly nervous, sensitive man; and his irritation at Ready's absence knew no bounds." Ready finally returned several excruciating days later and worked his magic, whereupon "Smith took the tablet and began to read over the lines which Ready had brought to light; and when he saw that they contained the portion of the legend he had hoped to find there, he said, 'I am

the first man to read that after more than two thousand years
of oblivion.' Setting the tablet on the table, he jumped up and
rushed about the room in a great state of excitement, and, to
the astonishment of those present, began to undress himself!"
There is no way to know how far this disrobing actually went;
Smith makes no mention of it in his own books, speaking only
of methodical searching and careful decipherment. Perhaps he
was embarrassed to reveal the full intensity of his excitement,
or perhaps Budge's tale grew in the telling over the years before he recorded it; the surprising state of "undress" may have
been little more than a loosened collar.

George Smith certainly had good reason to be flushed with
success: this discovery was the turning point of his life, and
he knew it. He had just made one of the most sensational
finds in the history of archaeology, and he became famous
overnight. Yet this discovery was only one of many achievements in his meteoric career, for George Smith was a genius.
He became the world's leading expert in the ancient Akkadian language and its fiendishly difficult script, wrote the
first true history of the long-lost Assyrian Empire, and published pathbreaking translations of the major Babylonian literary texts, in between expeditions to find more tablets in
Iraq. Though this would have been the lifework of an eminent
scholar at Oxford or the Sorbonne, Smith's active career lasted
barely ten years, from his mid-twenties to his mid-thirties.
Far from holding a distinguished professorship, he had never
been to high school, much less college. His formal education
had ended at age fourteen.

If you were a genius, in the Victorian era, but through the
luck of the draw you had found yourself born into a working-
class family, your chances of achieving such scholarly success
would have been vanishingly small. A brilliant scullery maid

or coal miner would earn the same meager wages as a competent drudge, and would enjoy the same poor prospects for advancement. The twentieth century's major engines of upward mobility, higher education and the armed services' officer corps, were essentially closed to the children of the working classes, and if your genius lay in artistic or intellectual directions, you would likely achieve, at most, a local reputation as a rare hand at the fiddle or "a deep one" at the pub.

As a genius, of course, you wouldn't really need much formal instruction: you could find your way to books, dictionaries, and grammars, teach yourself ancient and modern languages, and enter the world of ideas on your own; it could even be an advantage to have escaped the limiting routines of everyday instruction. But what then? As late as 1895, the novelist Thomas Hardy portrayed with grim irony the reception accorded his stonemason hero in *Jude the Obscure*, who manages to teach himself Greek and then boldly applies for admission to "Biblioll College, Christminster" (clearly modeled on Balliol College, Oxford). The head of the college replies with a well-intentioned but heartless note:

> Sir—I have read your letter with interest; and, judging from your description of yourself as a working-man, I venture to think that you will have a much better chance of success in life by remaining in your own sphere and sticking to your trade than by adopting any other course. That, therefore, is what I advise you to do. Yours faithfully,
>
> T. Tetuphenay.
>
> To Mr. J. Fawley, Stone-mason.

Hardy's irony is hidden here in the professor's rather implausible name: "Tetuphenay" echoes the Greek verb *tetúphōmai*, "to be shrouded in conceit and folly, to be silly, stupid, absurd." The world, however, was very much on Tetuphenay's side, and it was Jude who was destined to remain shrouded in obscurity.

George Smith's parents had no such academic illusions for their son, who was born in 1840 in the London district of Chelsea, at that time a seedy area of grimy tenements and high unemployment. They belonged to London's large, anonymous pool of unskilled labor—even after George became famous, no one ever bothered to record his parents' occupations, or even their names. When George turned fourteen, his father took the sensible route of apprenticing the boy to a skilled trade. Apparently George's literary and artistic interests were already becoming evident, and so his father did the best he could, articling his son to the printing firm of Messrs. Bradbury and Evans, where he was put to work learning to engrave banknotes. A modest step up from the father's own position, and as much as one could realistically expect—a good income, sufficient to marry and raise a family fairly comfortably, ideally enabling the next generation to take a step further, through high school perhaps and on to greater prosperity thereafter.

Working amid the clattering din of the printing presses and the smell of damp ink on paper stock, Smith took to his engraving with pleasure. He developed the patience, the keen eye, and the delicate hand that would later serve him well in his work with cuneiform tablets. His work also exposed him to a wider literary milieu, for Bradbury and Evans had branched out from printing into publishing; they owned the comic magazine *Punch* and published Dickens and Thackeray in lavishly illustrated editions. Smith was employed in the banknote division that had been started by Henry Bradbury, a son of the firm's senior partner. Henry Bradbury was deeply interested in the problem of producing paper money that would be difficult to forge, and he wrote several studies on this topic, culminating in 1860 with an encyclopedic volume soberly titled *Specimens of Bank Note Engraving*, on which Smith likely worked.

The young and innovative Bradbury would have been a natural mentor for his talented assistant. According to Wallis Budge, the firm's partners considered Smith a rising star, destined to become one of England's leading engravers, and they "regarded Smith's abandonment of a well-paid trade and regular employment, in order to follow his literary bent, as an act of pure folly." Yet it may have been a tragedy within the firm that shook Smith out of his expected trajectory: after publishing his magnum opus on banknotes, Henry Bradbury committed suicide in September 1860, at the age of twenty-nine. That fall, the twenty-year-old Smith began to haunt the Near Eastern collections at the British Museum.

Biblical studies drew George Smith to the museum, as a long-standing hobby turned into his passion. Like Hardy's Jude the Obscure, he had developed an early fascination with the Bible (one of the few books, if not the only book, that would have been in his household as he grew up). Yet unlike Jude, who got nowhere by learning the Greek language that many high school graduates knew better, Smith found his way into the brand-new field of Assyriology—the study of ancient Mesopotamia, so called because the first excavations in Iraq had focused on the ruins of Nineveh and other ancient Assyrian cities north of Baghdad. Assyriology was hardly an established field at all, with just a few researchers scattered about in British and Continental universities and museums. They had only recently succeeded in cracking the code to the region's history: the complex cuneiform (wedge-shaped) script in which most of the ancient Mesopotamian texts were written. Much of the ongoing work in deciphering the cuneiform inscriptions was still being carried on by amateurs—army officers posted to Persia or Iraq who fell under the spell of the antiquities there, or rural parish priests with time on their hands; a leading early decipherer was Edward Hincks, who served for fifty-five years as rector of the Irish town of Killyleagh.

Assyriology was, in short, a field in need of workers, with few established protocols or vested interests: a rare chink in the armor of the British class structure. An inquiring mind with a fresh perspective could be welcomed into the enterprise, without needing a single credential, letter of introduction, or family connection. Resources were still pitifully slim, and full-time employment in the field was almost unattainable, so it would be an exaggeration to speak of this as a window of opportunity; it was more of a mouse hole of opportunity at most, but it was just the route George Smith took into the British Museum.

More precisely, he began spending many of his lunch hours walking down Fleet Street and then up to the museum at Great Russell Street, roughly a mile from his workplace, threading his way among the dense press of carriages, horse-drawn streetcars, window-shopping pedestrians, and hand-drawn carts full of cabbages and potatoes. It was natural for Bradbury and Evans to have located their printing firm just off Fleet Street, the center of the London newspaper industry, and this location made all the difference in Smith's life. If Bradbury and Evans had situated themselves another mile away from the museum, then Smith wouldn't have had the time to get to it during business hours, and he never would

Gustave Doré, *Ludgate Hill*, from *London: A Pilgrimage*, 1872. The scene shows a bustling Fleet Street near Bouverie Street, where Smith had worked. Obelisks on each side of the street reflect the fascination with recovered Near Eastern antiquities. Billboards advertise several of the Fleet Street newspapers, including "LLOYD'S NEWS, SALE OVER HALF A MILLION, ONE PENNY."

have made the discoveries that led to his new career. But from the firm's offices at 11 Bouverie Street, a young man in a hurry (as Smith certainly was) could walk to the museum in twenty minutes, probably eating as he walked, with half of a ninety-minute lunch break left to pore over the enigmatic tablets in the museum's collection.

Smith may have gone to work early in order to buy more time for his lunch hour. In a letter to his fiancée, Mary Clifton (away on a seaside holiday), he warned her lovingly that "unless things alter you may often have to breakfast alone after we are married and I do not regret this so much, not because I do not enjoy your company but because in earning more I am doing good to us both. Today if I work as I anticipate I shall earn 11 shillings." Of course, this letter may simply suggest that even at an early age Smith was a workaholic, a trait encouraged by the fact that his income would rise with his output of engravings.

For several years, Smith had been reading everything he could find about Mesopotamia, but now he was determined to take an active part in studying the primary materials. What he encountered when he made his way to the museum's cuneiform collection was a kind of barely controlled chaos. Thanks to Layard and Rassam's efforts, the museum possessed the world's largest cuneiform collection by far, over a hundred thousand tablets and fragments in all, together with many paper "squeezes"—impressions made of immovable inscriptions by pressing damp paper onto their surfaces.

This was an extraordinary trove, if only it could be read, but the problems were not only linguistic. The squeezes deteriorated upon handling, and were further damaged when mice got into the storage area through some literal mouse hole and nibbled away at them for nesting material. Unbaked clay tablets could crumble. Many tablets had been baked, giving

them the heft and durability of terra-cotta roofing tiles, but
most of them had been broken amid the ruins of Nineveh, so
the collection consisted of a myriad of fragments. Even the
largely intact tablets were often encrusted with dirt and cal-
cified deposits and had to be cleaned with great care before
they could be read. Today the tablets reside in their own spacious, well-lit reading room with an ornate arched ceiling, its
walls lined with fifteen-foot-high oak cabinets holding ranks
of wool-lined drawers of tablets, but in Smith's day conditions
were haphazard. The tablets were stored loose in boxes and
sometimes damaged each other; items under active consideration were laid out on planks set on trestles in a dimly lit room.

At any given time, there might be two or three researchers
visiting from the provinces or the Continent, trying either to
help or to compete against the two professional staff members who ran the Department of Oriental Antiquities (Oriental
meaning Middle Eastern, in common Victorian usage). Everyone sensed that there were exciting discoveries to be made in
the chaotic mass of tablets, and papers like the *Illustrated London News* published dramatic reports of every new confirmation of a biblical name or establishment of a date in Israelite
history. Yet the museum's professional staff were not particularly well qualified to make these discoveries themselves. The
head, or "Keeper," of the department was a learned Egyptologist, Dr. Samuel Birch, D.C.L., L.L.D. Birch had no direct ex-
pertise in Mesopotamian studies and left the supervision of the
cuneiform collection to his sole assistant. This was a young classical scholar named William Henry Coxe, whose prizewinning
undergraduate career at Oxford had earned him the lasting
nickname "Coxe of Balliol"—the real-life version of the college
that rejects Jude in Hardy's novel.

In college Coxe had studied not only Greek and Latin but also Sanskrit, the classical language of India, and Birch had hired him with the (mistaken) idea that this knowledge might prove useful in helping to decipher the cuneiform tablets. Coxe had begun to learn Akkadian after joining the museum's staff, but both he and Birch deferred in practice to the dominant figure in British cuneiform studies, the formidable Sir Henry Creswicke Rawlinson. Not a museum employee, Rawlinson was a frequent presence in the department's workroom. Haughty, ambitious, and accustomed to command, Rawlinson had been knighted after a distinguished military career in India, Persia, and Iraq. He became a member of Parliament, ambassador, and director of the East India Company, then was appointed to the government's powerful Council on India. When he could spare time from his official duties he was often at the museum preparing a pioneering series of publications of cuneiform inscriptions. An odd avocation, perhaps, for a politician and military man, but Rawlinson had a genuine passion for ancient languages. He saw too that he could make a name for himself as a pioneer in this new field of study, an arena in which he could establish an unrivaled sway.

It was Rawlinson who had made the decisive breakthrough in the decipherment of cuneiform writing, thanks to an exceptional combination of insight and sheer physical daring. As a young lieutenant in India and Persia, he had become famous for feats of strength and endurance, making great journeys on horseback in record time, such as a ride of 750 miles within 150 consecutive hours. His two sons inherited his prowess, and both of them joined the army as well. Rising to the rank of general, the elder son achieved a major victory in World War I when he broke the Hindenburg Line along the western front. Somewhat less gloriously, the younger son was

known in sporting circles as "the best polo player in India."
Their father, however, was distinguished by his intellectual
passion as much as by his athleticism, rapidly learning Eastern languages during his tours of duty and making himself
welcome at the Persian court with his ability to recite long
passages of Persian poetry from memory.

While in Persia, where he helped reorganize the shah's
army, Rawlinson visited the ancient ruins at Behistun in the
mountains of western Persia. With his talent for languages,
the young officer was intrigued by the mysterious cuneiform
writing that the early Persians had borrowed from neighboring Mesopotamia. The intricate wedge-shaped marks seemed
to be completely unreadable. A German high school teacher
named Grotefend, working in the quiet college town of Göt-
tingen, had proposed some tentative readings in 1802, but his
ideas had not been widely noted and were unknown in England. Rawlinson, however, learned of a trilingual inscription on a monument to the Persian king Darius the Great. A
decade earlier, the Frenchman Jean-François Champollion
had deciphered the Egyptian Rosetta stone, also a trilingual
text, written in Greek and in two forms of Egyptian hieroglyphics. By identifying names in both languages, Champollion had been able to reconstruct the sounds of many of the
hieroglyphs: working back from the Greek, which he could
read, he gradually began to reconstruct the Egyptian text
and its grammar, and published his translation to great acclaim in 1824.

Rawlinson realized that a similar feat might be accomplished with Darius's inscription, but first it would have to be
copied for careful study. This presented a further difficulty:
the inscription was all but unreachable, carved on a cliff
three hundred feet above the valley floor. The site featured

monumental reliefs of Darius receiving tribute from subject
kings, but the accompanying inscriptions had been addressed
to the gods rather than to mortals, and they couldn't be read
from the ground far below. The only access to the carvings,
after a harrowing climb up an almost sheer rock face, was a
narrow, crumbling ledge.

Undeterred, Rawlinson made the climb with a few equally
bold friends and copied what he could. On subsequent trips,
they took along a ladder, and with this Rawlinson was able to
reach more of the inscriptions. He described his method some
years later, in the understated style favored by Victorian explorers when recounting particularly hair-raising adventures.
"Even with ladders there is considerable risk," he wrote,

> for the foot-ledge is so narrow, about 18
> inches, or at most 2 feet in breadth, that . . .
> the upper inscriptions can only be copied by
> standing on the topmost step of the ladder,
> with no other support than steadying the body
> against the rock with the left arm, while the
> left hand holds the note-book and the right
> hand is employed with the pencil. In this posi-
> tion I copied all the upper inscriptions and the
> interest of the occupation entirely did away
> with any sense of danger.

New dangers appeared farther along the ledge where the
path had broken away. Rawlinson tried to bridge the gap by
laying his ladder across it, but at the far side of the break the
edge curved and only one of the ladder's sides could hold; the
other side hung down. Rawlinson then began inching across

Monumental relief of Darius the Great at Behistun. Two tribesmen are perched on the ledge where Rawlinson precariously worked.

the gap, holding on to the secure side of the ladder and setting his feet on the lower side between the ladder's rungs. But it turned out that the rungs weren't firmly fastened. When Rawlinson was partway across,

the vertical pressure forced the bars out of
their sockets, and the lower and unsupported
side of the ladder thus parted company from
the upper, and went crashing down over the
precipice. Hanging on to the upper side, which
still remained firm in its place, and assisted by
my friends, who were anxiously watching the
trial, I regained the Persian recess, and did
not again attempt to cross until I had made a
bridge of comparative stability.

Farther along, the resourceful Rawlinson was stymied by
a looming overhang, and so he resorted to a classic imperial
move: he delegated the job to a native. No local tribesman
would agree to risk his life for the sake of scholarship, but "a
wild Kurdish boy, who had come from a distance, volunteered
to make the attempt, and I promised him a considerable reward if he succeeded." (The price of failure, apparently, was
not discussed.) The boy squeezed himself up a cleft alongside
the overhang, then inched across the cliff "by hanging on
with his toes and fingers to the slight inequalities on the bare
face of the precipice, and in this he succeeded, passing over a
distance of twenty feet of almost smooth perpendicular rock
in a manner which to a looker-on appeared quite miraculous."
Once in position, the boy made a paper pressing of the desired
passage.

Rawlinson slowly began to make sense of the inscription
during the next several years, though he had to interrupt his
work to serve in the Afghan Wars of 1838–42. Appointed
British Resident in Baghdad in 1843, he pursued his researches
in the time he could spare from his diplomatic activities, in

which elaborate dinner parties figured prominently; his large staff included specialists in coffee brewing and the tending of water pipes. In time, a small group of scholars around Europe began to build on his work. By the early 1860s they had penetrated the mysteries of the world's oldest script and had achieved a working understanding of Akkadian, the language most commonly used in the cuneiform tablets.

Their task was much harder than the daunting challenge Champollion had faced. The pictorial quality of Egyptian hieroglyphs meant that at least some signs showed clearly what they meant, whereas the cuneiform symbols were all highly abstract. Even when the symbols once represented something concrete, the visual reference had been obscured over time. A head could be represented by two upright wedges that had once been the neck, topped by a cluster of wedges that distantly recalled an eye, nose, and head of hair. A triangular sign might have originally signified a basket or a vagina. Even when a sign's visual origin could be guessed, this information was rarely useful, as the signs were usually used for their phonetic value rather than as pictures.

Furthermore, while one of the Rosetta stone's parallel inscriptions had been in ancient Greek—which Champollion could readily read—all three inscriptions from Behistun were in cuneiform script. Rawlinson was faced with a choice of enigmas. Fortunately, one of the three was a simple script used for Old Persian, with only thirty-six characters, and Rawlinson knew two early Persian languages. He shrewdly guessed that the monumental reliefs portrayed the dominant ancient Persian king Darius the Great, together with a line of captive or subordinate kings, and by a process of trial and error began to derive the sound values for many of the names on

the monument, along with formulaic phrases such as "king
of kings."

Fortunately, the sound values of the three dozen Old Persian characters held good for the Akkadian text, though it
had hundreds of different characters and so posed a far more
difficult challenge. It took fifteen years of steady work before
Rawlinson could declare, in 1850, that he had deciphered
most of the inscription. In this task, he was greatly aided
by Akkadian's close relationship to Hebrew and Arabic;
"dog" for instance, is *keleb* in Hebrew, *kalb* in Arabic, and
kalbum in Akkadian.

Such commonalities provided a crucial doorway into the
language, but the task of decipherment was complicated by
the intricacy of the Akkadian cuneiform system. Rawlinson
gradually realized that the Akkadian system must represent
sounds, as it had only six hundred different characters, far
too few for each sign to represent a discrete object. Since
six hundred characters were far more than would be needed
for an alphabet, Rawlinson concluded they must represent
syllables.

So they often did, though a character could also be used
for an entire word. The star symbol, ✳, pronounced *an,*
could represent Anu, god of the sky, yet it could also be the
first syllable of the pronoun *annûtim,* "these," among many
other words. (Like many ancient writers, the Mesopotamian
scribes didn't bother to leave spaces between words, so it was
always a challenge to decide where a word might begin and
end.) Moreover, a symbol could be used for more than one
sound, much as in English the letter *c* can have the sound *s*
or *k*. On the other hand, one sound could be represented by
several different characters, much as the letters *k, q,* and
sometimes *c* can all represent the same sound, but cuneiform

developed with many more complications than are found in simple alphabets. Finally, the individual signs often changed in form from one region to another and from one era to the next during the three thousand years of the script's use. One sign, to take a typical example, was originally written ▷ in Babylonia and was often pronounced *ni* or *ne*; but it could also be written as a more open triangle in the form ▷ or ▷ and it could be written more simply as ⊳; in Assyria, it was written ⚏, with the uppermost wedge set horizontally instead of slanting down. In any of its forms, the sign could convey a variety of sounds: not only *ni* and *ne*, but also *i*, *il*, and *shu*.

Rawlinson spent years making lists and charts of signs, looking for patterns that might suggest grammatical elements such as pronouns or verb endings. Since the Assyrians had extensive dealings with the peoples of Palestine, the royal inscriptions provided many names known from the Bible, whose representation in Akkadian could be worked out. Rawlinson and his fellow researchers painstakingly built up their knowledge, using known characters in one name to guess at unknown characters in another name that had some overlap with the first. A typical progression can be seen in the following selections from a chart in Austen Henry Layard's *Discoveries in the Ruins of Nineveh and Babylon*, which gives a series of Hebrew names and their cuneiform rendering:

NAME	CUNEIFORM	HEBREW
Jehu..	𒂍𒅁 𒀯𒈠 𒅁	יֵהוּא
Judæa	𒂍𒅁 𒀯𒈠 𒐊𒅁 𒅁	יְהוּדָה
Dagon	𒐊𒅁 𒂍	דָּגוֹן

Once the decipherer had arrived at the first name, Jehu ("ye-hu" in Hebrew, "ie-u" in Akkadian), it was possible to guess at the unknown character in the next name, "ie-u- -a," and arrive at "ie-u-da-a" or Judea. Having determined the sound of the *da* character, the linguist was halfway to unraveling the name of the god Dagon. It must have taken Rawlinson thousands of trial-and-error attempts to build up a reasonable certainty for at least the most common characters.

Another major complication in the process of decipherment was that cuneiform had originally been developed in southern Mesopotamia by people who spoke Sumerian, an ancient language completely unrelated to any other known language. The script had then been taken over by speakers of Akkadian, which became the most commonly written language for much of Mesopotamian history. Yet the Akkadian scribes continued to learn Sumerian as they mastered the script, and they often employed Sumerian loan words amid their Akkadian texts. It is as though, in reading an English text, we would often have to pause and determine whether *pain* meant "suffering," as in English, or "bread," as in French.

Conversely, a sign might have the same meaning in Akkadian as in Sumerian but a completely different sound: when used to mean "sky," the star symbol is pronounced *an* in Sumerian, but is *shamû* in Akkadian. Names in particular could be tricky, for Assyrian names often included Sumerian elements, along with Akkadian symbols. This would lead George Smith, for example, to misread the name Gilgamesh as "Izdubar"; he didn't realize that what looked like two Akkadian characters, *iz* and *du*, were actually Sumerian signs pronounced "giš-ga" or "gil-ga." He then guessed incorrectly on the final syllable, which was Akkadian as he assumed, but which can be pronounced either "bar" or "mesh." So "gil-ga-mesh" became "Izdubar," among other renderings by different Assyriologists of the day. The reading of "Gilgamesh" was finally established twenty-five years later by Smith's friend and successor Theophilus G. Pinches, in an article triumphantly entitled *"EXIT GIŠTUBAR!"*

Rawlinson had begun studying the Behistun inscriptions in 1835, and by the late 1850s his reputation was firmly established as the world's leading authority on cuneiform. Yet he realized there was much he didn't know. He had long hoarded his transcriptions—and often borrowed without acknowledgment from rivals such as the Irish priest Edward Hincks—but now he decided to publish a set of oversized volumes that would offer clear and accurate texts for other researchers to use. Rawlinson was engaged off and on with this labor of love for many years, up through the publication of the fifth and final volume in 1884; fifty years of age in 1860, he had just published the first volume of *Cuneiform Inscriptions of Western Asia* when George Smith began to frequent the museum.

At first, Dr. Birch and "Coxe of Balliol" paid little attention to the quiet but persistent young engraver who kept coming to examine tablets. The British Museum was open to the public only three days a week, and the trustees had been reluctant to allow that much access, protesting that crowds of uneducated laborers could damage the artworks, which should be reserved for study by art students and appreciation by a refined clientele (who could be admitted on the other days by special appointment). An outsider with no academic standing would ordinarily have been tolerated at best, but soon it became apparent to Birch and Coxe that George Smith could read the tablets better than they could, and Birch brought him to Rawlinson's attention.

As he got to know Smith, Rawlinson was strongly impressed by his ability to piece tablets together, a task requiring an exceptional visual memory and manual dexterity in creating "joins" of tablet fragments. A given tablet might have been broken into a dozen or more pieces, now widely dispersed among the hundred thousand fragments in the museum's collection. Rawlinson persuaded the museum to hire Smith to work on sorting and assembling tablets—a job involving more manual labor than scholarship. In fact, his salary was that of a semiskilled laborer; as Budge remarked, Smith "worked for some years for a salary that was smaller than that then received by a master carpenter or master mason." From a purely

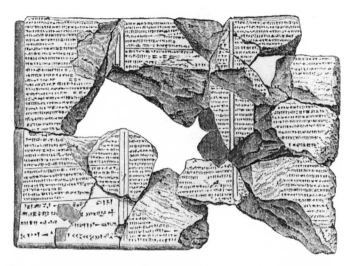

George Smith's engraving of a portion of the Flood story tablet, from *The Chaldean Account of Genesis* (1875).

financial standpoint, Professor Tetuphenay gave sensible advice to "Mr. J. Fawley, Stone-mason."

Smith made the fullest use of his new position to increase his command of the language and its script, and by the mid-1860s he was making real discoveries among the tablets: identifying Hebrew monarchs mentioned in Assyrian inscriptions and giving new detail and accuracy to the chronology of Israelite history. In 1866 he published his first article, and he received an important promotion when Rawlinson persuaded the museum's trustees to hire Smith as his assistant for the next volume of his *Cuneiform Inscriptions.* "Thus, in the beginning of 1867," as Smith later recalled with quiet pride, "I entered into official life, and regularly prosecuted the study of the cuneiform texts."

Smith always revered Rawlinson, even as he began to surpass him in mastery. The language of Smith's dedication for his 1875 book *The Chaldean Account of Genesis* is instructive:

TO

SIR HENRY CRESWICKE RAWLINSON,

K.C.B., D.C.L., ETC. ETC. ETC.,

MY TEACHER AND PREDECESSOR IN MY PRESENT

LINE OF RESEARCH,

IN REMEMBRANCE OF MANY FAVOURS,

THIS WORK IS

Dedicated

By naming Rawlinson his "predecessor," Smith places his teacher's influence in the past and directs our attention to the fruits of "my present line of research." By this time, Smith had eclipsed his mentor in public recognition, thanks to his electrifying discovery of "The Chaldean Account of the Deluge"—*The Epic of Gilgamesh.*

This discovery was just what Smith needed to achieve his life's ambition. For years he had been offering to go to Iraq to excavate, but the museum had no intention of sending him out. The trustees were mostly interested in classical and European art and culture and felt that the museum already had more than enough "primitive" Assyrian and Babylonian artifacts. (As the museum's sculpture curator opined when Austen Henry Layard shipped back his first finds, "It is very bad art.") Desperately eager to become a full-fledged archaeologist, Smith wrote to Layard, "If I cannot raise the money any other way I would if possible take any temporary employment out there (provided the Museum allowed it) so that by any means I might reopen the scene of some of your labours." The museum, however, wanted him at work on the premises, and Smith had no way to secure "temporary employment" in a distant province of the Ottoman Empire or even to pay his own way out there, as he was now supporting a wife and a growing family on his slender wages. Discouraged, he wrote to Layard in February 1872, "Government will not assist the movement in the least, at present, in fact I think they will not give a penny until something is discovered."

Smith therefore began to systematically survey the museum's collection for historical and mythological texts that might make some dramatic contribution to biblical studies. His chancing upon the Flood story in November of that year followed nine solid months of searching for something that could arouse enough public interest to justify an expedition east. Among a hundred thousand fragments, Smith had now found the passport to the land of his dreams.

✳

Word of the find spread rapidly, and Prime Minister William Gladstone was in the audience when Smith presented a translation in a lecture to the Biblical Archaeology Society on December 3, 1872. "This must be the only occasion," the Assyriologist Andrew George has dryly noted, "on which a British Prime Minister in office has attended a lecture on Babylonian literature." During the discussion following Smith's presentation, Gladstone rose to offer extensive remarks, as reported the next day by the *Times* of London. He began by praising the new discoveries in Mesopotamia, not so much for their relevance to the Bible but for giving "a solidity to much of the old Greek traditions which they never before possessed," bringing new understanding to the reading of Homer. Almost forgetting the occasion altogether, he extolled Homer as "the friend of my youth, the friend of my middle age, the friend of my old age, from whom I hope never to part as long as I have any faculty of breath left in my body." According to the *Times*, the assembled archaeologists warmly applauded this stirring statement.

Gladstone later proved to be as good as his word: after retiring as prime minister he went on to write books about Homer as well as probing essays on religious issues, which prompted Lewis Carroll to rearrange the letters of his name, William Ewart Gladstone, into a pointed protest: "*Wilt tear down all images?*" Interestingly, Lewis Carroll—a devout Anglican deacon as well as a mathematician and writer—clipped out the *Times*'s first report of Smith's discovery and pasted it into a scrapbook, a few months after he'd published *Through the Looking-Glass*. The Bible's images were being refracted in unexpected ways in the newly translated tablets.

Gladstone's praise of Homer was greeted with applause by the assembled archaeologists, but the prime minister went on to frustrate their hope that his administration would underwrite a new expedition in search of further artifacts. Smith had been careful to stress the importance of such an expedition, noting in particular that the Flood story tablet remained incomplete. Gladstone, however, refused to bite. Instead, he roundly declared, "It has been the distinction and the pride of this country to do very many things by individual effort that in other countries would only be effected by what Sir Robert Peel used to call 'the vulgar expedient of applying to the Consolidated Fund'"—the national Treasury. The *Times* doesn't record any applause by the archaeologists in response to this endorsement of private enterprise.

With Gladstone having craftily stifled the call for government support, it was left to a more openly vulgar institution to take up the challenge. Edwin Arnold, editor of a popular London newspaper, the *Daily Telegraph*, promptly put up the sum of a thousand guineas to fund Smith's expedition, and the next month Smith was at last on his way. It was a nice touch to set the figure in guineas, rather than in their functional equivalent, pounds sterling. The guinea had been a gold coin worth twenty-one shillings (one more than a pound), but it hadn't been minted for sixty years; the term had survived to price luxury goods, often including books. Arnold's thousand guineas thus suggested the tablets' cultural value as much as the direct cost of recovering them.

Appropriately, the guinea took its name from the British colony where it was first minted, since Arnold's dramatic gesture was inspired by imperial interests as much as by antiquarian concerns. From the very start of the century, archaeological exploration had been closely bound up with the

romance—and the politics—of imperial exploration and conquest. The French had taken an early lead in this enterprise
when Napoléon invaded Egypt in 1798, taking with him a com-
mittee of 167 scholars and scientists to survey the country and
its antiquities; the famous Rosetta stone, key to the decipherment of hieroglyphics, had been unearthed during Napoleon's
three-year adventure in Egypt. He had then been driven out
by a combined Ottoman and British force, and it was a matter
of British cultural pride that the Rosetta stone itself now
resided in the British Museum.

As the century wore on, the territories precariously held in
the Middle East by the declining Ottoman Empire became a
matter of intense competition among the major European
powers, which sought every possible advantage over their
rivals in gaining influence and control in the region. The
Crimean War was only the most bloody of a whole series of
open conflicts, but with military ventures rarely proving
decisive, the imperial contenders sought advantage in cultural enterprises as well, part of the larger civilizing mission intended to bring open markets and Christianity to the
"backward" countries of the Middle East. The excavation and
preservation of antiquities was a frequent area of competition, a way of asserting that Europeans could take better care
of the region's heritage than the natives themselves. As one
historian has written, the players in "the Great Game in the
Middle East . . . would wage conventional warfare and messy
diplomatic effrontery not only over Ottoman territory, but
over the very proprietorship of the past."

The prestige brought by cultural recovery and dominance
had important political effects. This point was made by no less
a figure than Sir Henry Rawlinson, in an 1867 speech to Parliament: "I look on 'prestige' in politics very much as I look on

credit in finance. It is a power which enables us to achieve very great results with very small means at our disposal. 'Prestige' may not be of paramount importance in Europe, but in the East, sir, our whole position depends upon it." Reports of archaeological finds in the Middle East regularly emphasized the natives' awe and wonder at the Europeans' ability to discover long-hidden treasures beneath their feet. Even as they furthered Western interests abroad, archaeological expeditions had value back home as well: the search for ancient artifacts made for great news reports and travelogues, providing European readers all the excitement of imperial derring-do and mastery—Rawlinson scaling the cliff at Behistun—without the recovered antiquities putting up any resistance or forming contrary alliances on their own.

Archaeology and empire are constantly intertwined in the period's accounts. On the day that the London *Times* reviewed Smith's 1875 book *The Chaldean Account of Genesis*, the column directly beside the review contained an article on Serbia ("Servia") and Montenegro, which begins: "Affairs in the East have again a gloomy aspect. It is caused by the doubtful attitude of Servia and Montenegro." The article goes on to describe the uncertain status of these Balkan states, uneasily situated within the overlapping spheres of influence of the Ottoman and Austro-Hungarian empires. In this troubled context, it is no coincidence that the reviewer of Smith's book enjoyed using triumphant language of legal control and military advance: "The deciphering of Assyrian cuneiform is marching at a pace that must astonish its most ardent admirers and surpass the expectations of its most devoted followers. . . . Assurbanipal had been cross-examined, and now Bel and the Dragon have been brought into court . . . the mythology, or

rather the religion, of the Semitic polytheists has been conquered."

In funding Smith's expedition to find the missing portion
of the Flood story, Edwin Arnold was following up on the
success of another imperial search-and-rescue operation. His
Daily Telegraph had sent Henry Morton Stanley to find the
explorer-missionary Dr. David Livingstone in Central Africa
when his contact with England ceased during a long journey
of exploration begun in 1866. Stanley located Livingstone
late in 1871, and after spending several months with him
searching for the source of the Nile, Stanley returned in triumph. In October 1872, two months before Smith's lecture,
Stanley was received by Queen Victoria, who graciously gave
him a gold snuffbox in thanks for his labors.

Ironically, the British obsession with finding the missing
doctor impeded Smith's earlier efforts to make his way East.
When he appealed to Henry Rawlinson for help in raising
funds, Rawlinson replied that he couldn't be of assistance as he
was too heavily involved in trying to raise money to find
Livingstone—a project "which I think is useless," Smith remarked in disgust in a letter to Layard, not long before news of
Stanley's success reached London. Yet as Smith's fame grew,
he became widely regarded as the archaeological equivalent of
Livingstone, discovering the sources of the Flood rather than
of the Nile. Smith's American publisher, Scribner, played up
the connection in the back of his *Assyrian Discoveries*, listing
several titles of related interest, including *Modern Doubt and
Christian Belief*, a book on *The Supernatural Origin of the
Bible*—and Stanley's recent bestseller, *How I Found Livingstone*. The identification persisted even in death: writing an
obituary of Smith for the *Times*, his friend A. H. Sayce noted,

"His name has become a household word among us, much as that of Dr. Livingstone; and I feel sure that the same sympathy that was aroused by the death of the great African traveller will be aroused also by the death of the great traveller and explorer in the Biblical lands and ancient Empires of the East."

Sayce was right to speak of Smith as a great explorer of "ancient" empires; the modern Middle East, on the other hand, baffled and frustrated him in many ways. As eager as Smith had been to follow Rawlinson and Layard's footsteps to Iraq, he was completely unprepared to deal with life in a radically foreign culture. He couldn't speak Arabic, Turkish, or Persian, and apart from a couple of brief research trips to Paris, he had probably never set foot outside England before leaving for Iraq in January 1873. He was about to confront a profoundly unfamiliar world.

Smith detailed his adventures in a book entitled *Assyrian Discoveries: An Account of Explorations and Discoveries on the Site of Nineveh, During 1873 and 1874*, published in 1875 in a handsome edition with dozens of engravings and a fold-out map showing his route across "Asiatic Turkey." Smith modeled his book on Layard's best-selling *Nineveh and Its Remains*, framing his excavation report in the popular modes of travelogue and imperial adventure tale. In the process, Smith cast himself as a kind of raider of the lost ark—Noah's Ark, in his case, rather than the Ark of the Covenant that Indiana Jones would one day pursue across the silver screen. A scholar rather than an adventurer at heart, Smith realized that this presentation had the best prospect of engaging not only his readers' interest but their financial support as well. He brought this agenda forward in his concluding chapter, as can be seen from the summary headings in the table of contents. "Difficulty of work.—Short time.—Good results," the headings begin encouragingly, going on to "New light on the Bible.—Origin of Babylonian civilization.—Turanian race.— Semitic conquest.—Flood legends.—Mythology.—Connection with Grecian mythology," before announcing the book's concluding theme: "Importance of future excavations."

Not reprinted since Smith's day, *Assyrian Discoveries* reveals both the fascination and the disquiet that foreign customs aroused in him. His sensibilities were challenged as early as Italy, where as a loyal English Protestant he was shocked at the sight of confession being openly practiced in church: "Service was then going on in the cathedral, but the point that seemed most painful to English eyes was the confessional,

George Smith, around 1874.

which was carried out during the service and in church."
Catholic monasticism seemed equally peculiar: seeing an iso-
lated monastery on a cliff, he remarks, "The feelings which
prompted men to build on these rugged rocks, and to inhabit
such lonely and inaccessible spots, must have been in marked
contrast to the spirit of intercourse and activity now so universal."

If Catholic southern Europe was alien to Smith, the Islamic Orient was completely disorienting. In the Turkish
city of Smyrna, his first Middle Eastern port of call, he was
jostled by crowds, upset by noise and confusion, and thrown
for a loop even by shish kebab: "Here and there were Eastern
refreshment houses, where natives were cooking dirty-looking
messes; one of these dishes appeared to me particularly re-
pulsive, it consisted of small portions of meat and intestines
of kids strung on skewers like cat's meat, and roasted before
a charcoal fire. This dainty appeared in particular request,
and the sellers were calling aloud to the passers-by not
to miss the opportunity of trying it, as it was then in perfection."

Dirt was everywhere, a deeply disagreeable fact for a fas-
tidious man. A main road was "nothing but one long mud-
pudding," and life aboard ship wasn't much better: in
Smyrna, "we took on board a number of Asiatics going on
pilgrimage; they travelled fourth class, living on the deck at
the fore part of the vessel: they were exceedingly devout and
equally filthy, and from the time they took possession we
avoided that part of the vessel." The very places where people
might get clean were sites of particular filth: in the town of
Hammum Ali, "people of both sexes bathe in the pool, of
which the water is of an inky colour, with lumps of bitumen
floating in it. The interior of the building round the pool has

been used as a convenience"—a toilet—"and is in a state of indescribable filthiness."

Hygiene aside, local customs rarely appealed to Smith. When he was treated to a banquet "served with the politeness and gravity of the East," the effect was soon spoiled by after-dinner entertainment involving "a series of coarse jokes," an exploding cigarette, and a seductive dance by an effeminate youth. The boy was robed in a faded dress, "fringed all round, flounced, and coloured red and blue. His movements were rather odd than graceful: he swung about, waving his arms, and rattling some little brass bells attached to his fingers, jumped, capered, and rocked his head backwards and forwards on his neck, as if it was loose on its joint. . . . I was glad when the entertainment came to an end, and I was able to retire to my couch."

A low point in Smith's travels came at a Syrian village whose inn "consisted simply of rough wooden rooms and benches, with a strong suspicion of vermin." After a miserable dinner and dreading an uncomfortable night to come, Smith and two fellow travelers were privately enlightened through a deceptive guest book:

> Yakub, the proprietor, brought to us a book, in which his various visitors had written their experience of this place. Yakub, who could not read, thought that these entries were all praise, and begged us to add some notice of our satisfaction to the collection. We took the book and looked it through; it was full of the richest and most appropriate remarks about the "hotel": one discoursed about the age of the fowls, another about the vermin; others gave

cautions to the travellers who might come
after; one advised his successors not to fall
through the holes in the floor, as they would be
astonished at the appearance of the apartment
below, another wrote that the place was comfortable, and the holes in the floor "very convenient." After inserting some remarks in this
book, Mr. Forbes left, and Mr. Kerr and myself commenced a battle with the fleas; ultimately our weariness got the better of us, and
we fell asleep.

Though Smith chafed at the discomforts of Eastern travel,
he loved the landscape and the sense of connection to the ancient history he had studied so long. As he traveled through remote villages on his way to the ruins of Nineveh, he was struck
by a sense of continuity with the past: he saw clay-brick houses
whose style he recognized from ancient reliefs and encountered a threshing machine "similar to those which are found in
prehistoric deposits. The use of such an instrument shows the
small amount of change produced by thousands of years in the
East." In a humorous vein, he rated his dinner at Yakub's inn
as an all-too-perfect example of a persisting antiquity: "The
single course consisted of a tough fowl that might have remembered the Assyrian empire."

Landscape and local lore combined to make Smith feel as
though he were almost in touch with Gilgamesh (or Izdubar)
himself:

Some of the scenery along the river is beautiful, the rocks especially are very fine, one of
them is crowned by the ruins of an old castle;

in another place, where the cliffs tower up straight out of the stream, there is a cave in the rocks attached to which is a curious legend. It is said that a griffin or monster in the old times lived in this cave, and took human victims from the surrounding districts. The wild desolation of the spot, the romantic and inaccessible position of the caves, combine to make this a fitting place for such a legend.

Passing this place on my raft, I watched the Tigris roaring and foaming round the fallen masses of rock at the foot of the cave, and I could not help remarking the striking similarity of this story to one of the Izdubar legends. I believe this is a modern version of this ancient story, and that the legend has been handed down in this country since the days of Izdubar.

Yet even the landscape had an ambiguous effect on Smith: after praising the "romantic" desolation of the scene in terms that Byron or Coleridge might have used, he admits to a growing unease: "The river was now rapidly rising, and its swelling, sweeping flood seemed almost the only thing of life in the whole picture, the cities which lined its banks are now most of them in ruins . . . the solitude of the scene, and the remembrance of the difference between the past and the present, have a depressing effect on the traveller, and he seems almost exiled from all the life and activity of the world."

Smith's uncertainties melted away as he finally approached his life's goal, the ruins of Nineveh outside the provincial capital of Mosul. On his last night before reaching the site, he was

too excited to wait until dawn before starting out: "Next day
(2nd of March) I started before sunrise, and arrived about nine
in the morning at the ruins of Nineveh. I cannot well describe
the pleasure with which I came in sight of this memorable city,
the object of so many of my thoughts and hopes." The ruined
city consisted of the vast, flat mounds whose featurelessness
had so moved Henry Layard when he first saw them. The
largest of these mounds, known as Kouyunjik, was forty feet
high and a mile long by a third of a mile wide. It was pitted
with various trenches and holes dug by Layard and Rassam
years before, when they had uncovered the palaces containing
Ashurbanipal's great library, along with more than two miles'
worth of sculptured reliefs.

Smith knew that Rassam hadn't been able to finish excavating the library in the "North Palace" built by Ashurbanipal, from which he thought the *Gilgamesh* tablets with their
Flood story had probably come. He had sold the idea of the
expedition to the *Daily Telegraph* on the rather slender hope
that he might be able to find a missing piece of the Flood
tablet, some three inches on a side, which should still be lurking among the tons of accumulated rubble at the site. Yet he
had to know that this quest would be as hard as looking for a
needle in a haystack, or even a straw in a haystack. The fragment of baked clay would be almost indistinguishable from
the masses of rubble around it, even supposing it hadn't been
pulverized in antiquity or tossed out by Rassam's men during
the excavations twenty-two years earlier.

Actually, the difficulty of the quest was a positive advantage for Smith: the longer the missing piece stayed missing,
the more excavating he could do. He had a *firman*, or decree,
from the Ottoman government authorizing him to excavate
for up to a year. The *Daily Telegraph*'s thousand guineas

wouldn't last that long, but he could hope for a new infusion of funds from the British Museum if he started making significant finds. Since he had already had extraordinary good fortune in discovering most of the Flood tablet in the museum's collection, he really didn't need lightning to strike twice; he was now just as eager to unearth historical and administrative tablets that would help him clear up gaps in his growing understanding of Assyrian history.

Smith wanted to begin digging the day he arrived, but he was delayed by local officials. Suspicious of his purposes or desiring bribes, they refused to accept his firman allowing him to dig. He had to travel two hundred miles down the Tigris to Baghdad to straighten things out, on the way passing through Saddam Hussein's future birthplace, Tikrit, "a miserable-looking town." On returning with his authority confirmed, he hired laborers from Mosul and surrounding villages and began to enlarge Rassam's old pit at the site of the library, setting other groups to work at likely spots where tablets or sculptures might be found. His men worked in groups of six or seven, one or two doing the digging, one or two filling baskets with rubble, and the others carrying the baskets to a dumping ground. All was chaos and confusion at the site, and not only because of the ancient trauma of the palace's destruction. Hormuzd Rassam's methods had been highly unsystematic, and in addition the pit had been used more recently as a quarry for stone, so ancient walls had been torn apart and new rubble added on top of the old. Work began at the site on May 7, 1873, and, remarkably in just a week lightning did strike again: Smith found a scrap of tablet containing the missing part of the Flood story. He telegraphed word of his find back to the *Daily Telegraph*, giving Edwin Arnold the scoop he wanted, and his feat was reported in newspaper stories around the globe.

It is appropriate that the recovery of this ancient text was announced to the world by the most modern of means. The world's first telecommunications system, commercial telegraphy had been pioneered by Samuel Morse in the 1840s. It came into wide use around the world in the 1860s, and the first successful transatlantic telegraph line was laid in 1866, just seven years before the *Daily Telegraph* sent Smith to Iraq. On the day that Smith made his great discovery, the *New York Times* ran an article reflecting on this convergence of ancient and modern modes of communication: "It is hardly possible to conceive of two more opposite literary productions than the modern newspaper and the crumbling and mysterious records found among the ruins of antiquity. . . . There is something startling in associating the two together, in thrusting them into sudden and unexpected juxtaposition; and this is what has just been done by a London journal, which has sent Mr. GEORGE SMITH, the well-known archaeologist, to puzzle out the antique inscriptions of Assyria." The ancient tablets were joining forces with the latest technology as they circulated out into the world.

Smith described his find in *Assyrian Discoveries* in sober scholarly terms—no running about, no undressing:

> On the 14th of May my friend, Mr. Charles Kerr, whom I had left at Aleppo, visited me at Mosul, and as I rode into the khan where I was staying, I met him. After mutual congratulations I sat down to examine the store of fragments of cuneiform inscription from the day's digging, taking out and brushing off the earth from the fragments to read their contents. On cleaning one of them I found to my surprise

and gratification that it contained the greater portion of seventeen lines of inscription belonging to the first column of the Chaldean account of the Deluge, and fitting into the only place where there was a serious blank in the story. When I had first published the account of this tablet I had conjectured that there were about fifteen lines wanting in this part of the story, and now with this portion I was enabled to make it nearly complete.

Smith is almost excessively matter-of-fact here—he was famous for his modesty, and once blushed to the roots of his hair when a woman asked him if she could shake hands with "the *great* Mr. Smith." Yet Smith's account carries fascinating historical and imperial resonances. Having triumphed over corrupt Ottoman officials to begin his excavation, Smith found the lost fragment shortly after he unearthed "half of a curious tablet copied from a Babylonian original, giving warnings to kings and judges of the evils which would follow the neglect of justice in the country." All too appropriately, this Babylonian text would have been broken apart by the Babylonians themselves in 612 BCE, when they stormed Nineveh and sacked its palaces.

As his workmen dug further into the library's ruins, Smith found the other half of the tablet on misrule, and almost as though a magic key had been fitted into a lock, the missing Flood fragment suddenly appeared. Its discovery was made in a social as well as a political context. In describing the scene, Smith uses impersonal language ("On removing some of these stones . . . there appeared") that avoids mentioning his native laborers. In their place appears Smith's visiting friend

Charles Kerr—his companion in suffering at Yakub's ill-favored inn—and the great discovery is made immediately after the "mutual congratulations" of the two Englishmen as they are reunited. Rescued from the wreckage of ancient history and modern misrule, the cuneiform tablet finds a very English audience ready to take it up and carry it off to its new imperial home.

❋

Smith's return to England took place much sooner than he wished. To his deep regret, as soon as he announced his quick find of the Flood passage, the *Daily Telegraph* recalled him, perfidiously altering the phrasing of his telegram to suggest that Smith had chosen to end his mission. Still fuming over this deception two years later, Smith protested in *Assyrian Discoveries*, "from some error unknown to me, the telegram as published differs materially from the one I sent. In particular, in the published copy occurs the words 'as the season is closing,' which led to the inference that I considered that the proper season for excavating was coming to an end. My own feeling was the contrary of this, and I did not send this." As it happens, the fragment Smith so rapidly found wasn't from *Gilgamesh* at all but was the opening of a still older version of the Flood story. Had he realized this, Smith might have been able to argue that his assignment hadn't been completed, even though he had gotten what he was sent to find, the opening of the story.

Ordered home, Smith faced the difficulty of getting there. Violence was flaring up around Mosul, with warfare between rival Arab tribes; refugees were streaming around the mounds where Smith was digging. Smith was oddly unperturbed by these events. He regarded the region's violence as a feature of the landscape, even a point of continuity with ancient times: "The hand of the wandering Arab is to-day, as ever, against every man's hand, and their hand against his," he remarks, reading the culture around him through biblical spectacles: he is paraphrasing the Bible's depiction of Ishmael, Abraham's rejected son, father of the Arab peoples (Genesis 16:12).

Smith reserved his outrage for the Turkish government's refusal to protect the antiquities in the lands under its rule. Modern warfare was actually less destructive to his sites than everyday life, since for centuries the local villagers had been mining the old mounds to extract stones and bricks for their own building projects. At the ruins of Babylon, "I used to see this work going on as it had gone on for centuries, Babylon thus slowly disappearing, without an effort being made to ascertain the dimensions and buildings of the city, or recover what remains of its monuments." Meanwhile, "the Turkish officials, while always ready to oppose researches and prevent the discovery or removal of monuments, never hinder the natives from destroying antiquities."

Smith's hostility toward the Turkish officials was matched only by their growing suspicion of him. Indifferent toward the ancient history of the lands they were occupying, and even less interested in parallels with the Bible, the officials Smith dealt with simply couldn't believe he was genuinely interested in the shattered clay tablets he showed them. He finally got permission to leave Mosul, at the head of a caravan of mules laden with boxes full of his precious tablets, but then he was stopped in Aleppo by customs officials who tried to impound his collection.

Smith produced his firman proving his right to the antiquities, but the officials insisted that he unpack them all for inspection. "The Turkish officers laughed at the appearance of the old fragments of inscriptions, and called them rubbish, making fun at the idea of taking care of such things." They then gave Smith a letter authorizing the goods to be cleared at the Mediterranean port of Alexandretta, "but although the things were worthless in their eyes, they could not resist the temptation to play me false, and I found later, on presenting my letter, that it was an order to seize my boxes. . . . The Turkish officials having made me the bearer of a letter directed against myself."

"Such was the conduct of the Turkish officials," Smith remarks with asperity, "to the agent of a nation which had been foremost in upholding Turkey." Smith had to sail in July 1873 without his treasures; they were released weeks later, after the British ambassador in Constantinople intervened, and were safely shipped to England. Consumed with indignation in recalling this episode, Smith fails to note the poetic justice of the situation: the guests' trick on the illiterate innkeeper Yakub of writing insults in the guest book was mirrored by the customs officials' reliance on Smith's own inability to read Turkish or Arabic. The world's greatest living authority on cuneiform writing was caught in a web of scripts he couldn't read. Thanks to the ambassador's help, there were no disastrous consequences this time out, but the comedy of errors would not stay comic for long.

CHAPTER 2

EARLY FAME AND
SUDDEN DEATH

Landing place with ferryboats on the Tigris at Mosul.

BACK in London, Smith found himself famous. The *Daily Telegraph* had run articles trumpeting

"THE DAILY TELEGRAPH" ASSYRIAN EXPEDITION
COMPLETE SUCCESS OF EXCAVATIONS
THE MISSING PORTION OF THE DELUGE TABLET DISCOVERED.

The *Daily Telegraph* and many other papers ran follow-up articles on "the well-known explorer" or "the distinguished Assyriologue," as Smith was now anointed in the press. He was suddenly in demand as a speaker, and the British Museum experienced an upsurge in attendance in its Near Eastern galleries. As Smith had hoped, the acclaim surrounding his Stanley-and-Livingstone success finally induced the museum's trustees to provide further funds—which they set at a prosaic thousand pounds, rather than the more elegant thousand guineas Arnold had given. Smith left London in November 1873, determined to make the most of the several months that his firman still allowed for excavation.

Enjoying his new stature as one of England's leading archaeologists, he took to his renewed explorations with gusto. Though he deeply missed his family, his letters to his wife overflow with excitement over his adventures and discoveries. "I have all sorts of treasures," he wrote to Mary after several months of work, "historical, mythological, architectural &c &c. I expect to bring home from 3,000 to 4,000 objects, you must come to the Museum and see them, it will be nothing to me if you do not share my success." Looking forward to his return home, he confided, "I do not come by Paris this time and cannot bring you a present, but I bring my noble and glorious self that will be the best present in the world. My face is in all the glory of whiskers and moustaches and resembles a good stiff broom with the bristles turned the wrong way." He had thought of shaving it all off, "but I remembered your taste for such billygoat's appendages and spared them for your sake."

Writing regularly and at length, he continually begged for letters in return from Mary. Few replies reached him, partly because mail delivery was erratic but also because she rarely wrote, either because she was overwhelmed in caring for their six children or because she felt awkward as a writer. Probably having had even less formal education than her husband, she may have been a little intimidated by his superb grammar and penmanship, honed during his years as an engraver; he did have a weakness for run-on sentences, but he wrote a lovely italic hand, with never a blot and almost never a crossing-out.

Smith continually sent love and kisses to "the little cherubs," Charley, Fred, Cissie, Arthur—nicknamed "Twopenny"— Bertie, and "Effel." He asked after the older children's studies and the younger ones' progress in walking and talking (Ethel was obviously pronouncing her name with a lisp). To amuse them he often drew comic sketches: his seasickness when crossing the English Channel, "Papa off to Assyria" on horseback brandishing a sword, or precariously perched atop a camel.

As attached as he remained to thoughts of his distant family, Smith made the most of his second trip, including the opportunity to live in a higher style than he ever could at home. He dined with ambassadors in Constantinople, wealthy travelers in Aleppo, and military officers in Baghdad, and even at his mound outside Mosul he was able to make a comfortable home away from home. He built a house near the site, marking out its foundations and then directing its construction, and he had an English servant who was an excellent cook. "I have wished you were with me today," he wrote Mary not long after his arrival. "We live capitally and Joseph says he is sure the Prince of Wales could not live better—we have splendid venison, ducks, tongues and every delicacy, with milk, cream and coffee in abundance—we have ceased work at the mound until the weather improves and have nothing to do but pamper our appetites. I shall return as fat as a pig and a good deal saucier." He ended the letter by saying that "I hear our dinner quacking."

Pets provided something of a substitute family: "I have

The final page of one of George Smith's letters home to his wife, Mary, in 1875, written in Constantinople. Signing himself "Your loving hubby," Smith sketches himself galloping off to Assyria, sword in hand, pursued by two of the stray dogs that were always lounging around Constantinople's streets.

kept no end of pets, a tortoise, some bats, lizards and now a little hare, he is a very pretty little fellow, and we feed him on milk as he is too young to eat, he runs about the room, and hides himself in Joseph's or my bed, Joseph pulls him about quite as much as any child." Smith closed by asking Mary to "kiss all my little pets at home, and many for yourself." Though he missed his family, he hardly seemed to miss England, writing that he intended to delay his return home in order to avoid the chilly English winter—not the most tactful announcement to make to a young wife cooped up with six children in a raw English February. But Smith was quite unself-conscious in his enjoyment of his surroundings, and he was developing a taste for the unaccustomed pleasures of colonial power. "Except that I have not you with me," he wrote Mary, "I am as much at home as in England and like it a good bit better and I can here do as I like and have power and influence."

The local officials he dealt with, however, were not pleased to have Smith doing as he pleased. Convinced that he must have spirited away some ancient treasure on his first trip, they delayed his work with a succession of bureaucratic road-blocks. In the end, they impounded several hundred tablets, and Smith had to return home with much less than he had found. In his 1925 *Rise and Progress of Assyriology*, the British Museum curator Wallis Budge was inclined to lay the blame at Smith's own feet. "His guileless soul did not understand the use of *Bakshîsh*," according to Budge; the local governor (pasha) needed to supplement his erratic income by such informal fees:

> No salary had been paid him for many months and he wanted money. He expected Smith to buy back the tablets that he took from him; but Smith did not do so, and now no one knows what became of them. The loss of these tablets is much to be regretted, and it might so easily have been avoided. Smith would not take the advice of the French Consul, who implored him to "make an arrangement" with the Pâshâ, who did not want the tablets and had no means

by which to send them to Constantinople. But
Smith never understood the native mind or native ways.

Budge may have a point, though anyone who speaks so confi-
dently of "the native mind" may himself have a limited grasp
of complex colonial situations. Smith did in fact grudgingly
pay baksheesh on at least some occasions, but the conflict
seems to have spiraled beyond the reach of ordinary bribery.

The core of the dispute was that Smith expected to take
home almost everything he found, while the pasha insisted
that Smith give the government half of the artifacts. Matters
were made worse when Hormuzd Rassam, the site's first excavator, appeared in Mosul during this time, visiting his family
there. Rassam agreed to advise the pasha on a fair division of
the finds. He and Smith had been on cool terms for some time,
with Rassam regarding himself as the seasoned excavator and
Smith as an amateur at fieldwork. Rassam had been disappointed that the *Daily Telegraph*'s editor had sent Smith to
find the balance of the Flood story in Rassam's old trenches,
after first broaching the idea with Rassam himself. Smith was
enjoying his sudden, newspaper-driven fame as a prominent
archaeologist and explorer, and felt he had every right to
press his opportunities to the fullest. As Smith wrote to his
wife in a passionate run-on sentence, "The Pacha is determined to have half my antiquities and has appointed my bitter enemy Hormuzd Rassam as his agent to divide the things,
he is calculating most securely on his gain and thinking only a
few days separate him from his object but I did not come here
to be made a fool of by him or Hormuzd, either."

Rassam's role in helping the pasha confiscate tablets must
have particularly infuriated Smith because he had been col-

lecting tablets and fragments that Rassam had missed twenty years before. Dividing up half the items before they were even studied would undercut the whole purpose of his expedition, to piece fragments together into coherent wholes and to identify multi-tablet sequences. As the dispute simmered on, Smith's anger at Rassam mounted, and on top of everything else, his servant got into some scrape that only made the situation more tense. As he wrote to Mary:

> The incaution of Joseph has involved me in a serious difficulty the details of which I cannot send to you now. Before you receive this all will be settled for if the English government does not support me in the meantime I shall sacrifice the collection and leave this place, the abandonment of myself by our government has been most scandalous and most of my difficulties have arisen from their want of support—my little hare is dead I had so many troubles that it got neglected.

Bereft even of his favorite pet, Smith began to think of resigning his post at the museum, a remarkable prospect for him to contemplate after all he'd gone through to achieve his position. He ended the letter by assuring his wife: "Trust me I will fall on my feet wherever I am thrown, and I am determined I will not incur any more worry for people who do not deserve it."

✳

There is no question that Smith exacerbated his difficulties by his characteristic impatience, even pigheadedness, but it is clear as well that Rassam and the British Museum were slighting him, and he felt such slights keenly. Then, too, political and cultural tensions were mounting throughout Iraq at this time. A new pasha had been installed in Baghdad and unlike his predecessor took a strong and suspicious interest in Smith's work—a suspicion only increased, to Smith's surprise, by familiarity with European culture: "I was told that Rajid Pacha understood French and was acquainted with something of European civilization, but instead of learning from the West I was informed that his policy at Baghdad was hostile to all foreigners." The pasha was further emboldened by reports that Smith was not in fact an agent of the British government at all but "only a newspaper correspondent and he might do as he liked with me."

Smith tried to stand his ground by relying on the letter of the law: he repeatedly pointed out that his firman from Constantinople said nothing of dividing up the finds, and he stressed that in any event his goal was not sculptures but clay tablets, which would have no value to the Turks. In an attempt at compromise, he offered to take the officials into his trenches and point out any large sculptures he might come upon, so that they could excavate them once he had completed his work. "At this reasoning the Turks laughed; they said they did not understand antiquities, and if I pointed anything out I should point out worthless things to them and they must have half the things I collected to make sure they had good ones." The meeting ended with both sides dissatisfied, "and from that time I was subject to perpetual annoyance."

Writing to Mary about his difficulties, Smith used language of open combat: "I have had a hard fight here for the governor of the country and the Pacha have set their heads

against me but I am carrying my will against them. . . . They
however have made a mistake in opposing me and I know I
shall have the victory." Smith didn't employ such belligerent
terms in print, yet in the preface to *Assyrian Discoveries* he
suggests the larger political stakes involved in his archaeological work, linking his difficulties with those encountered by
Christian missionaries in the region: "I have not the smallest
doubt that in the government of Asia the Turks are not alive
to their own interests, and particularly in the oppressive laws
and persecution of the Christians. The American missions in
Asiatic Turkey are doing a noble work in the country, but
they can only be useful in proportion to the amount of official
support they receive from England and America." Smith
pointedly noted that the British presence in Iraq was less
than that of their rivals the French, adding that "it is extremely unfortunate that in the wide extent of country between Aleppo and Baghdad there is not a single British
representative."

Though Smith had to leave a good number of tablets behind, he arrived home in early June 1874 with a large collection. He began to decipher the full Flood story and the epic in
which it appeared. Though the Flood occupies only one of
the epic's twelve tablets, Smith entitled his translation *The
Chaldean Account of the Deluge,* so as to capitalize on public
interest in the epic's early version of the Noah story. Working
at a furious pace, he published his translation at the end of
1874, and the next year he finished no fewer than four more
books, including his 450-page *Assyrian Discoveries* and a
large collection of translations of all the major literary texts
he had found. No longer able to link this more varied group of

texts to the Flood story alone, he simply expanded his biblical frame, titling his new book *The Chaldean Account of Genesis: Containing the Description of the Creation, the Fall of Man, the Deluge, the Tower of Babel, the Times of the Patriarchs, and Nimrod; Babylonian Fables, and Legends of the Gods; from the Cuneiform Inscriptions.*

Smith's treatment of *Gilgamesh* was informed by his political concerns. He read "the Chaldean account of the Deluge" not only for its parallels to the Bible, but also in terms of nineteenth-century European ideals of national identity. As he began to reconstruct the body of the epic leading up to the flood narrative, Smith sought a unifying theme in Gilgamesh's adventures. Smith believed that Gilgamesh was the same person as Nimrod, identified in Genesis 10 as Noah's great-grandson. The Bible describes him as a mighty hunter and founder of Babylon, Nineveh, and Erech—the biblical name for Uruk, Gilgamesh's city. Smith decided that the epic must have been "a national poem to the Babylonians, similar in some respects to those of Homer among the Greeks. Izdubar [Gilgamesh] himself was often afterwards esteemed a deity, and at Nineveh I found part of a tablet with a prayer addressed to him."

So far, so good, but what was this national epic really about? Smith located the heart of the epic in Gilgamesh's journey to a distant cedar forest in Tablet 5, where he and his companion Enkidu defeat a demon called Humbaba. Piecing this account together as best he could, Smith saw Humbaba not as a monster but as a king who had invaded the region and oppressed its people. "It appears that Izdubar did not assume the crown until after he had slain the tyrant Humbaba, and this leads to the conclusion that it was Humbaba, or at least the race to which he belonged, that conquered and tyrannized over Erech and probably over the whole of Babylonia . . . the death of the oppressor being the signal for the proclamation of Babylonian freedom and the reign of Izdubar." Smith was completely wrong in this reading. Humbaba is no invading tyrant but a solitary giant, living alone in his Cedar Forest and oppressing no one, least of all Gilgamesh's subjects in distant Uruk. Gilgamesh is the ruler of his city from the very outset, and defeating Humbaba has no effect on his political status: he ends the epic as he began, not a "national" hero but the ruler of his own local city-state. There were no nations at all in Mesopotamia, in the modern sense, but larger or smaller social units: empires, city-states, and nomadic tribes.

Though it was fundamentally mistaken, Smith's interpretation was nonetheless a brilliant piece of detective work, building plausibly on external evidence to help him make sense of the fragmentary text before him. His writings are full of discoveries that have stood the test of time, often involving intuitive leaps beyond the literal surface of the text. His accomplishment is all the more impressive given that he built some of his interpretations on guesses about words that no one had ever deciphered, in lines that often were only fragments of their full selves. In *The Chaldean Account of Genesis*, Smith begins his chapter "Destruction of the Tyrant Humbaba" by frankly acknowledging, "I have had considerable difficulty in writing this chapter; in fact I have arranged the matter now three times, and such is the wretched broken condition of the fragments that I am even now uncertain if I have the correct order." The chapter has some connected passages, but many others that look like this:

George Smith's photograph of the major piece of the Flood story tablet,
c. 1873.

  7. Humbaba . . . .

  8. he did not come . . . .

  9. he did not . . . .

     (Seven lines lost.)

  17. heavy . . . .

  18. Heabani opened his mouth . . . .

  19. . . . . Humbaba in . . . .

  20. . . . . one by one and . . . .

     (Many other broken lines.)

Where Smith had reasonably well-preserved tablets to work with, he was often able to produce highly accurate translations. First he would transcribe the cramped characters, and then he would determine what syllable each character represented; next, he would fashion a word-by-word translation, as with the following description of Uta-napishtim's reaction when the rain has ended and he sees the devastation wrought by the Flood:

uk - tam - mi - is - ma	at - ta - šab	a - bak - ki
crouching down,	I sat,	I wept

eli	dūr	ap - pi - ia	il - la - ka	di - ma - a - a
on	wall	of my nose	streaming	tears

Rendering this into polished English, Smith translated this passage as: "I sat down and wept, over my face flowed my tears."

One of Smith's most admirable traits was his constant effort to improve his understanding and to revise or discard theories as necessary. As he says at the end of *The Chaldean Account of Genesis* concerning his theories about the epic: "I have changed my own opinions many times, and I have no doubt that any accession of new material would change again my views respecting the parts affected by it . . . for certainly in cuneiform matters we have often had to advance through error to truth." His reconstruction was a tour de force, certainly more successful than any other scholar of his generation could have achieved, yet the text's very obscurity aided him in conforming the work both to biblical history and to

modern national concerns, constructing Gilgamesh as the
king who had given the Babylonians "that unity without which
they were powerless as a nation."

George Smith was now at the height of his career and at
the peak of his powers, with ambitious plans to write a long
series of books on Assyrian and Babylonian history and culture. He had left Iraq, moreover, vowing never to return, and
could very well have spent thirty years working at the British
Museum with his thousands of tablets, with no need ever to
venture abroad again. Yet he was nagged by the sense of opportunities not yet taken for further discoveries. Popular interest in his finds continued unabated, and when the museum
decided to mount a third expedition at the end of 1875, he
agreed to make one final trip out. Hooked as he was on the
thrill of archaeological discovery and the pleasures of colonial
life, it is hard to imagine that this would really have been his
last trip. Hard to imagine, except for one thing: this third
trip killed him.

The fullest account of this fatal expedition has always
been the one given in 1925 by Wallis Budge in *The Rise and
Progress of Assyriology*. Budge says that Smith traveled out
with a Scandinavian archaeologist named Eneberg, whose
limitations matched his own:

> The truth is that no two men who were called
> upon by Fate to travel in Mesopotamia, con-
> sidering what travel was in those days, were
> ever more unfitted for their work. Both were
> enthusiastic, excitable, and optimistic; and
> both were sadly chafed in mind by the petty

daily annoyances of the natives, and by their
difficulty in obtaining food and good sleeping
accommodation. Smith had little Arabic, and
Eneberg's Arabic was that of the Kur'ân,
which does not help a man in buying dates,
sugar and bread, or in chaffering with greedy
natives about the hire of camels and asses.

Smith encountered months of delay, first in Constantinople to get his firman authorizing his work, and then in getting
it honored in Mosul. Interestingly, an obituary article in the
London *Times* suggests that Smith's own books may have con-
tributed to his difficulties: the article says that Smith was
"not a favorite with the Ottoman authorities, owing to certain
strictures upon their misrule in his books. . . . At every turn
he was baited with the most pettifogging quirks and scruples
as to the meaning of the Imperial concessions, until he could
bear it no longer and resolved to return home." In the notebooks from his journey, Smith's fractured jottings in Constantinople succinctly convey the frustration of weeks of
evasions and obscure delays, tactics the Ottoman government
had honed to a fine art over the centuries. Even a single entry
speaks volumes:

Firman . . . ask aid, promise books—dragoman
leaves, apply at embassy—nothing done—
promise of Turks—telegraph Baghdad & Mosul,
2nd teleg.—renewed applic.—promise telegr.
again . . . delays—propose law of 1876. Turkish law, French travel—I object, refuse to
sign—Firman offered, dispute new promises—
offer to give up sculptures—Grand Vizier's

promise—tablets free—sculptures at valua-
tion . . . . agree—renewed difficulties.

He finally got permission to go to dig, but his travels east
through Syria and Iraq were greatly delayed by civil unrest
and spreading disease. Tragically, his companion Eneberg
died of cholera as they were heading down to Baghdad. When
Smith reached Mosul he encountered still more bureaucratic
obstructions, and by the time he was allowed to start digging
it was July and the heat was too intense for excavations to
proceed. Smith gave up in frustration, having collected only a
single trunk's worth of items. According to Budge:

> Weary and disappointed, he left Môsul at the
> end of July, and set out for Aleppo. In spite of
> the warnings of the French Vice-Consul and
> of natives experienced in travelling, he in-
> sisted on marching during the day, which no
> native ever does in the summer; and he tried to
> live on the coarse hard bread-cakes of the
> country and dates, like the natives. I was told
> in Môsul in 1888 that he was badly provisioned
> for the journey, and that he had no medicines
> with him.

Budge's explanation has been the received account for the
past eighty years, often cited in the brief discussions of Smith
that dot the literature on Middle Eastern archaeology. It is
inadequate at best. Budge's basic approach is to blame the victim, in terms very much in keeping with his overall portrait
of the naive young Smith. Budge begins this episode with the
statement "Smith never understood the native mind or native

ways," adding, "and his inability to do so in the end cost him his life." Can this be the whole story?

It is known that Smith died suddenly of dysentery in a Syrian village while on his way home from this trip, but the question remains why this intestinal disorder would have felled a man in his mid-thirties blessed with an iron constitution. It is unlikely that Budge was right to imagine that eating pita bread and dates hastened Smith's death—what better to eat, in the desert, than Bedouin staples?— but there is some plausibility in the theory that Smith weakened himself by traveling by day: dehydration, or even sunstroke, would then have been contributing factors. Indeed, traveling through Syria on his second trip, Smith had found the heat in this area to be particularly troublesome: "This region is so shut in by mountains that the air seems still and oppressive, and on this day the sun appeared to give an intense heat here, which was difficult to bear; the air seemed luminous, and floated in waves before the eyes, while any little wind that arose appeared as if it came from an oven."

The only problem with Budge's theory is that it is wrong. Smith traveled mostly at night during the hot months; in one of several published passages on the pleasures of night riding, he says, "The road here at this time of year is excellent, and the riding by night enjoyable. . . . During these nightly rides I enjoyed magnificent views of the heavens; Venus rose each morning like a lamp, and all the stars had a brilliancy with which people in northern climes are not familiar." In the final surviving letter to his wife, written as he began his fatal journey home, Smith specifically remarked, "The weather is so hot that we cannot go out in the day and having to travel at night our progress is slow and I feel the fatigue very much."

What, then, brought about Smith's death? One factor was surely the disease itself, which deserves more credit, or blame, than Budge gives it. In its virulent bacterial form, known today as shigellosis, dysentery is a dangerous illness, and its causes and treatment were poorly understood until the end of the nineteenth century; it was the leading cause of death in the American Civil War. How would Smith have acquired shigellosis? Probably not from a common source, vegetables grown in dung, because he was—wisely—eating bread and dates. Another source is water tainted by fecal matter, and in his field notebooks Smith spoke of the unsanitary water he was encountering on this final journey: "Cross river mules & donkeys to Baghdad, cesspools fetid smells dead animals green & red water foul state of district."

Smith's unlikely career had come about because he happened to be just the right person at the right time and place; he died because he was caught at just the wrong time and place. A few years later scientists realized that cholera and dysentery are caused by bacteria that can be killed by boiling water; if Smith had known to take what soon became an elementary precaution, he likely would have reached home alive.

Smith's difficulties were compounded by a host of problems brewing around him: there was tribal warfare in the north, rioting in several cities, the cholera in central Iraq that had killed Eneberg, and plague in the south. The reason Smith was making the difficult midsummer ride through the desert was that plague quarantine had stopped him from taking the simpler way out, down the Tigris from Baghdad and then home by steamer. He would have had to cool his heels for some weeks while waiting out the quarantine, and he would have been housed with many travelers from plague-ridden areas. Smith judged that the quarantine lodgings were the like-

liest place of all for the plague to spread, and so he opted to
chance the overland route instead.

Smith had begun to get word of these problems as he
first approached Iraq in March. Writing home to Mary from
Aleppo in Syria, he tried to make light of cholera and plague,
though as usual his prose accelerates as he gets wound up:

> The plague is sweeping part of the very district
> I ought to visit; now do not be alarmed, you are
> not aware that the plague was in the country
> when I was here last although then it was not
> spreading so fast but as it is I am very cautious
> although there is no real danger, I have stopped
> my journey & remain for the present at Aleppo
> to see how it goes—people here are alarmed and
> naturally so for last year they lost in this city
> 8,000 people out of a population of 100,000 by
> cholera, that however has disappeared.

Clearly realizing the panic this information could cause in his
wife, he added—now throwing all punctuation to the winds—
"I tell you these things because you ought to be my confidant
and I should not hide anything from you but do not have
unreasonable fears I never run any danger but I shall have
considerable difficulty from these causes and they may even
suspend my journey."

These problems would certainly have left anyone "sadly
chafed in mind," as Budge put it, but Smith's letters reveal
that his spirits were further depressed by still another cause:
the recent death of an infant child. Writing from Constantinople after his arrival there at the start of the expedition, Smith
speaks of arranging for a headstone, then as the memories well

up he abruptly changes the subject to clothing purchases: "I will see about our little pet's stone. I never forget him, I see his little cradle put away in my room just as it was in those bitter days when he lay dead. I often dream of him but I do not like to write about it—If you have to get my outfit I will pay you the money by check."

In Smith's mentally fragile condition, he may not have been exercising the best judgment in his anxiety to get home. Yet still other factors were at work. Some can be seen from the eyewitness account of an English dentist, John Parsons, who was in Aleppo when Smith took sick on his way back through Syria in August. Smith had an assistant with him, Peter Matthewson by name; as Smith weakened, he gradually became unable to ride his horse, and they halted at a village called Ikisji, forty miles from Aleppo. Matthewson then rode ahead to Aleppo, where he encountered the dentist Parsons, the closest thing to an English-speaking doctor he could find. Parsons went to Ikisji with Matthewson and did what little he could for Smith, then helped transport him in a conveyance called a tatravan, a kind of mule-drawn sedan chair used to allow women to travel in secluded comfort. They got Smith to Aleppo, where he died shortly after arriving in town. Parsons was making an extended Middle Eastern tour, and he wrote of his experiences in a book-length manuscript entitled *Travels in Persia and Turkey in Asia*. Never published, this narrative now resides in the British Library's manuscript collection, and it includes ten pages describing Smith's final days.

Parsons's manuscript could easily have been buried in the archives, forever unknown to anyone interested in George Smith. It was saved from this fate by the efforts of several library employees, working over the course of the twentieth century. In June 1918, some years after the manuscript was given to the library, a cataloger named "G.J.E." read through all 464 pages, and noticed the ten pages on Smith's death; he or she then made a cross-reference on an index card. Seventy-five years later, a restorer named "D.N." repaired several pages with laminate and "mylar coated with texi-cryl," carefully noting these substances for the benefit of any future restorer. Then at some quite recent date, a cataloger transferred G.J.E.'s cross-reference to the library's electronic database, making it possible for a contemporary researcher to learn of its existence. This is the kind of attention that generations of the British Library's staff have expended on tens of thousands of documents in their care; Parsons's narrative is number 39,300 in the library's "Additional Manuscripts" collection. The library's catalogers and restorers had no way to know whether anyone would ever benefit from their attentiveness to an obscure dentist's unpublished travelogue, and quite likely no one ever has before now, but thanks to their work a direct window can be opened onto Smith's final days.

Parsons was no specialist in infectious diseases, but he thought that Smith could have recovered with proper food and care. In his manuscript he says that Smith was so consumed with his mission that he hadn't taken proper care of himself, but Parsons's real emphasis lies elsewhere. His explanation? *Blame the Bulgarian.* When Matthewson took him to Ikisji, Parsons was shocked to find Smith lying feverish on the floor of a hut, with no bedding other than a blanket, no food, and only "a small tin etna to boil a little water with, and about a handful of tea"—named after the volcano, an etna was a portable burner. Parsons couldn't believe that any

true Englishman would leave his comrade in such circumstances and was shocked to learn that Matthewson had taken
ample supplies with him for his ride into Aleppo, together
with much better bedding than he had left for Smith. The
mystery was solved, however, when the dying Smith informed Parsons "that Mr. M was *not* an Englishman at all,
but a _Bulgarian_." Parsons concludes the story of Smith's
death by stating soberly, "I consider he was sacrificed to the
negligence of his Bulgarian Assistant."

It is hard to know what to make of this theory. "Peter
Matthewson" is hardly a Slavic name, and Smith's letters and
notebooks are silent on his nationality. Parsons took Matthewson for an Englishman until the moment of Smith's revelation, or at least until he heard something from the dying man
that he could interpret in such a way as to relieve his wounded
national pride. (Could Smith have described Matthewson as
"vulgar," or "a vulgarian"?) Whatever Matthewson's national
origin was, Parsons shows that Smith suffered in part from
the negligence of his traveling companion. Perhaps Matthewson was remorseful at having left Smith so poorly supplied;
Parsons reports that as they headed off to Ikisji, "the cook at
the consulate had put into my hand 2 or 3 mutton cutlets,
which Mr. Matthewson did not wish shd. be eaten, remarking,
that Smith would like a little meat perhaps."

Matthewson may have been remorseful, but Parsons was
anxious to deflect blame from any English source, and this
would later be Wallis Budge's strategy as well in *The Rise
and Progress of Assyriology*. Yet one indisputably English
culprit does emerge from the museum's archives: the British
Museum itself. It turns out that as the delays and difficulties
mounted, Smith decided to cut his losses and come home

early. The romance of imperial adventure had faded away, as
he wrote to Mary:

> I do not enjoy my stay here, although I live
> well I am certainly thin, and often I feel I
> would sooner have cold mutton!!! at home than
> be here, the truth is I do not do very well as a
> single man, I have been married too long, it
> was all very well in the first expedition, but
> the gilt was soon off the gingerbread and if I
> had not been pledged I would not have come
> now. . . . Kiss all our pets and tell them Papa
> will soon come back and look one of these days
> to see my cab drive up to the door. If I am suc-
> cessful this year I will come home in July and
> leave the excavations in charge of my assistant
> who is a very good and likely party.

Smith then wrote to the museum, announcing this plan; the
letter hasn't survived, but the museum's reply did. Writing in
the tone one might use to scold a lazy servant, the secretary of
the museum, McAllister Jones, expressed his surprise that
Smith would consider leaving his post prematurely. "This the
Trustees consider to be very objectionable," Jones wrote. "It is
not stated that Mr. Matthewson's labours would be equally efficient with your own, and if not equally efficient it is clear
that such excavating ought not to be left to his superinten-
dence excepting in cases of absolute necessity. The Trustees
will be glad to receive your explanation for this."

Jones tried to close in a more sympathetic vein, though
even here a note of reproof creeps in:

> I am very sorry to hear from your last letter that
> the plague is increasing to so great an extent. This
> will require every precaution on your part.
>
> Believe me
>
> > Very truly yours
> > S. McAllister Jones

Jones orders Smith to take every precaution, short of taking
the precaution of leaving the plague-ridden area immediately. A carping tone had become common in Jones's letters.
In June, Smith wrote to Mary from Baghdad, where he was
unsuccessfully trying to avoid quarantine and book passage
home by boat, adding a cautionary postscript: "Do not say
anything to Museum people of the presents I gave you"—
probably some cylinder seals or other small keepsakes from
his site—"they are very critical and rude in the letters to me."

No doubt many in Victorian England were inspired with a
sort of imperial bravado, risking death as a matter of course,
even for fairly optional purposes. Yet it is hard to imagine
McAllister Jones writing in such tones to Sir Henry Creswicke
Rawlinson or Sir Austen Henry Layard. How might his reply
to one of them have run? "By all means, dear sir, come home
at once! Never think of lingering until July—the Trustees
cannot allow you to hazard your life for a few tablets when we
already possess so many. . . . Do not hesitate to employ all the
Bulgarians you may need to secure the sites in your absence."
Something along those lines, most likely, suitable for a gentleman with a title and names derived from two or three prominent family lines. Sternly reprimanded for his plan to come
home early, George Smith stayed on in Iraq far too long, to no
useful purpose, and died.

In *The Rise and Progress of Assyriology*, Wallis Budge

closed his account of Smith's career by saying how little
Smith was missed in death. In the very same paragraph, he
shifts into extolling Sir Henry Rawlinson's elevation at the
museum that same year:

> Smith . . . died on August 19, and was buried
> in the cemetery of the Levant Company.
> Thanks to the large amount of work helpful to
> students that Smith had done, his untimely
> death at the age of thirty-six did not greatly
> delay the progress of Assyriology, for several
> young men in England had begun to work at
> the subject; and fortunately Rawlinson was
> enabled to carry on his great undertaking of
> publishing new material for study. It may be
> noted in passing that Rawlinson was elected a
> Trustee of the British Museum in 1876; and
> thus, in addition to being the "Father of As-
> syriology," he became the official head and di-
> rector of Assyriological studies in England.

At least Smith's loss was deeply regretted by others, if not
by McAllister Jones or Wallis Budge. Writing an obituary in
the scientific journal *Nature*, his friend and colleague A. H.
Sayce noted sadly: "Scholars can be reared and trained, but
hardly more than once in a century can we expect a genius
with the heaven-born gift of divining the meaning of a forgotten language." Praising Smith as "the intellectual pick-
lock," Sayce went on to recall his personal qualities as well:
his enthusiasm, his "obliging kindness," and his modesty. He
concluded that "his loss is an irreparable one."

Another friend, a young German scholar named Friedrich

Delitzsch, had a more direct experience of loss. At the very hour when (as he later learned) Smith died in Aleppo, Delitzsch was in London, on his way to visit a mutual friend, William St. Chad Boscawen. On passing Smith's street, he heard a ghostly voice call out his name. The *Times* thought enough of this coincidence to print a report of this communication from across the Mediterranean—or beyond the grave:

> In passing the end of Crogsland-road, in which Mr. George Smith lived, and within a stone's throw of the house, his German friend and translator says he suddenly heard a most piercing cry, which thrilled him to the marrow, "Herr Dr. Delitzsch." The time—for as soon as he had got over his shock he looked at his watch—was between 6:45 and 7 p.m. Mr. Parsons gives the hour of Mr. Smith's death at 6 p.m. Dr. Delitzsch, who strongly disavows any superstitious leanings, was ashamed to mention the circumstance to Mr. Boscawen on reaching that gentleman's house, although on his return home he owns that his nervous apprehension of some mournful event in his own family found relief in tears, and that he recorded all the facts in his note-book that same night.

Even as he avowed his freedom from "superstitious leanings," Friedrich Delitzsch couldn't help telling this story, and the usually sober *Times* couldn't resist printing it: in death as in life, Smith provided good copy. In return, the newspapers that had made Smith famous served him well in death, keeping his name in the public eye and emphasizing the dire circumstances of his widow and six children, until the government finally offered her a pension—a modest £150, but enough to enable her to scrape by.

The museum's "Smith Personalia" folder still holds the black-edged note card on which Prime Minister Benjamin Disraeli personally wrote to Mary Smith, signing it with his new title, Lord Beaconsfield, which Queen Victoria had just bestowed on him in the month of Smith's death:

> Madam,
>
> The Queen, sympathizing with you in your bereavement, & with the loss of one, whose interesting and devoted labors have shed fresh light on ancient history, has been pleased to confer on you a pension of one hundred & fifty pounds per annum.
>
> I have given directions, that Her Majesty's gracious intentions shall be carried forthwith into effect.
>
> I have the honor to be,
>
> > Madam,
> > Your faithful Servant,
> > Beaconsfield

In the brief decade after he "entered into official life" in 1867, Smith had written eight important books, including linguistic studies, pioneering historical works, and translati ns of the major Mesopotamian literary texts. All modern scholarship on Babylonian literature stems from his pathbreaking work, and at the time of his death he at least knew that his accomplishments would live on, both in his own books and in the work of those who would follow in his footsteps.

These considerations figure prominently in the last entries in his final field journal. This is a small black notebook, three and a half by six inches in size, bound along the
short side. The inside cover bears the proud label "Henry
Penny's Patent Improved Metallic Books." The label an-
nounces that Henry Penny's notebooks employ "BEST PRE-
PARED PAPER," and assures us, "They will be found of good
advantage for travellers and all persons who wish to preserve their Writing."

This notebook indeed preserves Smith's final writing, his
beautifully clear script only occasionally wavering in his last
entries. As they have never been printed, I give them here in
full. In these entries, his mind wanders between family, duty,
Assyrian history, and two bronze statuettes that he has stored
inside his boots. Amid premonitions of death, he expresses his
hopes for the future of his life's work.

> Night 9–10 from Biradjik to Ikisjah ill all the time
> 10 send Mathewson for taktarava
> 11 better rest—decided improvement
> 12 Not so well, purge brought low, if Doctor pres-
> ent I shou. recover but he has not come, very
> doubtful case if fatal farewell to my dear Mary
> and all the little ones. My work has been en-
> tirely for the science I study. I hope the friends
> protect my fami. My collection includes some
> important specimens includ. the two earliest
> bronze statuettes known in Asia before the Se-
> mitic period. They are in my long boots beside
> in my trunk there are about thirty-five tablets
> and fragments about twenty valuable some
> unique including the tablet of Labir-bari-Kurdu

the Laborssoarchus of Berossus, there is a large
field of study in my collection, I intended to
work it out but desire now that my antiquities
and notes may be thrown open to all students. I
have done my duty thoroughly. I owe Mathewson £38 and 20£ I was going to make him a present up to the end of August in all 58£ salary and
present.

I do not fear the change but desire to live for
my family perhaps all may be well yet

Vul-bal-idin the early Babylonian monarch
associated someone perhaps his son with him on
the throne. I have however no means of proving
this because I am away from the Museum. People here are kind after their fashion but make a
great noise so I cannot rest.

Trying to shake myself up and feel a little
better, better still, might attempt to sleep out
strong wind bitter cold go in again sleep

13 better going on well, require rest and good food
My neighbors at Ikisjah male and female, men
little to do now but smoke, women generally
spin cook draw water from the well with a rope
tied round their waist ~~recruiting~~ officer collecting tithes of corn, long disputes, disagreeable
to me

13 August Mathewson returned and Mr Parsons
dentist at Aleppo decided improvement *bottle* of
Beer appetite returning—fail a little in evening—
takaravan

14 Caracos bad

15 Caracos little better
at night 15–16 to Chibombek

To the last, Smith observes what he can, even correcting his first impression that a tax collector is an army recruiting officer. Then the entries trail off in the final few broken phrases, appropriately enough for the great restorer of fragments. These are the last words Smith wrote. Three days later he died in Aleppo, four years after he had been the first person to read *The Epic of Gilgamesh* after two thousand years of oblivion.

CHAPTER 3

THE LOST LIBRARY

Excavation tunnel.

GEORGE Smith made a dazzling discovery when he found the missing portion of the Flood story at Nineveh, but the search process itself was straightforward enough: he simply combed through the rubble in the trenches dug by Hormuzd Rassam twenty years earlier. Rassam had uncovered Ashurbanipal's palace and its great library in 1853 thanks to a combination of shrewd intuition, sheer obstinacy, and random good luck that included a stretch of several clear nights under a full moon, allowing him to conduct a daring series of midnight probes at the decisive locale.

Rassam was working in secrecy because he didn't actually

have the rights to explore the site. The French consul in Mosul, Victor Place, had begun conducting excavations in 1851 on behalf of the Louvre. Place had made a gentleman's agreement with Henry Rawlinson, then serving as British consul in Baghdad, to divide the mounds outside Mosul into areas of British and French responsibility. This arrangement was a miniature version of the imperial powers' political "spheres of influence," helping them to divide and conquer the world without becoming embroiled in unnecessary battles over individual locales. Yet Rassam chafed under the terms of this agreement, for among Place's territories was a large mound known as Kouyunjik, just across the Tigris River from Mosul.

Kouyunjik was part of the ancient center of Nineveh. Over several thousand years the mound had gradually built up as mud-brick buildings decayed and were leveled, with new ones built on top of the compacted debris. In the centuries after the city was abandoned, erosion cut the city's artificial mesa into several different mounds, bare elevations rising as much as ninety feet above the surrounding desert. Nomadic Arab tribes would pitch their tents beneath the mounds, and sheep and goats would scramble up them to forage for grass in the spring. The Kouyunjik mound was the largest of these remnants, a roughly oval mass a mile long by a third of a mile across at its widest point. There was a cluster of huts at one end of the mound, but its only other use had been as an occasional burial site. Kouyunjik's ruins had remained undiscovered and undisturbed, just a few feet below the surface of the earth.

Rassam thought of Kouyunjik as his own territory. A native of Mosul, he had been hired by Nineveh's pioneering excavator, Austen Henry Layard, as paymaster for his excavations in 1845–47 and 1849–51. One of Layard's most important finds had been the palace of the Assyrian king Sennacherib, located in the southwest corner of the Kouyunjik mound. Layard had made a few probes elsewhere nearby, but Rassam had always felt that the north end of the mound deserved more attention. The British Museum's trustees asked Layard to go out a third time in 1852, but Layard had become involved in British politics and wanted to pursue a career in Parliament, so he persuaded the trustees to send Rassam instead. When the British Museum sent Rassam out to excavate late in 1852, he was intensely frustrated to learn that Victor Place had secured the rights to dig at Kouyunjik.

During the following year Rassam jockeyed with Place for access to new sites, often getting the better of his French rival thanks to his local contacts; he secured possession of one site with the timely gift of half a pound of coffee to a local chieftain. Rassam dug in many places with some success, but made no remarkable finds. It was particularly irksome that Kouyunjik was off-limits, as Place was directing his efforts elsewhere and there was no work going on at Rassam's coveted mound. Finally, as the time and money allotted for his expedition began to run out, Rassam couldn't bear the situation any longer and decided to take direct action. As he describes his dilemma in his book *Asshur and the Land of Nimrod*, "My difficulty was how to do this without getting into hot water with M. Place. I feared if I did so, and failed, I might displease Colonel Rawlinson, and get into trouble with the British Museum. . . . So I resolved upon an experimental examination of the spot at night, and only waited for a good opportunity and a bright moonlight for my nocturnal adventure."

Rassam and his Albanian assistant Lateef Agha—an actual Albanian, not a fantasized Bulgarian—assembled a crew "from among our most tried and faithful Arabs, who could be depended upon for secrecy. . . . The best of the joke was, not one of the men knew where they were wanted to work until they commenced digging." On the night of December 20, 1853, he divided his men into three small groups and set them to work. On the first night, one of the crews came upon some broken remains of an ancient building, and in the morning Rassam excitedly telegraphed Rawlinson and London to announce a major find. Digging deeper on the second night, his men unearthed the remnants of an Assyrian bas-relief on a wall, yet the stonework petered out after a few feet, "and there was nothing to be seen save ashes, bones, and other rubbish." Rassam comments wryly that "this put a damper on my spirits," but he must have been devastated, as he would be publicly humiliated if his unauthorized dig yielded nothing but Victor Place's wrath. He had been counting on making some great discovery, since actual finds would trump Place's neglected territorial claim, but if he came up empty-handed Rawlinson and the British Museum would be furious, and his newfound archaeological career would end in disgrace.

Rassam knew that news of his clandestine work would soon reach Place's ears, for by the second day "the fact of my digging at night had oozed out in the town of Mosul." With no time left to lose, he greatly expanded his operations on the decisive third night, setting numerous crews to work all around the area. At last his efforts were crowned with success, as his men unearthed a beautifully preserved carving of a king standing in a chariot. This proved to be Ashurbanipal, in a relief panel from his long-lost palace. As the men dug farther, a fifteen-foot stretch of earth collapsed, revealing an entire wall of sculptured scenes. "The delight of the workmen was naturally beyond description," Rassam reports, "for as soon

as the word 'Sooar' (images) was uttered, it went through the
whole party like electricity. They all rushed to see the new
discovery, and after having gazed on the bas-relief with wonder, they collected together, and began to dance and sing my
praises, in the tune of their war-song, with all their might."
The workers' war song caught the tone of the moment well:
Rassam's victory over the oblivion of antiquity was also a minor triumph in a modern imperial competition.

Even by the swashbuckling standards of the mid-
nineteenth century—when it could be hard to distinguish
archaeologists from grave robbers—Rassam was sometimes
unconventional in his methods, but he was unusual in many
ways. One of the most extraordinary figures in the history of
archaeology, Rassam was the only prominent archaeologist of
his era who was of Middle Eastern origin. Well into the twentieth century, archaeology was a European obsession and pastime; local residents in places such as Egypt and Iraq were
employed at low wages to do the hard work of digging, but
they worked for the archaeologists who came out from London, Paris, or Berlin to conduct excavations and bring
trophies home. The Imperial Ottoman Museum in Constantinople might perhaps receive some share of the finds—but even
the Imperial Museum, in Rassam's day, was directed by a
Frenchman.

Descended from ancient Assyrian stock, Hormuzd Rassam
was alone in crossing this ethnic barrier, and he rose rapidly
from a subordinate position to make a career as an archaeologist and diplomat, employed by the British Museum as director of major expeditions and by the British Foreign Office as
a political agent. He became an author as well, writing papers

for learned societies and publishing two engaging books—one about his archaeological career, the other about his most dangerous diplomatic adventure, a mission to rescue hostages from the king of Abyssinia. Yet well before the end of his long life, Rassam found his books forgotten, his achievements credited to others, and his very name erased from the plaques where it had once been prominently displayed in the British Museum.

Assyriologists in recent years have made amends for these sins of omission, and Rassam is now properly credited with an important role in the archaeology of his homeland. Even recent investigations give an incomplete picture, however, in part because fire and flood have decreased the once extensive unpublished material that Rassam left behind. Letters home to Iraq were lost when the Rassam family home in Mosul burned down around 1950, and an unpublished autobiography, long preserved by a descendant in England, fell victim to mold and damp while stored in a cellar. Although Rassam's published works tell a good deal, he was typically discreet and circumspect in print and often played down the tensions and difficulties he encountered.

Fortunately, Rassam maintained an active correspondence with Henry Layard from the 1840s onward. A warm friendship grew between them, and they wrote each other scores of letters over a fifty-year period, until Layard's death in 1894. These letters provide an invaluable supplement to Rassam's books, and they reveal the full complexity of his situation. Both a loyal son of Mosul and a proud participant in the British imperial enterprise, Rassam spent his life mediating between the two cultures he loved.

The affection, however, was not always returned by his British associates, who were often unprepared to treat an

"Oriental" as a social or intellectual equal. Never entirely sure of his acceptance in his adopted land, Rassam in turn could take offense quickly at real or perceived slights. His bicultural identity was crucial to his success, and yet it also exposed him to misunderstanding, mistreatment, and outright slander, culminating in a disastrous lawsuit that he filed against E. A. Wallis Budge. Rassam was, in fact, more adept in dealing with the violent and unpredictable King Theodore in Abyssinia than with the gentlemanly, guarded, and self-protecting old boy network at the British Museum.

Hormuzd Rassam grew up in a mixed cultural situation. He was born in Mosul in 1826 as the youngest of eight children of an Iraqi father and a Syrian mother. Mosul was then a sleepy provincial city, its dusty streets unpaved and its medieval minarets in various stages of disrepair. Mosul was home to Arabs, Kurds, and Chaldean Christians, all under the alternately harsh and indifferent rule of the Ottoman Empire. The Rassams were Chaldeans. They were descended from the area's early Assyrian inhabitants; many had converted to Christianity around the fourth century and had remained distinct from the Arabs and Kurds among whom they lived.

The Chaldean Christians were often regarded with suspicion, not only by Muslim Arabs and Turks, but also by Westerners who felt that some of their practices were not strictly orthodox. The Chaldeans, however, stoutly maintained that their ancient sect with its simple liturgies was a pure reflection of early Christianity. Various European missionaries were active in the region when Hormuzd was growing up, including an Anglican missionary named George Percy Badger. As an adolescent Hormuzd had followed the lead of his older brother Christian and had converted to Anglicanism; Christian then married Reverend Badger's sister Matilda. Through this English connection, Christian came to be appointed as the British vice consul in Mosul, the town not being viewed as important enough to merit a British-born representative.

When Layard began his excavations outside Mosul in 1845, Christian Rassam assisted him in assembling a crew of workmen and recommended his nineteen-year-old brother as paymaster. Hormuzd was well suited for this post, as he had been working as his brother's clerk, and Christian's mother-in-law had taught him English. He was also fluent in Arabic as well as in his mother tongue, Aramaic—the language spoken by Jesus, which had been widely used in the Near East before Arabic began to spread along with Islam. Quite apart from his linguistic skills, the young Hormuzd stood out in several ways that Layard appreciated. He was gregarious, curious, and interested in everything; he had exceptional stamina; he was scrupulously honest; and finally, not least of all, he was deeply impressed with the romance of antiquity and the excitement of the chase after ancient artifacts.

In the 1840s, this passion was shared by few people in the region. On the rare occasions when erosion would reveal Assyrian or Babylonian sculptures at some ancient mound, the Arabs typically regarded them with deep distaste as graven images from the benighted days before the foundation of Islam. Some considered it their pious duty to smash such idols to pieces. The Turkish officials in charge of Mesopotamia showed less religious concern, but they were consumed with the thankless chores of suppressing tribal warfare and squeezing taxes from their impoverished, resentful subjects. The Turks took a keen interest in buried treasures made of precious metal, but, as George Smith found, they couldn't see the point of worrying about dirty items of clay or stone. In his

Asshur and the Land of Nimrod, Rassam speaks of one such
official, who "was at least seventy years of age, and conse-
quently of the old school, who considered searching for antiquities a silly occupation, and those who valued them were only
fit for a lunatic asylum." Many of the Europeans in the area
held similar views, combining religious hostility toward pa-
gan artifacts with an aesthetic disregard for art that didn't
conform to Greek norms of beauty.

Rassam, however, was enchanted with everything that he
and Layard found, and he became Layard's right-hand man
and his principal confidant in the field. When the time came
to return to England at the end of 1847, Layard offered to
take Hormuzd with him and help him enroll at Oxford. Hormuzd's father was deceased, but Christian and Matilda had
taken responsibility for him and would be able to cover his
expenses. They also had missionary contacts in England who
were happy to help a talented young Iraqi absorb Anglican
doctrines at the source. So off Hormuzd went with Layard,
though Matilda warned Layard royally that her young
brother-in-law "requires a strong hand to rule him."

At first Layard felt fully in control of his protégé; as he
wrote to his friend Henry Ross, a British trader in Mosul, "I
think I see a possibility of employing Hormuzd in the East
and if he behaves well of pushing him on in time." Yet a growing note of exasperation soon began to enter into subsequent
letters. Hormuzd "is quite well, and as obstinate as usual," Layard wrote after they'd been in England a few weeks. A
month later, Layard wrote, "I only wish he would apply his
mind seriously to something—he is too frivolous." Even so,
Layard allowed, "He is a general favorite and he is very good-
natured. He will pick up many friends." Henry Layard was
only thirty at the time, just nine years older than Hormuzd;

headstrong and impetuous himself, Layard probably wasn't
the most persuasive model of sober maturity to his young
charge. Before long, any vestige of English authority over a
colonial subordinate had melted away, replaced by a dynamic
of sibling rebellion. As a frustrated Layard complained to
Ross: "He no longer listens to me and looks upon me as he
used to do his brother at Mosul. I am sorry for this as I think
I have a little more experience in the civilised world than he
has, but he is far from thinking so. The fact is he has been
spoilt—and then (as is his habit you know) he does things
which he is well aware I would not approve and then makes a
very lame attempt to hide them and deceive me."

That winter Hormuzd got himself involved in a poten-
tially serious romantic misadventure in Oxford, and only
when it was all over did he confess everything to Layard. For
several weeks in a row he had seen an attractive young lady
looking at him in church at his Oxford college, Magdalen, and
then he began noticing her at the sacred music concerts held
at the Magdalen chapel on Sunday afternoons. "About a
month ago," he wrote Layard in February 1849, "when I left
the Chapel about five o'clock to come home, I found the same
lady walking behind me, and before I reached the house she
came so close to me that her left shoulder touched my right
one & then I was obliged to ask her what she wanted, but she
only replied, I do not know, Sir! Then I prayed her to leave
me alone and if she wished to speak to me I would meet her at
the same place at half past six o'clock; she replied Perhaps."

Hormuzd had blurted out this suggestion as he was petri-
fied that people might see him talking to a strange woman,
while at dusk they'd have some degree of privacy. Excited but
wary, he was in a complete quandary, for he couldn't decide,
he wrote, "whether she was a Lady or not." And if not? He

feared that "she might turn out to be a bad woman who would put me in troubles and disgrace my name in the University." Hormuzd was so flustered he hadn't been able to look at the girl as she walked beside him: "Although I spoke to her those few words, yet I did not move my head half an inch to look at her, for you know that I am known in this place and I did not like to speak to her in that time of the day when all the University people were going about from one College to another. When I returned home I thought a while about it and did not know what to think of it."

He decided that the best plan would be to have a friend come along in the evening and view the young lady—if lady she was—from afar. Unsure of Englishwomen's codes of behavior and dress, Hormuzd hoped that an English friend could assess the girl's character from her appearance and body language. His plan misfired, however, for the young woman saw them together at the trysting spot before his friend took up his observation post, and she passed by them without a word. The adventure was suddenly over, and she never reappeared in church after that day.

There is no way to know whether Hormuzd's admirer was indeed a "bad woman," boldly trolling for customers in the aptly named Magdalen Chapel. Perhaps she was simply a young girl who had developed a crush on the handsome foreigner, but then was embarrassed when she saw Hormuzd and his friend awaiting her in the dusk. All in all, Hormuzd was relieved. He persuaded himself that he, not she, was the one who had called things off: "I am very glad I got rid of her, for she would have quite ruined my name amongst my pious friends; she had the finest figure I have seen for some [time], and her face was quite attractive. Two young men the sons of very respectful gentlemen have just been turned out of the University for the same thing which was going to happen to me."

As revealing as this letter is, it doesn't yield its secrets easily, since Hormuzd had a habit of writing across his own pages: upon filling up a page, he would rotate it ninety degrees and fill up the page again, lattice-style. This practice was used occasionally by members of his family and by Henry Layard when in the field; it saved paper and also reduced the high cost of postage, an important consideration for someone on a tight budget, as Hormuzd was at Oxford. At the same time, this mode of writing meant that a letter's contents wouldn't be obvious on a casual glance and could be read only with care.

This particular letter contained an exceptional weight of emotional content, for in addition to detailing Hormuzd's romantic misadventure, it also described his reactions to a piece of terrible news from home, which arrived after he caught a severe chill while out riding in rainy weather: "The next day I could not move any of my joints and they seemed just as if any one had tied them together. I remained in that state two or three days, and when I went down to take a little luncheon I had by the afternoon Post a note from Messrs. Hanson & Co. enclosing the melancholy letter from Mrs. [Matilda] Rassam conveying the mournful intelligence of the loss of my dearest Mother." The shock of this news must have been increased by Hormuzd's distance in time and space from his mother's death. The recently invented telegraph hadn't yet reached Iraq, and so Matilda could only write. Her letter would have taken several weeks to travel three thousand miles by post-horse, Mediterranean steamer, the slow French wagon-poste, channel ferry, and the coaches of the Royal Mail. Hormuzd had had trouble finding an afford-

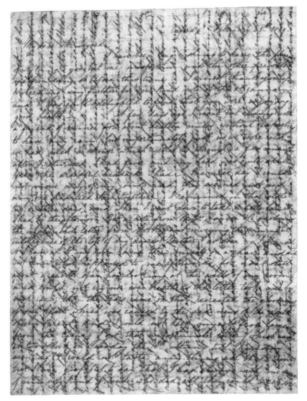

Hormuzd Rassam's letter to Layard, 25 February 1849, describing his mother's death—and an ice-skating expedition.

able living arrangement in Oxford, and Matilda wasn't even sure of his address, so her letter was conveyed at a second remove by the London solicitors who were handling his finances. Messrs. Hanson & Co. probably had no idea what news they were forwarding on to a feverish young man in his foreign rooming house.

Hormuzd was overwhelmed. "I ran up to my room and threw myself on a chair and did not know what happened to me afterwards, for I sat still about a quarter of an hour looking at the walls of my room and could not cry nor even breathe as the letter took me by surprise; then the tears came on that recreated the gloominess of my heart." Still a little awkward in writing English, Hormuzd expressed his grief in a touching mix of personal outpouring and the bureaucratic phrases he'd learned while working as his brother's clerk: "I could not keep myself from lamenting from the time I got that unfortunate letter which came at two o'clock on Tuesday the 16th ult.," he continued, "and till Thursday evening I could not taste any thing all that time, but I am grateful to say that I had always with me some of my very kind friends who did all they could to comfort me."

It is fortunate that by this time the outgoing Hormuzd had developed a network of friends, because his first weeks at Oxford had been a time of profound dislocation. As he had written to Layard in December 1848, he was making good progress in improving his English, thanks to a kindly land-lady who "does all she can to instruct me in both tongue and soul." Yet he felt he was losing his Arabic at almost the same rate, and he was struggling with his university studies: "It is very curious, whenever I wish to begin to study I get some thing which puts me quite out and perplexes my head. I be-lieve if I should stay in England one century in this kind of unsettledness I should make no improvement whatever. I know not whether I have improved on my coming to England or not, but my notion is that I have not only gained nothing but lost that which I knew, into the bargain."

Before long, though, Hormuzd was enjoying such novel pleasures as ice skating, unfazed even when he and his friends plunged through a weak patch: "We were nearly dying from laughter to see ourselves sticking in the ice." He gave his friends gifts of Arabic calligraphy, and was proud to have one of his compositions hung in Oxford's venerable Bodleian

Library. Best of all, the Bishop of Oxford took a liking to him
and started inviting him to his palatial residence. Three
months after his ambiguous encounter with the young lady at
Magdalen Chapel, Rassam wrote to Layard of his friendship
with the Bishop, adding slyly, "There is a report all over Oxford that I am going to marry his daughter who was presented to the Queen a few days ago; but I cannot say whether
this report is true or not." The rumor wasn't true at all, but it
was delightful testimony to the elevated social circles in
which Hormuzd was becoming at home.

Just at this time Rassam's Oxford idyll came to an end.
The British Museum's trustees asked Layard to return to Mosul for further excavations, and he secured their agreement to
hire Rassam as his formal second-in-command, a significant
promotion from his earlier role as paymaster. Layard wrote to
Rassam congratulating him on this coup, but to his surprise
Rassam balked at the prospect. After a year and a half at Oxford, Rassam was in no hurry to return home any time soon—
if ever. Yet he could hardly turn down a direct request from
his patron and benefactor. He wrote Layard in tones of sor-
rowful resignation,

> No doubt you will think me quite mad were I
> to tell you that I was as much sorry (when I
> had the pleasure of receiving your intelligence
> about my return to Nineveh) as I ought to have
> been glad to go and see my family and many
> dear friends; but really my dear Mr. Layard I
> cannot bear to leave England and I have a
> great horror for returning to the East; but still

a man must do what he can in this miserable world and run from the East to the West to find himself an employment. I know you will laugh at my little sense if I [were] to say that I would rather be a Chimney Sweeper in England than becoming a Pasha in Turkey. Perhaps you will think it unnatural that I should feel so, but what can I do! I will sacrifice myself for England and worship forever the pure religion of Great Britain. Notwithstanding the very thought of having the pleasure of traveling with you again, is a great consolation to me, and I trust that my dutiful services will always prove fervent to you, and hope to be your companion wherever you wish me to go with you. I shall always look for your advise and be under your rule.

Though Rassam stressed his dutiful loyalty to Layard, he then went on to ask whether Layard could help him find a post in the British diplomatic service once the excavations were done. He clearly feared being stranded in Mosul at the conclusion of the museum assignment, his academic career derailed along with any hope of securing a government post on the strength of an Oxford degree. So even as he reluctantly agreed to return home, Rassam was laying the groundwork for getting away again.

Mosul was certainly not a promising place to come home to at this time. It had long been the center of trade in northern Iraq, but tribal warfare and widespread banditry in the countryside had depressed the flow of goods into and out of the decimated much of Iraq—half the population of Baghdad died—and the economy hadn't yet fully recovered from the severe depression that ensued. Many irrigation canals had ceased to be maintained and were in disrepair; food was often scarce, and hunger fueled the lawlessness in the countryside. Even at the best of times, the Ottoman administration was rarely focused on developing infrastructure, and the government's ability to spark a recovery was seriously constrained by the lasting decline in tax revenues in the plague's aftermath. European travel writers in the 1840s typically painted a picture of timeless stagnation in Iraq, with no awareness that they were often seeing the lingering effects of the severe health crisis of the decade before.

If the overall picture in Mosul was unpromising in 1849, things were little better within the family. Rassam's parents were now both dead, and he and his brother Christian had never been close. In print, Rassam would later make a point of praising "the kind demeanor" of his "amiable" sister-in-law, but in reality he found her censorious and disagreeable. Matilda was increasingly unhappy with the life she had fallen into in Mosul. Her marriage was not prospering, and she had become angry and bitter; in a letter of 1850, Layard referred to "her jealous & vindictive temper" as her leading quality. Eventually Christian initiated divorce proceedings against her, a move that only further strained Rassam's relations with both of them. As he wrote Layard at that time,

> As for my oldest brother his disgraceful affairs with his wife have been a source of great anxiety to me. . . . I have tried all I could to keep clear from mixing myself in his anything but pleasant disputes with his wife; but I find

if I do not advise him what to do with regard to the laws of this country he will get into a mess and his disgrace and ruin will naturally affect me. . . . He thinks that he has merely to express a wish to dissolve his marriage and the thing will be done. His wife has very scheming friends and relations and she is herself not a dunce; as while he is shilly-shallying they are fortifying themselves to ruin him.

Long before that crisis erupted, a stiff formality had marked the letters between Rassam and his brother and sister-in-law; there was no warm family nest awaiting him. Yet he did go with Layard, gaining new skills and confidence as an excavator.

After the expedition ended in 1851 they returned to England, laden with treasures from Nineveh and its environs. Some of their finds were major pieces, such as a fierce pair of huge winged lions, so heavy that it took three hundred men to drag each one from the site to the rafts constructed to ferry them downriver. They used penknives to free the surrounding earth from more delicate items, such as naked ivory figurines of goddesses and dozens of beautifully decorated dishes used at Assyrian banquets.

Back in London, proud of his successes in Iraq and also increasingly at home in England, Rassam sat for a pair of parallel portraits, in formal English attire and in an elegant set of robes from home. He became sought after as a dinner guest, and he enjoyed the role of mysterious stranger: "I was very much pleased with the Lord Mayor's dinner," he wrote Layard, "and no one could make out of what nation I was." His London stay was fairly brief, however. Layard had written a

Hormuzd Rassam in European and Assyrian dress, painted by his friend
F. C. Cooper, 1851.

bestselling book about his first expedition and crowds were
coming to the British Museum to view the new treasures he had
brought back, and so the trustees determined to fund a third
expedition. With Layard beginning a political career, the
trustees accepted his suggestion that Rassam would be the man
to send out, since Rassam had become fully conversant with
the sites and was uniquely qualified to handle the complexities
of working with (and against) the many competing interests in
the area. The trustees hesitated to bestow full authority on a
twenty-five-year-old Iraqi, so they arranged to have Henry
Rawlinson supervise Rassam's work. Rassam consulted regularly with him, but Rawlinson was a linguist with no experience in excavation. Living two hundred miles away in Baghdad,
he rarely came to see what Rassam was doing.

     With this trip, Rassam came into his own. At last, he was
the accredited agent of the British Museum, conducting a major archaeological expedition. On his arrival back at Mosul,
he was treated like a conquering hero, with the city's elders

coming out to meet him as he approached the city. As Rassam reports in his memoirs, "a Moslem butcher of the town, with whom I used to deal, killed a fine ram in front of my house, the flesh of which he said he had vowed to distribute amongst the poor for my safe return." Rassam's welcome was all the warmer as he had ample funds to hire workers—prudently stretching his funds further than expected, thanks to his ability to bargain directly with the locals, whom he often persuaded to work for lower rates than they charged the French.

Moving from one site to another, he would ride grandly at the head of a long file of workers clad in flowing robes and turbans, who passed the time on the road by singing songs of love and war. When he had to travel through unsettled areas, the splendor of his retinue would often be increased by a caravan of camels and donkeys, as dozens of traders attached themselves to his party for protection against bandits. It was widely known that Rassam enjoyed an unusual degree of double protection: by the Ottoman government and by many of the local sheikhs, who often cared little for Turkish authority but knew Rassam and his family. Remarkably, in all his travels Rassam was never once attacked or robbed, thanks to his hosts' watchful care of him: "I was sometimes told in the morning that the chief who felt himself most responsible for my safety kept watch all the night around my tent, for fear of some stray robber entering and stealing some of my belongings. The fact is, wherever I encamped I felt that all the Arabs around me knew who I was, and that no one would attempt to do me any injury for fear of revenge of my Arab friends."

Dressed as a proper British gentleman in jacket and vest, Rassam on hot days would ride under the shade of a parasol, constantly scanning the surroundings for likely mounds to

explore. He perfected the art of staying comfortable in the
sort of rest house where George Smith was tormented with
vermin and bad food: he knew to stay upstairs whenever possible (fewer fleas), and by having water sprinkled on the walls
and floor he could lower the temperature by ten degrees. Often he avoided rest houses altogether, simply riding directly
to the largest house in a village and relying on his charm and
prestige to win the owner's hospitality. Sometimes the owner
insisted on giving over his own bedroom to Rassam, and on
one occasion he was graciously accommodated in the women's
quarters when the owner was away, fed by his hostess with
crushed melons and "small, but extremely luscious" figs.

He generally traveled with an excellent cook and good supplies of his own, supplemented by such fresh food as he could
procure en route, and often cemented his relations with local
leaders by sharing his plenty with them. He charmed one
group of nomads by introducing them to an unheard-of delicacy: cake. "I had a supply of Baghdad cakes with me, of which
I gave them some to eat. They seemed very much amused in
tasting them, as they had never eaten such a dainty before; 'actually,' they exclaimed to each other, 'bread flavored with
sugar and butter!' "

Not that travel in Mesopotamia was easy, even for Rassam.
In his book he good-humoredly details all kinds of irritations
and inconveniences: "I do not think there can be anything
more annoying and discomforting than to arrive at a dirty
village in wet weather. Everything seems to be smeared with
mud and dirt, to say nothing about the noxious odors which
emanate from the filth that surrounds every hut, especially if
there are any buffaloes in the place." Sometimes he was attacked by thick swarms of mosquitoes—"horrid irritators," he
called them—and on one memorable night a multitude of

crawling creatures descended on him from the thatched roof
above his head: "The great discomfort I experienced . . . was
from the dirty state of the ceiling, which every now and then
sent down showers of unwelcome insects and smut. . . . Moreover, as the roofs of all the houses are connected with each
other on the same level, and easily mounted, they become the
resort of dogs and goats, which are continually rambling about
on them. The consequence is, every time any of these animals
move on the roof, they send down a shower of dirt, fleas, flies,
and spiders."

Discomfort could suddenly turn into danger. Horses could
miss their footing when fording swift-moving rivers, bags
and even riders could be swept away, and the rickety, flat-
bottomed boats that served as ferries across the Tigris and
Euphrates were floating death traps, thanks to shoddy construction and serious overloading: "They are generally ankle-
deep with bilge-water; and as they take in as many laden
animals as the boat can hold, the unhappy passengers have to
keep out of the animals' way by hanging on anyhow to the
rough timber which is rudely nailed to the sides of the vessel.
No sooner does the boat get into mid-channel than the beasts
begin to get restive; and if there should happen to be a vicious
horse or mule amongst them, a regular stampede follows."

One night, Rassam almost drowned on dry land. Camp-
ing out on his beloved mound at Kouyunjik, he unwittingly
pitched his tent over a poorly covered trench left from Layard's earlier excavations. A violent hailstorm came up during
the night, releasing torrents of rain that undermined the
ground beneath him. "All of a sudden I felt myself going down
in a pit, with bed, tent, and everything else I possessed. My
plight at that time can be better imagined than expressed.
Taken so by surprise in a very dark night, with rain and hail

pouring down in torrents, and I being ingulfed in a pit with a deluge of water rushing down upon me and bringing with it heaps of the debris of the excavations, I could not for some time realize the true state of my position." Panicked and groggy, Rassam felt himself suffering the fate of the wicked Korah, a rebel against Moses whom God caused to be swallowed up by the earth. "I did not collect my senses," Rassam says, "until a number of my faithful Arabs came to my rescue, and quickly raised me out of the ditch half-drowned and covered with mud."

Bandits and floods were bad enough, but Rassam's most persistent problems were with his French rivals. At one point, Rassam's workmen were outraged to learn that a French team was hastening to one of their sites in their absence; Rassam's men "were seized with inexpressible frenzy, and began . . . to sing the war-cry and dance about as if they were demented." Rassam calmed them down, but then as they approached the contested site, the workmen raced ahead to confront their opponents. Rassam came behind them on horseback, pushing through tangled branches and bushes. He and his men disturbed an entire Eden of animals in the process: "Our rapid march drove in utter confusion from their haunts the wild boar, hares, hyenas, jackals, foxes, and the other wild animals inhabiting that thicket, and disturbed the roosting of the francolins, partridges, and quails." Rassam managed to reach the site just in time to avert outright bloodshed.

As the rivalry heated up it wasn't only the Arab workmen who turned to violence. In a letter to Layard, Rassam detailed an astonishing and near-fatal encounter between the Europeans themselves. He was returning from Kouyunjik to Mosul

together with several people, including his assistant Lateef
Agha, a friend named Berrington, and William Kennett Loftus, an archaeologist of considerable talent but explosive
temper who was conducting some excavations with private
funding. About to cross the unstable bridge of boats that
spanned the Tigris, they were overtaken by the French consul
and an Italian doctor. The doctor swore at the Englishmen's
guide and ordered him to make way. The guide paid no attention, and so the doctor struck the guide with his whip "and
used a shameful language to us all." Matters quickly deteriorated once the French consul's party crossed the bridge and
headed into Mosul. Enraged, Loftus jumped from his horse
and chased after the doctor, brandishing his horsewhip as he
ran. Bringing up the rear, Rassam encountered Mosul's pasha,
who asked what was going on: "As I was telling him that a European Doctor had insulted us," Rassam reported, "a man came
to me running & said 'Your friend is killed.'"

Fortunately, it turned out that the report of Loftus's
death had been somewhat exaggerated.

> Berrington & myself ran as fast as we could
> but Lateef Agha outran us & reached the spot
> just in time to keep the enraged Dr. from stab-
> bing Mr. Loftus. It appears Mr. L. had horse-
> whipped the Doctor but his companion & the
> Chancellor came down upon poor Loftus & all
> three began to beat him. The Dr. who insulted
> us got in such a rage that he dragged [out] his
> knife & ran after Loftus to stab him. Luckily
> there were [a] great many people collected
> there at the time who got hold of the Dr. &
> pulled him on one side.

As outrageous as the incident was, the aftermath was equally strange. The Englishmen lodged a criminal complaint against the murderous Italian doctor, whom the pasha duly arrested. Yet Victor Place managed to have the doctor freed by the remarkable ruse of having him renounce his Italian nationality and declare himself a French citizen. As French consul, Place then insisted that the doctor was now his responsibility, and he persuaded—or bribed—the local jailor to release the doctor into his custody, whereupon he quietly let him leave town. The Englishmen protested bitterly, to no avail. Even if he wasn't pocketing a share of the jailor's bribe, the pasha was probably relieved not to have to bother adjudicating the claims of the brawling Europeans.

Rassam makes no mention of this bizarre episode in his book, perhaps because the Englishmen too were hardly behaving well. The jostling at the bridge was just one incident during months when each party kept trying to shoulder the other aside, and Rassam was lucky that "the best of the joke" of outwitting Place didn't turn out to be the stabbing death of Kennett Loftus. In his book, Rassam presents himself as rising above such petty rivalries, remarking sadly, "it is a known fact that, whenever the British and French interests clash in foreign lands, there is sure to be jealousy and ill-feeling; and, although I always avoided such unhappy results, my public duty forced me sometimes to brave it out." Yet he used highly confrontational language in private, as in a letter he wrote to Layard in 1860 from Muscat, on the coast of Arabia: "The Mohammedans of this country are certainly the most liberal in the world, and even the religion of the Hindoos is tolerated amongst them. I believe this is owing to the non-existence of French interference and bigoted Papists in these parts; as you know these two evils are always at the bottom of all discord! . . . Now Brigadier Coghlan having gone to Zanzibar there is no fear of the frog eaters getting any influence there or here." Directly after Rassam praises religious toleration, he shifts into denouncing French "frog eaters" and their "bigoted" priests, showing no sense of the irony of his own language.

Ardently pro-British and anti-French as he was, Rassam nevertheless constantly struggled to counter his British colleagues' condescending attitudes toward the peoples of the Arab world. Most European travel writers of his time portrayed the "Orientals" they encountered in terms of colorful quaintness and childlike simplicity, spiced with lurking hints of barbaric cruelty. Outright racism was not uncommon in their accounts, often sugarcoated with feeble attempts at humor. Kennett Loftus's *Travels and Researches in Chaldea and Susiana*, for instance, is filled with hostility toward the region's inhabitants. While he too passed over the embarrassing episode of European fisticuffs at the Mosul bridge, he didn't hesitate to amuse his readers by comparing a group of Persian tribesmen to apes: the tribe was "the most extraordinary assemblage of animals bearing the human form that I ever set eyes upon. They had high shoulders, long legs, pucker-faces, and (if the Lamarckian theory of transmutation of species be true) perhaps also long tails, although I will not vouch for this fact, not having had an opportunity of making a minute zoological examination." Loftus was writing in 1857, two years before the publication of Darwin's *Origin of Species,* and he had to fall back on Lamarck's older theories for his rancid little witticism, but in 1874 George Smith had the benefit of evolutionary theory to underscore a comparison of Arab and ape: "The chief of Durnak was a wretched-looking old specimen of humanity, whose appearance lent some colour to Mr. Darwin's theory, and he had a son as good-looking and well clothed as himself, but these people thought much of themselves because they were Mahometans."

In deliberate contrast to such accounts, throughout *Asshur and the Land of Nimrod* Rassam emphasizes the kindness and fair dealing he regularly met with during his travels. On a trip in the 1880s he became involved in mediating disputes between different groups in Armenia, but despite his own Christian sympathies, he reports, "I must say that I always found the Moslems more easy to pacify than the Christians. Although the former are considered the most bigoted, I found them, on the whole, more tolerant than their Christian neighbors." Rassam agreed with many observers of the time in seeing the declining Ottoman Empire as rife with corruption and misrule, remarking at one point that "the system is rotten to the core, and requires a thorough cleansing." Yet in that very passage, he goes out of his way to give a warm portrait of the governor of Baghdad: "I was never so struck with any Ottoman official as I was with this Albanian nobleman. He is a thorough gentleman, and most courteous. . . . Doubtless there is no lack of high-minded men with administrative talent in Turkey, who are competent to rule justly and uncorruptly, if they are only allowed to have their own way."

As early as the preface to his book, Rassam makes his cultural agenda clear: "In describing fully my travels and the conduct of my archaeological work I had one aim in view, and that is to show how easy it is to get on with all the inhabitants of Biblical lands, especially the Arabs, provided they are not treated with unbecoming hauteur and contempt." He returns to this theme in summing up his experiences at the book's end: "With all the minor annoyances and childish obstructions thrown in my way from time to time, mostly through ill-designed intrigues, I can not but acknowledge that, with unfeigned sincerity, generally speaking, the Ottomans are good-natured, courteous, and obliging; and, as far as I am concerned, I owe all officials my gratitude and cherish for them a most friendly feeling; and, though sometimes I was bothered in connection with my explorations, I, nevertheless, in the majority of cases, received from them most unremitting kindness and help in all my undertakings." The body of Rassam's book actually describes as many obstructions as kindnesses from the Ottoman officials, who stymied him at several points much as they did George Smith. Yet Rassam's insistence on the officials' "unremitting kindness" underscores his commitment to countering the common Victorian hostility toward the benighted denizens of the mysterious Orient.

Far from mere propaganda for his native land, moreover, Rassam's perspective helped him enormously in surmounting the annoyances and obstructions he encountered. A timely compliment or friendly appeal could open doors that would never budge before George Smith's bluster or Kennett Loftus's contempt. A recurrent bone of contention with officials in Mosul, for instance, was that many of the ancient mounds had been used off and on as graveyards. While pre-Islamic burials posed no problem, it was against the law to disturb Muslim cemeteries. Rassam, however, soon became aware that local officials' definitions of a graveyard were elastic, depending on whether they were favorably or unfavorably disposed toward a proposed excavation. A pound of coffee, offered at the right moment, could be far more effective than the flourishing of a firman from distant Constantinople.

The hired workmen sometimes objected to digging amid old graves, either from purely religious motives or because the graves crystallized an uneasy sense that they were being taken advantage of by foreign treasure hunters. As Rassam learned, after a dispute arose among his workmen: "While I was spending Sunday quietly at Mossul, the Shabbak workmen were arguing amongst themselves whether it was right to allow their graves to be desecrated for the sake of paltry gain, especially as there was no lack of mischievous men ready to upbraid them for their stupidity in allowing me to excavate amongst their dead. They were told that for every piaster they received I was carrying away antiquities worth more than their weight in gold." Rassam had no patience with such arguments made by "mischievous men"; his goals were scholarly and artistic, he felt, not grubbing after buried treasure. Yet his impoverished workmen knew that there was a vast disproportion between their meager daily wages and the high prices the ancient artifacts could command on the growing private market. Even on behalf of the British Museum, Wallis Budge and George Smith sometimes paid private dealers in Baghdad a hundred times what the dealers had paid for ancient items brought to them.

On hearing of the work stoppage, Rassam went out to the site and defused the situation with a surprising tactic: humor. He pretended to be entirely willing to stop the excavation, declaring that "if those who were adverse to digging out the remainder of the chamber would swear that the bones belonged to their forefathers, I would stop digging at once. For all I knew the bones might belong to murderers or enemies of their forefathers, which had been rotting there for hundreds of years. This made them laugh, and forthwith they all resumed work."

The capstone of Rassam's work was the discovery of Ashurbanipal's palace. One of the greatest monarchs in Assyria's history, Ashurbanipal had been forgotten for two thousand years; his very name had been lost because he had not been mentioned in the Bible or any surviving Greek source. But even by the half-light of the moon when his men first came upon the wall of relief carvings, Rassam could tell that he had stumbled upon some great king's palace. In the morning, news of his discovery spread "like wildfire," and Victor Place hurried to Kouyunjik from the site south of town where he had been fruitlessly excavating. He confronted Rassam, protesting that the site was his to exploit, but Rassam calmly replied that Layard had been the first to obtain permission to excavate on Kouyunjik, and "Sir Henry Rawlinson had no power to give away ground which did not belong to him." Fuming, Place stiffly congratulated Rassam on his find, and the excavation proceeded.

In the ensuing weeks Rassam's men uncovered one spacious stateroom after another, some completely ruined but others with walls still lined with dramatic scenes carved in stone. Rassam was thrilled with the reliefs he found, as he knew they would attract the greatest public attention. Most spectacular was a room fifty feet by fifteen in size, lined with exquisite scenes of Ashurbanipal hunting lions. Among the masterpieces of Assyrian art, these reliefs dramatically portray lions attacking the king's chariot as he wheels among them, shooting arrows with unerring aim into their hamstrings and their throats. With every sinew boldly outlined, the lions are magnificent opponents for the great king, fearsome in their rage, pitiful in defeat as they die, coughing up

blood. "The suffering of one lioness in particular is beautifully portrayed," as Rassam remarks in his book: "resting on
her forepaws, with outstretched head, she vainly endeavors to
gather together her wounded limbs." The human figures are
represented with equally vivid realism. Ashurbanipal is at the
center of every scene, an image of balance and resolve amid
scenes of whirling chaos.

Ashurbanipal hunting, c. 660 BCE. This detail from one of the reliefs found
by Hormuzd Rassam exemplifies the dynamic realism of the art of Ashurbanipal's reign. The king's horse strains forward, every sinew taut, while
the king is an image of balanced poise, not one braided strand of hair out
of order, about to release the arrow at the point of maximum tension.

Left to himself, Rassam would have concentrated his efforts entirely on uncovering such eye-catching wonders, but at least in theory he was under Rawlinson's guidance. The great linguist had no real interest in art: what he wanted was more tablets. Rassam was as fortunate in this regard as in his discovery of sculptures. In his book, after several pages about the lion hunt reliefs, Rassam mentions almost in passing that the floor of the room was covered with thousands of cuneiform tablets: "In the center of the same saloon I discovered the library of Assur-ban-ipal, consisting of inscribed terracotta tablets of all shapes and sizes; the largest of these, which happened to be in better order, were mostly stamped with seals, and some inscribed with hieroglyphic and Phoenecian characters. Amongst these records were found the Chaldean accounts of the Creation and Deluge." Rassam had no idea he had stumbled upon a principal repository of one of the greatest collections of literature ever recovered from the ancient world. He couldn't read cuneiform himself and wasn't sure that Rawlinson really understood the tablets either. "At that time I was quite skeptical as to the true reading of Assyrian, or what is commonly called cuneiform," Rassam admits in his book, adding that he felt "surprise and satisfaction" when a visiting French scholar gave an inscription the same meaning as Rawlinson had proposed for it.

Rassam had been scheduled to leave Mosul at year's end, but he prolonged his stay for three months, excavating Ashurbanipal's great library and opening up room after room lined with splendid reliefs showing scenes of hunting and of battle. He reluctantly left Iraq in March of 1854, with the British Museum's funds completely exhausted, and the privately funded Kennett Loftus took over the excavation.

Rassam had made the discovery of his life, and yet in the

years that followed he made a much less pleasant discovery:
the British press, and even the British Museum, increasingly
failed to credit him for his finds. By the time Loftus crated
up a generous selection of reliefs to ship back home in 1856,
Rassam's major discoveries were mixed in with his own much
more modest finds, and on their arrival in England the sculptures were credited to Loftus. In France, furious at having
been upstaged by Rassam, Victor Place erased him from his
memoir of his excavations, substituting Loftus in his place.
Henry Rawlinson, moreover, began to publish articles on the
tablets, describing them and even the sculptures as *his* discoveries. Having actually discouraged Rassam from digging on
Kouyunjik, which he believed Layard had fully excavated,
Rawlinson retroactively decided that the finding of Ashurbanipal's palace had really been his inspiration all along, while
Rassam was only a "digger" supervising the work.

Almost alone among publications, the *Illustrated London
News* emphasized Rassam's role in finding the magnificent reliefs that Loftus shipped back in 1856. Yet even the writer of
this article couldn't resist patronizing Rassam. Noting Rassam's success in extending the excavations inaugurated by
Austen Henry Layard, the writer comments, "It must be not a
little gratifying to that pioneer of Assyrian research to find,
through his example, an Oriental—generally indifferent to all
works of art—so thoroughly interested in the undertaking and
impregnated with the English energy to carry his individual
labors to a successful conclusion." The Victorians tended to
see Orientals as passive and feminine by nature; naturally,
then, Rassam must have been "impregnated" with Layard's
English energy to get the job done.

Meaning to praise Rassam, the writer notes that he had
been under special pressure to succeed, since if he failed to

find anything, "no amount of energy, perseverance, or labor would have shielded the conductor of the expedition from undeserved blame, more freely bestowed, too, perhaps, because he was a foreigner in an Englishman's position." Rassam quoted this passage in his memoirs, saying nothing about the strangeness of being described as "a foreigner in an Englishman's position" as he excavated the mounds just outside his own birthplace. His lifelong friend Henry Layard, however, didn't hesitate to give a blunt explanation for the shabby treatment Rassam received from colleagues and the press alike: Rassam, he declared, was "one of the honestest and most straightforward fellows I ever knew, and one whose great services have never been acknowledged—because he is a 'nigger' and because Rawlinson, as is his habit, appropriated to himself the credit of Rassam's discoveries." Archaeologist or mere "digger," gentleman or "nigger"? The ambiguities of Rassam's identity would shadow all of his achievements, including his greatest success—or failure—in the diplomatic career to which he next turned.

CHAPTER 4

THE FORTRESS
AND THE MUSEUM

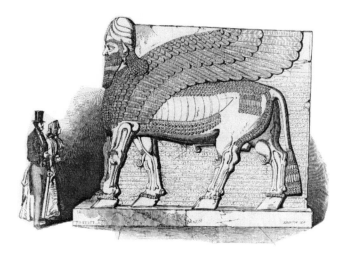

Bull and museum-goers.

Rassam was far from England by the time articles and books
began appearing that denied him credit for his work. Needing
employment on his return from Iraq, he succeeded in getting
a political appointment, as he had hoped. Layard was then a
member of Parliament and was able to ask the Foreign Min-
istry to offer his friend a position in the British consulate at
Aden, a colonial outpost in Yemen at the southern tip of the
Arabian Peninsula. Blasted with heat and subject to blinding
sandstorms, Aden was an enervated town that served mostly
as a port of call for ships passing out of the Red Sea en route

to India. Though this was not a sought-after assignment, it
was a full-time job and the first step in a diplomatic career,
and Rassam accepted it with pleasure. He was soon caught up
in his new responsibilities and for the next two decades gave
little thought to archaeology. Instead, he held a series of positions at Aden, from postmaster and police superintendent to
magistrate and political attaché, eventually becoming deputy
chief in charge of running the mission.

In his political work as in his archaeology, Rassam strove
to mitigate the high-handedness that the British often displayed in the Orient, even as he worked to bring the benefits
of European civilization to the tribal societies he encountered
in Arabia. He was proud that no one ever appealed any of the
decisions he rendered in thousands of cases as a magistrate. In
1860, on a diplomatic mission to help resolve a border dispute
involving the Arabian principality of Muscat, he succeeded in
persuading the imam of Muscat to institute some significant
reforms. As he wrote to Layard, "His Highness does every
thing I recommend, and indeed there is such good understanding between him and myself that I believe he will do any
thing I ask him." Rassam was distressed to find that thieves in
Muscat were punished by having their hands cut off, but as
soon as he explained to the imam that "such punishment was
looked upon now by the civilized world with horror, and I informed him that the British Government would be very much
pleased if this horrible law of maiming would be done away
with altogether, he immediately followed my advice in a most
cheerful way."

When the border settlement was reached and Rassam was
recalled to Aden, the imam wrote to Rassam's superiors in
terms of genuine regret: "We are grieved at the prospect of

this separation more than we are able to describe; for, since his residence with us we have experienced from him nothing but the most kindly interest, and his solicitous endeavours have always been exerted on our behalf. Hence our heart is sad, and we are greatly depressed; nevertheless your orders are supreme, and must be obeyed."

A few years after this success, Rassam's diplomatic skills were put to the test in the most dangerous assignment of his life. A civil war was raging in Abyssinia (known today as Ethiopia) in the Horn of Africa, just across the Red Sea from Aden. The country's king, Theodore, had come to feel that the handful of European missionaries and traders in his country were colluding with his enemies, and in 1864 he arrested them, along with their wives and children. He was particularly angry at the British consul, Captain Charles Duncan Cameron, who had become friendly with an Egyptian bishop whom Theodore regarded as a mortal enemy. It didn't help matters that the English missionaries—sent out by the London Society for the Conversion of the Jews—had written injudiciously of Theodore in a book and in letters home. One letter referred to the king as "His Savage Majesty," a phrase that sounded even worse when—inadvertently or maliciously—it was translated for Theodore as "King of Wild Beasts." Most likely maliciously: a French adventurer named Bardel was working for the king and had ferreted out the incriminating letter—one more small but vicious instance of European rivalries being played out in distant locales. Theodore had Cameron and several English and German missionaries arrested. They were held in chains, and Cameron was subjected to torture. As he later wrote, "I was doubled up until my head appeared under my thighs, and while in this painful posture, I was beaten with a whip of hippopotamus hide on my bare back, until I was covered with weals, and while the blood dripped from my reeking back, I was rolled in sand."

The British government was faced with a dilemma. England had no military force near Abyssinia, and it would be an expensive proposition to send an army thousands of miles from India. Once in Abyssinia, an army would have to struggle through four hundred miles of mountainous wilderness in order to storm Theodore's stronghold at Magdala, a fortified plateau rising a thousand feet above the surrounding landscape. All this in order to rescue a handful of prisoners, assuming that the defenders had not murdered them in the meantime.

Yet the 1857 "Mutiny" (as the British called it) had taken place in India only seven years before, almost toppling British rule, and Theodore's direct affront to British prestige could not be ignored. So the government opted to seek a diplomatic solution. By this time Henry Layard had become deputy foreign minister, and he felt that his friend Hormuzd would be the best person to send, given the king's suspicion of Europeans. So Rassam sailed by steamer across the Red Sea from Aden in July of 1864, bearing a letter from Queen Victoria that gently reproved the king for his ill-advised action but promised friendly relations if the hostages were released.

There was just one problem with the strategy of quiet diplomacy: King Theodore was insane. Born as Kassa, son of a minor chieftain, he had enjoyed early successes in gaining sway over his fellow warlords, and his rapid rise had bred a conviction that he was divinely appointed to fulfill God's will on earth. He began styling himself Emperor Tewodros, the Ethiopian version of the Greek name Theodore ("God's Gift"). He dreamed of invading his enemies to the north, Egypt and

King Theodore's fortress at Magdala.

the Sudan, and then intended to drive Islam from the Holy
Land and conquer India, following the footsteps of his supposed ancestor Alexander the Great.

The first part of this divinely ordained program had gone

well, and Theodore had succeeded in unifying Abyssinia. He was a shrewd strategist, an exceptionally skilled horseman, and a man of considerable personal charm and magnetism. He initiated various reforms in his country, including the abolition of slavery and the building of a rudimentary national governing structure. Yet the country's tribal chiefs resisted his efforts to reduce them to the status of salaried subordinates, and eventually their simmering opposition erupted into full-scale civil war. By the early 1860s Theodore was resorting to increasingly harsh measures against the rebels. A favorite tactic was to herd a rebellious village's entire population into a building, surround it with underbrush, and burn everyone alive. Individuals were often subjected to a more lingering death: the person's hands and feet would be carefully cut off, using a twisting motion to reduce loss of blood, and then the mutilated victim would be left lying outdoors, racked with pain, to die slowly of starvation and thirst.

Following the death of a beloved wife, the king began comforting himself with long drinking bouts and an almost daily succession of mistresses. He started to see plots everywhere, and his fears blossomed into outright paranoia. "A mere suspicion, or a mischievous report while he was heated with drink," Rassam wrote, "was quite sufficient to make him order hundreds of men to be executed for whom, perhaps a few minutes before, he had professed great friendship." According to one of Rassam's companions, Dr. Henry Blanc, "The expression of his dark eyes, slightly depressed, was strange; if he was in good humour they were soft, with a kind of gazelle-like timidity about them that made one love him; but when angry the fierce and bloodshot eye seemed to shed fire." Though Theodore was subject to savage rages, Blanc wrote, "even a few days before his death he had still, when we met him, all the dignity of a sovereign, the amiability and good-breeding of the most accomplished 'gentleman.' His smile was so attractive, his words were so sweet and gracious, that one could hardly believe that the affable monarch was but a consummate dissembler."

Few foreigners had ever met Theodore, and Rassam was optimistic as he steamed across the Red Sea, proud to enjoy the rank of "Envoy Extraordinary" on a sensitive mission. He and Dr. Blanc landed at the sweltering port of Massowah, on the outskirts of Abyssinia, and sent messages into the interior asking permission to bring the queen's letter. Then the waiting began. Theodore either had no interest in receiving Rassam's embassy or he had no way to ensure the diplomats' safe passage through his rebellious land. For almost a year and a half he kept Rassam marking time in Massowah, a fly-ridden, cholera-prone town noted for its intense heat, often 120 degrees in the sparse shade. While Rassam was there a German missionary, fresh off the boat, died of sunstroke after a single bareheaded walk; on the hottest days, Rassam took to wrapping a wet towel around his head for protection. Food was often in scarce supply, and for one entire month Rassam and Blanc had to subsist on rice and Hennessey's brandy.

Rassam spent his time sifting endless rumors about when and how he'd be allowed to approach the king. In the book he wrote about this period, *Narrative of the British Mission to Theodore, King of Abyssinia*, he described the intense tedium of the long wait, broken only by ominous reports of massacres in the ongoing civil war in the interior. Everyone he talked to urged him to give up on the mission. Even the captive consul Cameron held out little hope of success: "For God's sake," he wrote in a letter smuggled out to Rassam, "don't think of coming up here either with or without a safe-conduct. You will only get chains for your pains."

As the waiting wore on, the British government decided that Rassam's mission should be given the added weight of a military presence, and so a Lieutenant Prideaux was sent from Aden to join Rassam and Dr. Blanc. In October 1865 they finally got permission to proceed into the interior. At first they were well received, but then Theodore decided that Rassam's party was also in league with his enemies and he imprisoned them as well. For almost two years, Rassam, Blanc, and Prideaux were kept in chains at Magdala along with Cameron and the missionaries Theodore hated the most, while the other two dozen or so Europeans and their families were kept under house arrest.

Even before this disaster, during the long cat-and-mouse waiting game that preceded Rassam's arrest, questions had been raised in England as to whether Rassam was the right man for the job. Some speculated (on no evidence) that Theodore was annoyed that a true Englishman had not been sent to negotiate with him. Rassam had become a British citizen, but hostile members of Parliament persistently described him as "an Asiatic," "an Oriental gentleman," "an Ottoman," or even—quite incorrectly—as "an Armenian." Interestingly, though Lieutenant Prideaux was added to the mission precisely to give it British backbone, no one ever seems to have criticized him for failing to force the paranoid king to see reason.

Some in England questioned Rassam's character rather than his ethnicity. They wondered whether he was too mild or hesitant to secure the captives' release: was he man enough to be the right man for the job? One journalist later contrasted Rassam's "grovelling" approach to the "spirited and manly" letters written by his fellow captive Dr. Blanc—not pausing to reflect that he was comparing letters Rassam had written to King Theodore with letters that Blanc was getting smuggled out to friends in England. By contrast, one of the captive missionaries later wrote that Rassam had always comported himself "like a Christian and a gentleman" and had refused to be intimidated by Theodore. The missionary said that Rassam had aided their cause by mastering the Abyssinian style of flowery rhetoric, which he used to good strategic effect: "His epistles displayed a tact and ingenuity that won him the admiration of every one with whom he came in contact." Once they were published abroad, however, Rassam's letters looked to many readers like craven flattery. Six years after the final rescue of the hostages, Henry Morton Stanley published a book on the Abyssinian campaign. Missing no opportunity to speak slightingly of Rassam, Stanley emphasized Rassam's slavish submissiveness before Theodore: "Humble were his salaams. . . . With prodigious suavity and wonderful heartiness, Rassam drank the Emperor's health. . . . Many loveable phrases were interchanged, before they parted for the night."

Echoes of Stanley's stereotyping of Rassam as a passive, feminine Oriental could still be heard a century later in Alan Moorehead's classic account of the mission to Theodore in *The Blue Nile* (1962). Moorehead at first describes Rassam as "very able indeed . . . . a supple and persistent man, not at all lacking in bravery," but in the end he falls back on the old explanation: Rassam was just too feminine for the task. "There is something elusive about Rassam," Moorehead claims. "Helpless though they all were in Magdala, he seems at times a little too soft, too compliant, too yielding for his own good. His intimacy with Theodore was certainly not all of his own making, but it is a special sort of intimacy, he submits with a feminine passivity . . . and there is not much doubt that he was as strongly drawn to Theodore as Theodore was to him." In Moorehead's view, Rassam wasn't so much an embattled diplomat as a battered wife who was really asking to be abused all along.

Yet what could Rassam do? During the long wait at Massowah he had been persistent in trying to gain access to Abyssinia. His three-man mission could hardly invade the country on its own, and the British government preferred to exhaust all diplomatic means before contemplating the massive cost and danger of sending in an army. Once Rassam finally had Theodore's permission to meet with him, it required considerable courage to make the journey, in full knowledge that he would be putting his own life at risk. During his ensuing imprisonment, Rassam knew that his fate was "at the whim of the royal gamester." He was forced to engage Theodore in an endless game of wits, seeking the right mixture of flattery, moral pleading, and political pressure to save himself and his fellow prisoners.

Theodore, however, was unmoved by political arguments. When Rassam warned him that his actions were angering the British government and strengthening his enemies' hand, the king retorted, "Never mind your Government and my enemies, my friend. Your masters have already decided upon their treatment of me; and my foes would spread evil reports against me, even if I were to carry you on my head." Theodore could tell that the British government regarded his Islamic enemy Egypt as a more valuable ally than Christian Abyssinia. He imprisoned the consul after Cameron failed to get a reply to his proposal to send a delegation to England to discuss an alliance. Theodore understandably regarded this nonresponse as an insult—and a sign of support for Egypt, which was supplying more and more cotton for England's mills. As one British observer wrote, the foreign minister had quietly decided "to withdraw as much as possible from Abyssinian alliances. His policy was founded entirely on the desire to promote trade." Theodore was probably not the first warlord, and certainly not the last, to try to sway an imperial power by hostage taking when he had gained nothing by ordinary diplomatic means.

Rassam, Cameron, and several others were imprisoned in a round hut fifteen feet in diameter, often manacled with chains. Theodore's attitude toward the Europeans varied with his changeable mood. Approached by a beggar who asked for alms such as "the English masters" had earlier given him, Theodore declared that he was the master and the Englishmen were his slaves; he drove the point home by having the beggar beaten to death on the spot. Yet he also wrote notes to Rassam protesting undying friendship: "Oh! My beloved, send to me for whatever you need, and I will supply it. Don't fear." Visiting the prisoners, he would often harangue them for their many misdeeds, while later the same day he might bring them candles and beer, pouring drinks with his own hand. One day, Theodore smilingly told Rassam, "I used to hear that I was called a madman by my people for my acts, but I never believed it; now, however, after my conduct towards you this afternoon, I have come to the conclusion that I really am so."

As the stalemate dragged on throughout 1866 and into 1867, the opposition in Parliament began accusing the government of weakness and inaction, and newspapers printed lurid accounts of the captives' sufferings. Something had to be done, and finally it was. General Sir Robert Napier was ordered to assemble an invasion force in India, and after several weeks of hectic preparation arrived in January 1868 at Annesley Bay, a Red Sea port on the outskirts of Abyssinia. He was commanding a force of nearly five thousand English soldiers and ten thousand Indian soldiers; with support staff, the companies numbered more than forty thousand men, plus 2,538 horses, 16,022 mules, 4,700 camels, 1,709 donkeys, and—most impressive of all—44 Indian elephants, which were fitted with special howdahs for carrying artillery pieces through the mountainous terrain.

Napier's army included turbaned Sikhs, Punjabi sharpshooters, the Twenty-seventh Wing of Beluchis, explosives experts from Bombay and Madras, and a mounted regiment of the Sind Horse. His English forces included the Third Dragoon Guards, the Duke of Wellington's Regiment, and the Sherwood Foresters. The companies were commanded by seasoned British officers, many of them sporting formidable outworks of facial hair. Napier's army even included a company of naval artillerymen, brought along to man newly invented rocket mortars; they amused their land-based companions by persistently referring to their mules as boats, "wearing the ship round" to "tack through the crowd." The sailors became great friends with the Punjabis. They would dance in the evenings to the accompaniment of the Punjabi military band, whose melodies made up for the lack of any common language between them.

Bringing along a Punjabi military band might have seemed an extravagance to some, but Sir Robert was nothing if not thorough. No expense was spared—and much expense was wasted—in the scramble to outfit the invasion force. The expedition ultimately cost ten million pounds, the equivalent of

Major General Sir Charles Staveley, one of Napier's right-hand men.

perhaps a billion dollars today, three times what the government had forecast. Napier chartered almost seven hundred ships to transport his men, animals, and supplies, including 82,000 tons of coal, massive amounts of rum for the men and wine for the officers, and a case of champagne for the anticipated victory celebration. He even brought along two locomotives and ten miles of train track, just to transport everything from the shore to his base camp inland. To secure communications from the coast all the way to Magdala, he brought four hundred miles of telegraph wire, with poles to string it up—a system that worked only sporadically, as the wires were often snapped by baboons, who liked to climb the poles and swing from the wires by their tails.

Napier's army slowly pushed its way through the mountains toward Magdala, delayed for days at a time while their engineers constructed usable roads. The high mountain passes were particularly difficult for the elephants: "An ascent of

1,500 feet told seriously upon them, and their hard puffing
and loud trumpeting were eloquent of their sufferings." Food
and drink became painfully limited, and the quality de-
graded steadily as the army inched its way along. As one reporter ruefully wrote, "I have seen some rum drunk in which
several cockroaches had committed suicide.... As for cooking, I confess that I avoid the cooking-fires. I have seen sights
which have tried my philosophy to the utmost."

The army's physical problems were compounded by gnaw-
ing uncertainty. No one knew how many of King Theodore's
tens of thousands of troops had remained loyal to him. Would
the British be able to fight in open country or would they be
ambushed in mountain ravines? Would Theodore take refuge
in his fortress at Magdala, or would he simply disappear with
his hostages into the wilderness? Just as Rassam had discovered during his long wait at Massowah, it was impossible for
Napier to get clear information concerning Theodore's inten-
tions or even his whereabouts. According to Henry Morton
Stanley, who was embedded with the troops as a reporter,
"The literal truth was never told in Abyssinia. All Abyssinians are the most stupendous liars, and everything related of
the country ahead was certain to be found false as we jour-
neyed along.... It was passing strange, in such a deceptive
atmosphere and illusive mirage, how anybody could ever say
again one word of truth."

Napier's army finally reached Magdala on Good Friday,
April 10, 1868, after three full months of toiling through the
mountains. Riding ahead with an advance party, Napier
found the fortress a sobering sight. Its sheer cliffs rose above
the high plateau with only a single road up; there were
sturdy gates at the summit, with artillery pieces positioned to
fire down upon the invaders. Most of Theodore's army had

deserted him during the previous years of civil war, but he was left with some four thousand loyal troops, armed with rifles as well as spears and bows and arrows. Magdala could be taken, if at all, only with heavy casualties. To some of the old India hands Abyssinia looked all too similar to Afghanistan, where 4,500 British troops had been overwhelmed in 1842 by Afghan fighters who took every advantage of the terrain and succeeded in massacring almost the entire force.

Ironically, it was a major British blunder that saved the day for Sir Robert. As his weary, bedraggled force made its way slowly through a final valley leading up to the plateau around Magdala, a company of eight hundred soldiers that was supposed to precede the pack animals lagged behind them. "The whole of the baggage was therefore open to an attack from Magdala," as one reporter commented; "a more stupendous blunder never was made, and had we the most contemptible European force to deal with instead of savages, we must have sustained a crushing disaster." Elated at the opportunity to destroy the invaders' supplies and take large amounts of spoil, Theodore sent his men charging down toward the apparently helpless convoy two miles away. He had not observed, however, that Napier was already on a nearby hillside with a substantial body of soldiers, while the main force was hastening up the ravine just behind the pack train. The English succeeded in getting into position on the valley's slopes just as the Abyssinians came within range.

What then took place was either a glorious victory or a brutal slaughter. After peering down from Napier's hillside during the battle, Henry Morton Stanley described the conflict in the breathless tones of a boy's adventure story: "Onward, still onward they came, horsemen and foot soldiers vieing with each other. They flung their flowing symas, their bezans, and many flung their loin clouts away, and with lances and shields in rest they bore down the hill, reached the plateau, and inundated it with their dusky bodies. A clear open plain was before them, over which they rolled like a huge wave! . . . The fiery, hot-blooded, impulsive Sikhs came hand to hand with Ethiopian mountaineers, fierce and impulsive as they. Now came the tug of a genuine contest!"

Another reporter on the scene, G. A. Henty, described the Good Friday battle in far more sober terms:

> With my glass I could distinguish every fea-
> ture, and as we looked at them coming forward
> at a run, with their bright-coloured floating
> robes, their animated gestures, their shields
> and spears, one could not help feeling pity for
> them, ruffians and cut-throats as most of them
> undoubtedly were, to think what a terrible re-
> ception they were about to meet with. As the
> enemy poured down the ravine they were re-
> ceived by a withering fire from the deadly
> Snider. A portion of the Punjabees came down
> the ravine and took them in flank, and some
> of the guns of Penn's battery, getting upon a
> projecting spur, scattered death everywhere
> amongst them. . . . It was a terrible slaughter,
> and could hardly be called a fight.

The British pursued the Abyssinians onto the plateau as huge thunderstorms rolled overhead. Their breech-loading Snider rifles could fire ten rounds for every one round of the Abyssinians' older guns, and within three hours nearly two thousand of the Abyssinian fighters had been killed or

seriously wounded. The British army lost two men. As dusk
fell and the surviving Abyssinians reached the safety of Magdala, Henty went into the field, where his attention was
drawn to a dozen bodies lying in a little hollow: "Some had
died instantaneously, shot through the head; others had fallen
mortally wounded, and several of those had drawn their robes
over their faces, and died like Stoics." The corpses were not
the worst sight: "Some were only severely wounded, and these
had endeavoured to crawl into bushes, and there lay uttering
low moans. Their gaudy silk bodices, the white robes with
scarlet ends which had flaunted so gaily but two hours since,
now lay dabbled with blood, and dank with the heavy rains
which had been pitilessly coming down for the last hour."

Theodore tried to commit suicide that night, but his pistol
would not fire. His advisers wrestled the gun away from him,
and after a long debate as to whether they should kill the
hostages—as most urged—Theodore decided to sue for peace.
He released the captives the next day as a goodwill gesture,
but Napier demanded his unconditional surrender, and after a
day of indecision Theodore refused, at which point most of his
men deserted him and streamed down the road from Magdala.
Napier's troops then stormed up the roadway on Easter Mon-
day, with infantrymen providing covering fire for the sappers
who would blow up the gates. There was an embarrassing delay when the British reached the gates, however, for in a moment worthy of Monty Python the sappers discovered they
had forgotten to bring any gunpowder along and had to go
back down to the plateau to get some. By that time the gates'
few defenders were killed or driven back and the British were
able to climb over the walls before the hapless sappers returned. Inside, Theodore and his few remaining supporters
were soon driven into the king's compound. This time, the

revolver that Theodore put in his mouth did its job. It had been a gift from Queen Victoria fourteen years earlier, after he had hunted down a gang of bandits who had murdered Colonel Cameron's predecessor as consul. It bore an engraved plaque:

PRESENTED

BY

VICTORIA

QUEEN OF GREAT BRITAIN AND IRELAND

TO

· THEODORUS

EMPEROR OF ABYSSINIA

AS A SLIGHT TOKEN OF HER GRATITUDE

FOR HIS KINDNESS TO HER SERVANT PLOWDEN

1854

It had taken four years to achieve the hostages' rescue, but it took only a few days for the British to leave Magdala. First they held an auction of valuables recovered from Theodore's compound, the proceeds of which were divided among the enlisted men; a representative of the British Museum bought a large collection of illuminated Ethiopic manuscripts. Then they set all the plateau's buildings on fire. From Magdala they marched straight back to Annesley Bay, packed up the locomotives and the thirty-nine surviving elephants, and sailed back to India.

On the day after his failed suicide attempt, Theodore had written a dignified letter to Sir Robert Napier, refusing to surrender but urging him to stay long enough in Abyssinia to bring some order to the country: "God has given you the power. See that you forsake not these people. . . . My country-

men have turned their backs on me and have hated me, because I imposed tribute upon them, and sought to bring them
under military discipline. You have prevailed against me by
means of people brought into a state of discipline." Theodore
ended his letter with a melancholy farewell: "You people, who
have passed the night in joy, may God not do unto you as he
has done to me!"

Napier was unmoved by Theodore's letter; he had no
intention of staying a moment longer than necessary. One
of Rassam's Abyssinian friends—characteristically, Rassam
made many friends while in captivity—asked him whether the
rumor was true that the English were going to pull out without establishing any government in Theodore's place. "On my
replying in the affirmative, telling them at the same time that
they must learn to govern themselves, they rejoined, 'You
mean that we must cut each other's throats.' "

The Abyssinian campaign had a mixed aftermath. Gradually two of the country's warlords established themselves as
the dominant figures, one in the north and one in the south,
and a measure of peace returned by 1872. After one warlord
died some years later the survivor, Menelik II, gained control
over the whole country. He ruled until 1913, achieving the
centralized government that Theodore had attempted, and
was generally successful in resisting ongoing intrusions by
Egypt, Turkey, England, France, and then Italy. As for the
British, Sir Robert Napier returned with his troops to India
and then proceeded to England, where he was received in triumph. Queen Victoria elevated him to the title of Lord
Napier of Magdala, and glowing biographies were written
about him. The former hostages were besieged with offers
from publishers, and several of them wrote memoirs.

Hormuzd Rassam was welcomed home in England by his

many friends, and the government gave him a cash award of
£5,000 in recognition of his hard service. He was sure he had
done the best he possibly could amid the constant uncertainty
and fear of his four-year ordeal. He was shocked, though, to
find how widely the press had portrayed him as incompetent
or worse—someone who had succumbed to the evil king's
wiles, taken bribes, and gained advantages for himself at the
other captives' expense. He settled into the London suburb of
Twickenham, gradually regaining his health and writing his
book to set out his side of the story. In closing his account, he
quoted a testimonial from the foreign minister praising his
"prudence, discretion, and good management," adding:
"Proud of having been judged worthy of such a testimonial
from her Majesty's Government, I shall feel prouder still of
the approval of the British public, to whose verdict this Narrative of the Mission to King Theodore is now submitted. A
Chaldean by birth, Great Britain is the country of my adop-
tion; but although I cannot boast of being an Englishman, I
can glory in this—that, to the best of my ability, I have endeavoured to emulate the loyalty of her most loyal sons."

Rassam's 700-page *Narrative of the British Mission to
Theodore, King of Abyssinia* was brought out in 1869 by
John Murray, the leading publisher of imperial travel writing, but it had little impact. Too detailed in describing the
long wait in Massowah and the fruitless maneuverings in captivity, it did not appeal to general readers. Lord Napier of
Magdala emerged as the real hero of the episode, with Rassam
not even enjoying the status of exemplary victim. This was reserved for the missionaries, who had suffered nobly for their
faith. "The Saviour was indeed with me," as Rev. Henry
Stern wrote, "and His presence diffused peace and comfort
around the captive home of the crushed missionary."

Frontispiece to Henry Stern, *The Captive Missionary*. This engraving looks like an eyewitness portrait from the time of captivity, but it is actually an artful reconstruction after the fact. Looming over Rassam (seated second from left), Henry Stern offers comfort to the Madonna-like missionary's wife at the center of the group.

People who had long made up their minds against Rassam were unlikely to be swayed by his self-defense at this late date. Henry Morton Stanley, for example, shows no sign of having bothered to read Rassam's book before publishing his *Coomassie and Magdala*, with its insulting portrayal of Rassam, in 1874. Though the government praised Rassam's work, his mission could hardly be called a triumph of diplomacy, and the Foreign Office did not offer him promotion to new posts of greater responsibility. Rather than return to a low-level job at an obscure outpost, Rassam settled into semiretirement in England, attending meetings of archaeological societies and writing essays on religious affairs. He got married, at age forty-two, to Anne Eliza Price, daughter of a captain of the Seventy-seventh Highlanders; they eventually had six daughters and a son.

Rassam found his Abyssinian experience "fast fading away into the unreality of a dream," as he reported at the close of his book, yet it had profound effects on his life. Had his mission been more successful, he could have advanced in the diplomatic service to positions of real responsibility and, like his mentor Layard, never have returned to the archaeological work of his early days. The sudden short-circuiting of his government career left Rassam at loose ends, open to renewing his Assyriological interests and his contacts at the British Museum. As a result, the ambiguous end of the mission to King Theodore paved the way for what was to be the major phase of Rassam's archaeological career.

Less positively, Rassam's sensitivities to slights, insults, and accusations of misdealing were reinforced by the often hostile reception his diplomatic efforts had received in England, with disastrous results in his later dealings with the museum. For several years after his liberation Rassam seemed beyond the reach of any further controversy, for his professional life appeared to be over. The situation suddenly changed when George Smith met his untimely end in 1876, and the British Museum determined to continue and extend the work that Smith had so tragically left undone. Realizing the value of the local knowledge Smith lacked—or simply hesitating to risk the life of another museum employee so soon after his death—the trustees turned again to Rassam. This time they wanted him to conduct a series of excavations at multiple sites in Iraq, from Babylon in the south to Nineveh in the north. Rassam made annual expeditions from 1876 through 1882, and conducted excavations at thirty or more locations, several of which yielded important finds.

Most famous archaeologists have become known through their discoveries in one or two places—Layard at Nineveh,

Schliemann at Troy and Mycenae, Howard Carter at Tutankhamen's tomb—but Rassam had multiple successes. Iraq had hundreds of ruin mounds, almost all untouched, many in deserted areas that had not been overbuilt. Rassam was exceptionally skillful at assessing likely sites, and he was endlessly energetic at pursuing leads given to him by his extensive local contacts. Then, too, he was working under orders from the British Museum to find as many tablets and sculptures as possible, so he didn't stay too long at any one site. The modern discipline of archaeology was still in its infancy, only just developing the thorough methods that reward the patient sifting of a site over a period of years to uncover centuries of history layer by layer. Rassam regretted that he never had time for such basic work as tracing the full dimensions of Babylon's walls, but if he wasn't turning up objects the museum could acquire, he had to move on.

Rassam's energy impressed all who met him. As one of Layard's old Baghdad friends wrote in 1880, "This Rassam is . . . a Jackal of the Desert who goes from hole to hole and from place to place, really Rassam takes great pain and does great works but he is inadequately compensated in comparison to his trouble—he spends his life like the Basrah tide in going to England and returning to Arabistan." The writer was equally impressed by Rassam's nine-year-old daughter Theresa: "Rassam's eldest daughter proves to be a rare and uncommon Oriental type amongst the beauties of the sex in England." Perhaps reflecting on the transience of youth, the writer rather surprisingly turned to thoughts of Henry Rawlinson's wife: "Lady Rawlinson previous to her marriage was like a wild Gazelle, now she has become like an Iron Elephant."

Theresa, however, continued to thrive as she grew up, enchanting her parents with her abilities as a singer.

During these years of archaeological work, Rassam had teams of excavators working at a dozen or more sites at once, and he would visit them in turn, concentrating his time wherever the best discoveries were being made. His multiple digs yielded many treasures, including seventy thousand tablets from the ancient Babylonian city of Sippar and a pair of monumental bronze gates from Balawat in Assyria, on which rows of beautifully molded figures march in procession. These and other finds led to Rassam's being awarded a major prize by the Royal Academy of Sciences at Turin in 1882.

Rassam was now fully established as a leading archaeologist. Yet the sheer number of excavations meant that he couldn't supervise them in person even on a monthly basis, much less daily; so he had to rely on foremen to oversee the work and keep items from being pilfered from the sites. The situation was still more difficult during the several months each year when Rassam would return to England, as it was impossible to stop the workmen from continuing to dig on their own account, selling new finds to Baghdad antiquities dealers. From 1883 onward matters became murkier still as Rassam stayed in England while his foremen carried on excavating on the museum's behalf. As a favor to the museum, Rassam continued on an unpaid basis to coordinate the work as best he could from England, but he was far from the scene.

Rumors began circulating that some of Rassam's trusted foremen were actively colluding in taking sculptures from British Museum sites. Worse, some people suspected that Rassam himself might have a hand in the clandestine trade, perhaps because he had hired his nephew Nimroud as one of his

foremen. Concerned, the British Museum sent E. A. Wallis
Budge to investigate in 1887. Thirty years old at the time,
Budge was an ambitious assistant curator who felt he should
be managing the museum's Assyrian interests rather than Rassam, who might know the sites but could not read cuneiform.
Budge spent the winter of 1887–88 in Iraq. He discovered that
there was indeed a steady trade in illicitly excavated artifacts
from the museum's sites and decided that Rassam must have
some direct involvement. Either because his Arabic wasn't fluent or because he heard what he wanted to hear, Budge came
away with the impression that all the foremen were Rassam's
relatives and were taking their cues from him. Though he
couldn't prove anything, Budge spread the word at the museum that Rassam was not to be trusted.

When Rassam began to hear about these accusations, he
was no longer formally connected with the museum. Sixty-two
years old in 1888, he had retired to Brighton, where he and his
wife lived in a cozy semidetached house with elegant bay-front
windows. His diplomatic career had been stymied amid the
false accusations of bribe taking in Abyssinia, and he was hor-
rified to think that his renewed archaeological achievements
could be tainted as well. Insult was added to injury in 1890,
when Budge was assigned to revise the Near Eastern section of
the British Museum's visitors' guide, and in the process several mentions of Rassam's contributions were dropped. Thirty-
five years before, the credit for his initial finds had largely
gone to Rawlinson and Loftus, and now Rassam found history
repeating itself in a most unpleasant way.

Although profoundly upset, Rassam could do nothing until
Budge made the mistake of speaking scornfully about him during a visit that Austen Henry Layard made to the British Museum in July of 1891. Thanks to his early discoveries Layard

was still the most famous British archaeologist, and by now he was also a retired ambassador and former member of Parliament. A formidable ally for his old friend, Layard was shocked to hear Budge slandering Rassam in the museum's public galleries; Budge went so far as to claim that Rassam had sent the museum only worthless fragments of tablets, while the best tablets had been sold off on the side to private dealers. Layard wrote all this to Rassam, giving him the evidence needed to call Budge to account. Rassam then wrote to Maunde Thompson, the British Museum's principal librarian or chief executive officer, demanding an investigation and an apology. Thompson reacted by protecting Budge, a protégé of his. His investigation consisted of a conversation with Budge, who denied having said anything "in public" about Rassam, apparently hoping that his conversation with Layard could be written off as museum-related business. Thompson took Budge at his word and told Rassam that the case was closed.

Deeply aggrieved, Rassam sent Thompson a forty-eight-page complaint summarizing the long history of his work for the museum and insisting that he had always maintained the strictest standards of honesty. Layard and others weighed in on Rassam's behalf, and Maunde Thompson finally got Budge to produce a truculent letter of half-apology in December 1891. In it, Budge implausibly claimed that he hadn't intended to be understood literally when he remarked that "we got all the rubbish and other people got all the tablets." He then apologized for having stated that Rassam was related to the thieving agents, but in the process underscored the claim of widespread dishonesty having occurred on Rassam's watch.

Far from reprimanding Budge in any substantial way, Maunde Thompson promoted him to the position of acting head of the museum's Near Eastern division—passing over a

more senior Assyriologist who had annoyed him by supporting Layard and Rassam against Budge. Thompson considered
Rassam to be "unduly sensitive" and admitted to Layard only
that "Budge has certainly been most indiscreet"—a response
that seemed to endorse Budge's slander, merely criticizing
him for having voiced his suspicions openly. Thompson hoped
that the whole affair would somehow blow over; as he wrote to
Layard, "I think we need have no more of these storms."

Layard was livid. He went public with his criticisms, writing a letter to the London *Times* denouncing Budge for trying to sabotage the reputation of a rival, and accusing the
British Museum of a cover-up. As supporting evidence, Layard noted that Budge had deleted the most prominent mention of Rassam in the museum's guide. In reply, Thompson
rather weakly asserted, "It is true that the passage referred to
does not mention Mr. Rassam by name; but in a popular
guide-book to the galleries of a great museum it is impossible
to go into minute details. . . . No disrespect for Mr. Rassam
was intended by silently including him under the words 'and
others.'"

Rassam responded by suing Budge for slander. In a twenty-
seven-page affidavit in support of his complaint, Rassam referred with wounded dignity to the museum's years of justified
reliance on him. "The first time that I began to suspect that
some underhand intrigue was going on to prejudice the
Trustees against me," he wrote, "was after Mr. Budge's first
expedition to Baghdad in the beginning of 1888. I certai·ly
never thought that after my long devoted service that I should
be treated so unexpectedly with unmerited discourtesy." Suddenly, he found, "everything I had done seemed to count for
nothing." It was galling to Rassam to be accused of theft after
he had served as an unpaid adviser, visiting the museum and

writing from Brighton for several years, "without even charg-ing for traveling expenses and postages." He implored the court to clear his good name, and asked for damages of £1,000.

Rassam made a terrible mistake in filing this lawsuit, for he faced a wily and well-connected opponent. Fortified with an armature of upper-class-sounding names, Ernest Alfred Thompson Wallis Budge had emerged from circumstances of deep obscurity. Born in 1857 in a town in Cornwall, he was the son of a young woman whose father was a waiter at a local hotel; the identity of Budge's father is unknown. Budge left school at age twelve, becoming an articled clerk in a London law firm headed by a member of Parliament. As a boy, Budge developed a passionate interest in biblical languages and his-tory, and at age fifteen in 1872 he began frequenting the British Museum's Near Eastern reading room, just when George Smith was making his discovery of the Flood story tablet.

Throughout his life, Budge proved to be a passionate col-lector, of both ancient manuscripts and modern patrons. Samuel Birch, the head of the Near Eastern department, took a liking to him and helped him get lessons in Akkadian. George Smith gave him pointers as well, no doubt seeing Budge as a younger version of himself. Budge would often spend his lunch hours in Saint Paul's Cathedral, near the law firm where he was a clerk, to have a quiet place to study his languages. There he came to the attention of the cathedral's socially well-connected organist, who was tremendously im-pressed by the young man's diligence and evident talent. The organist persuaded Budge's employer and their mutual friend Prime Minister Gladstone to send Budge to Cambridge to study Hebrew.

On graduation in 1883, Budge was hired by the museum

as the "Assistant Keeper" in the Near Eastern department, and his career was launched. He shortened his weighty name to E. A. Wallis Budge, dropping "Thompson" outright. He worked at the museum until his retirement in 1924, and made many trips to the Middle East to acquire ancient manuscripts. A great raconteur, Budge was a popular dinner guest among the circle of wealthy patrons of ancient art. He excelled at writing flirtatious letters to society matrons, combining archaeological adventure with tactful appeals for funds in support of further work. Often signing his letters with the humorous nickname "Budgie" (short for the Australian term *budgerigar,* or parakeet), he looked a good deal like a five-and-a-half-foot budgie with a bristling mustache. He could be charming under the right circumstances, yet neither he nor his powerful patrons would ever forgive Rassam for making their dispute public.

The trial took place in late June and early July 1893 and involved extensive testimony from witnesses for both sides. There could be no denying that stolen artifacts were widely available in Baghdad. Some had likely been supplied by three brothers hired by Rassam, all sons of an untrustworthy old overseer named Fat Toma, so called after a mule collapsed under his weight. As far back as 1851, Christian Rassam had written emphatically to Layard that "I cannot place the least confidence in Fat Toma," and several months later Matilda asserted, "If I followed my own inclinations I would dismiss Fat Toma immediately." The sons seem to have taken after their father. Yet Budge was forced to admit that he had no evidence that Rassam had ever been involved in the illegal antiquities trade.

The press covered the trial with a kind of irritated fascination, not quite believing that so much passion could be stirred up over details of tablet fragments and stolen cylinder seals. As the London *Daily News* said in an editorial, "The trial was, in some respects, a sort of antiquarian festival. These distinguished persons have not been in the intimacy of Assurbanipal for nothing. Their measures of time are not as our measures. Otherwise, the better part of a week would hardly have been devoted to the settlement of such a case." In a vein of bemused reflection, the London *Times* regretted that despite the British Museum's appearance of quiet elegance, "an atmosphere of monastic tranquility does not always pervade the great building in Bloomsbury. The truth is that the combative instinct in man seems to be as constant, if not quite as active, in his nature now as in the days when the oldest of the mummies led his armies to victory or defeat." Scholars, the writer noted, "have always been particularly subject to its sway, and amongst the whole order of scholars the collectors and the antiquarians have not been the least pugnacious." The *Times* concluded that Rassam had a case, but that he should never have brought it; Budge's earlier apology should have sufficed.

The judge in the case, Mr. Justice Cave, took a more serious view of the matter. In its heavy folio volume labeled "Rassam v. Budge, 1893," the British Museum's Central Archive preserves his summation and instructions to the jury. Transcribed from a court reporter's shorthand notes, the typescript runs thirty-three pages. "Gentlemen of the Jury," Justice Cave began, "this is a Case of some considerable importance, and also of some little difficulty." He detailed the evidence of irregularities, Budge's exaggerated charges, and the museum's efforts to avoid responsibility for his remarks. The crux of the case, in Mr. Justice Cave's view, was that Budge had defamed Rassam and then had refused to admit he had been wrong. Cave was acerbic in discussing Budge's note of

apology to Rassam: "Now I cannot help saying that that
sounds to me to be as shabby an apology as ever I read in my
life. It is not a manly apology; to start with he does not retract
anything. . . . It is ridiculous and absurd to my mind, to call
that an apology which one gentleman ought to write to another." As Mr. Justice Cave realized, the fundamental issue
was the recognition for which Rassam had striven all his life:
the right to be treated *as a gentleman*.

People like Maunde Thompson, who thought that Rassam
was being unduly sensitive, were implicitly denying that an
Iraqi could merit "an apology which one gentleman ought to
write to another." Implicitly, or sometimes even explicitly
denying it. As the trial date approached, a German archaeologist wrote to Thompson to express his surprise that Rassam
had ever been entrusted with responsibility. Having met Rassam in Mosul in 1880, he wrote, "That man made—by all I
heard and saw of him—a very unfavourable impression upon
me. . . . I could not understand—nor can I so now—why the
Brit. Gov't had entrusted with the excavations of Ninive a
common sort of Levantine without the slightest education,
and not a gentleman as e.g. the then consul Russell. . . . [I] can
only say that the direction of such a work demands more conscience, character and education than the average of a native
of the East—in particular one without the least European
education—can muster."

Such attitudes were to have a long life in the field. It is
striking, for example, to see a mid-twentieth-century archaeologist display his prejudice against Rassam in the very act
of denying it: "There is something in Rassam's conduct as an
explorer which induces a peculiar distaste. . . . Without laying oneself open to a charge of prejudice, one may perhaps be
allowed to suggest that the picture of an Englishman like

Layard frustrating by patience and good-humour the impor-
tunities of oriental malice and bigotry appeals to one more
than that of Victor Place . . . being outwitted by a born Moslâwi
in what can only be described as an undignified scramble for
archaeological loot."

In 1893, there was a limit to how seriously a British jury
would take the quest of "a born Moslâwi" to clear his name,
and in the end Rassam both won and lost his suit. The jury
found in his favor, agreeing that Budge had unjustly ma-
ligned him. Yet instead of granting Rassam the £1,000 he'd
asked for, the jury awarded him token damages of only £50,
accepting Budge's claim that he had simply been repeating in
good faith what he'd been told in Baghdad. Rassam returned
to his retirement in Brighton, ostracized from the museum
and with substantial legal fees to pay. The newly promoted
Budge, meanwhile, kept his position at the museum, and a
group of friends raised a subscription to pay his legal fees.
The following year, he was made permanent head of his department, a post he held for the rest of his career. He went on
to become a prolific editor of Egyptian texts (his *Book of the
Dead* is still in print today) and to write popular accounts of
Egyptian religion. He developed an interest in paranormal
activities and spiritualism, and his books are often reprinted
now by publishers of esoteric wisdom. He was knighted in
1920, in recognition of his contributions to Egyptology and
his long service to the British Museum.

In a final effort at self-defense, Rassam published his archaeological memoirs, *Asshur and the Land of Nimrod*, pointedly subtitling the book with a long list of the places where he
had been most active: *Being an Account of the Discoveries
Made in the Ancient Ruins of Nineveh, Asshur, Sepharvaim,
Calah, Babylon, Borsippa, Cuthah, and Van, Including a*

Narrative of Different Journeys in Mesopotamia, Assyria, Asia Minor, and Koordistan. Yet he couldn't find a single British publisher to take the manuscript. After a long delay, he finally managed to publish the book in New York. It appeared in 1897, with a frontispiece showing Rassam holding photographs of panels from the magnificent bronze gates he

discovered at Balawat, as though they were exhibits in an unending legal case.

Signed "Your's sincerely," Rassam's final appeal went unheard: few took note of the book, and most of his finds continued to be credited to Layard, Rawlinson, Loftus, and even George Smith, who was a child when Rassam found Ashurbanipal's library and died before Rassam made his later series of expeditions. Rassam did have the pleasure of dedicating his book to his lifelong friend and greatest supporter, Henry Layard, "the pioneer of Assyrian explorers, whose friendship of fifty years' standing was as true in my youth as it proved constant in my advancing years." Even this pleasure was a melancholy one, as Layard died in 1894, when Rassam was still trying to get his book published.

Despite his disappointments, Hormuzd Rassam lived out his life as the English gentleman he felt himself to be. In one essay written in retirement, he even asserted a direct link between his two worlds: he argued that the English language was descended from his native tongue, "Aramaic, or what is commonly known as Chaldee." As examples he listed several similar-sounding words in both languages, and he observed that "the most quaint resemblance that I have seen between the English and Semitic languages is in the common phrase 'tally-ho'; because *tally* in Chaldean means fox. When a fox-hunter, therefore, calls out 'tally-ho,' it means, in Chaldean, the 'fox-ho.' . . . If this resemblance occurs only as a coincidence, it is certainly a very curious accident." On this theory, the very language of England's fox-hunting aristocrats had made the same migration he himself had performed.

Rassam was a devoted father, and he made sure that his seven children received excellent educations. He had always taken particular pride in his oldest daughter, Theresa—

named for his mother, who had died while he was first in England. A beauty since childhood, Theresa proved to have a lovely singing voice as well. Given her father's long struggle for acceptance in England, there is poetic justice in Theresa's successful career in that most British of all musical spheres: the theater of Gilbert and Sullivan. From 1902 to 1907 Theresa was a principal in the D'Oyly Carte Opera Company, performing the contralto lead in every Gilbert and Sullivan operetta in the company's repertoire. Theresa excelled in many roles, from *The Mikado*'s oriental Katisha to the noble Lady Blanche in *Princess Ida* to the winsome Little Buttercup in *H.M.S. Pinafore*. Her father surely appreciated the irony of her success.

Rassam lived on to a ripe old age in Brighton, dying in 1910 at age eighty-four, long forgotten by everyone. Or so he thought. It is probably just as well he didn't know how implacably Wallis Budge would pursue him even after death. In 1920 Budge published *By Nile and Tigris*, a two-volume memoir in which he reprinted without comment a set of newspaper articles about the trial, making sure to present only those that had been most favorable to him. In addition, in dozens of passing references throughout his book, Budge painted a portrait of Rassam as an incompetent who allowed rampant misdealings among his subordinates. For evidence, Budge cited rumors and secondhand reports from sources including the German professor who had disparaged Rassam as "a common sort of Levantine." As for Ashurbanipal's library, Budge unblushingly described its discovery as Layard's "great 'find' of tablets in 1854," despite the fact that Layard was thousands of miles away in England during the entire year of Rassam's pivotal expedition.

Four years later, Budge indulged in a final hatchet job

when he retired and wrote the history of Assyriology. Once again he tried to take some of Rassam's major finds away from him, attributing several of them to Rawlinson. He also described visiting the site where Rassam had found his famous bronze gates and claimed—quite wrongly—that they could not have been found where Rassam had said; the implication was that someone must have unearthed them elsewhere. In *The Rise and Progress of Assyriology*, Budge insistently portrayed Rassam as Layard and Rawlinson's feckless assistant, out of his depth once he tried to work on his own, and this was the view that held sway for most of the twentieth century. If history is usually written by the victors, it is clear who won the case of "Rassam v. Budge, 1893."

CHAPTER 5

AFTER ASHURBANIPAL,
THE DELUGE

Royal procession.

AMONG the thousands of artifacts that Layard, Rassam, and
Smith recovered from Nineveh, two images can serve to introduce life in the Assyrian empire: a picnic beneath a severed
head and a mongoose darting out from beneath a chariot. A
relief from Ashurbanipal's palace contains the first of these
images, a portrait in death of the luckless Elamite king Teumman, disloyal former ally of the Assyrians. His head swings
from the branches of a tree in Ashurbanipal's garden as
birds flit by, a woman plays a harp, and the king and his favorite queen enjoy an outdoor feast. Hormuzd Rassam, who

"The Garden Party," c. 645 BCE. King Teumman's head hangs from the tree on the left, suspended by a rope through his jaw, while a harpist plays nearby and attendants bring food to the king and queen, who are cooled by a pair of fans as they relax under a grape arbor.

unearthed this scene, named it "The Garden Party." Assyrian kings are usually portrayed in formal postures of piety and command, but here Ashurbanipal reclines as he eats, as if to emphasize his carefree pleasure in the scene around him— harp, head, and all. This is the public face of empire as the Assyrians projected it: ruthless, magnificent, supremely self-confident.

The mongoose is another matter. It makes its fleeting appearance in a letter written to Ashurbanipal's father, Esarhaddon, in about 675 BCE. This is one of more than two thousand letters that survived on clay tablets in the wreckage

of Nineveh's palaces. Cryptic, fragmentary, and less spectacular than the great palace reliefs that dazzled Layard and Rassam, these letters give an intimate picture of everyday life in the Assyrian court. In this letter, Esarhaddon's chief scribe was replying to an anxious message from the king. Evidently, Esarhaddon was riding out from Nineveh when something ominous occurred.

Usually the king stayed inside his heavily guarded palace, relaxing in his harem or sitting in state in his throne room, visited by his courtiers or foreign ambassadors, who would be suitably impressed as they were led to his chambers down long

corridors lined with scenes of slaughter. On the occasions
when Esarhaddon emerged from the palace for a trip beyond
the city walls—always a moment of public drama—he would
be surrounded by his sons and most loyal retainers, along
with the suppliants and sycophants who had been lucky
enough to get near the royal chariot. The chariot was a magnificent vehicle, carved and painted in glowing colors, drawn
by a pair of richly bridled horses. The king would stand
proudly in the center of the chariot, his braided beard flowing down over his embroidered robes, an ivory-inlaid bow in
his grasp if he was heading out for his favorite sport, a lion
hunt. With his charioteer before him and a servant shielding
him from the sun with a tasseled parasol, he would ride
through the great archway of one of the city's eighteen gates,
crowned high above with battlements and guarded by scores
of eagle-eyed archers.

Everything on this particular day was just as it should be
for the ruler of the world—until a mongoose suddenly ran beneath his chariot. Esarhaddon was unsettled by this sight:
Could it be a warning from the gods? Was there not a line
somewhere in the omen texts about the dangerous meaning of
an animal running between your legs? The king was planning
to crush a cluster of Arabian sheikhdoms at the edge of his
empire; now he hesitated. That mongoose . . . perhaps this was
not the best time to go to war? But then again—Esarhaddon
often had second thoughts—the omen text spoke about an animal running between a man's *legs*: in the case of standing in a
chariot, perhaps it could be said that the mongoose had not
run between the royal legs as such? These are the questions he
put to his chief scribe, a priest named Issar-shumu-eresh.

Issar-shumu-eresh would have none of this hairsplitting,
and replied in no uncertain terms: "As to what my lord the

king wrote to me: 'Does the omen "If something passes between the legs of a man" apply to something that came out from underneath a chariot?'—it does apply." The portent was indeed significant: "If a mongoose passes between the legs of a man, the hand of the god or the hand of the king will seize him." But who exactly was in danger? As one of Esarhaddon's trusted advisers, Issar-shumu-eresh could speak frankly, and he brusquely dismissed the king's hesitation about his upcoming campaign: "Let us say 'mercy' for the Nabataeans? Why? Are they not hostile kings? They will not submit beneath my lord the king's chariot!" As the priest understood the omen, the Nabataeans were only so many mongooses, nothing more than imperial roadkill. The king, however, was not so sure.

Esarhaddon and his son Ashurbanipal were monarchs of all they surveyed, and they received tribute from almost every land they had ever heard of, and even some they hadn't: Ashurbanipal recorded with pride that he received gifts and pleas for help from King Gyges of Lydia, "a distant country whose name the kings, my fathers, had never heard." The Assyrian kings had built the greatest empire on the face of the earth, stretching from Elam in western Persia across Mesopotamia and Arabia into Egypt, and up the Mediterranean coast through Palestine and Syria into Asia Minor. The royal title "King of the World and King of Assyria" was not just a figure of speech for them. And yet these lordly and rapacious monarchs were at the mercy of every passing mongoose or, rather, of the god or goddess who had set the mongoose in their path. The gods had given them everything in the world, and the gods could just as easily take it all away again—which happened a few years after Ashurbanipal's death, when the Assyrian empire came to its sudden, crashing end in 612 BCE, never to recover.

The Assyrian kings used all sorts of strategies to maintain their tenuous grip on absolute power. They developed elaborate bureaucracies to manage trade, diplomacy, and warfare, creating models of imperial organization that would be refined for centuries to come by the Persians, the Romans, and finally the Ottomans. Not at all a static, archaic society, the Assyrians were self-consciously modern, and their kings loved to boast in their annals of having done things undreamt of by their fathers, from conquering new lands to inventing a better water pump. They constantly improved their armies, introducing innovation after innovation in weapons and tactics, and they spent lavishly to build temples and to commission oracles and divinations, seeking to please the gods and learn their will. Yet they never relied on the gods alone for guidance: they employed spies and agents both abroad and in their own palaces, keeping their finger on the pulse of the region's constantly shifting alliances and their own courtiers' endless infighting. Ashurbanipal used all these methods, and for good measure he added a distinctive initiative of his own: he created the world's greatest library.

Libraries were a Mesopotamian invention. The first organized collections of texts were made by the Sumerians in southern Mesopotamia around 2500 BCE, and by Ashurbanipal's time archives could be found in many different locations. Priests consulted religious texts, palaces kept annals and diplomatic correspondence, and different branches of the bureaucracy maintained more specialized archives, such as those kept at Nineveh by "the Horse Department" and "the Wine Department." Collections could also be found beyond court and temple circles: merchant families maintained archives of contracts and business correspondence, and private individuals assembled small libraries of religious and literary texts for their own instruction and pleasure.

Ashurbanipal, however, went far beyond this. The nucleus of his collection was the archive held at the palace he inherited from his father and grandfather, but he added greatly to it, and he included a large library room when he built a palace of his own north of his father's palace. The temple of Nabu, patron of writing, became a third major repository, and together the three locations held Ashurbanipal's constantly growing collection. His library was not only the largest ever created, it was the most comprehensive, with important texts from all over his empire; the best organized, with tablets copied in standard formats, carefully numbered, labeled, and catalogued; and the most accurate, with great efforts taken to ensure the correct copying of older texts. Mesopotamian literature is known today chiefly from Ashurbanipal's collections.

Though pieces of *The Epic of Gilgamesh* have been unearthed in a dozen other locations, only Ashurbanipal's library has preserved a largely complete text of the epic, of which it had several copies. The epic was known either as the "Series of Gilgamesh" or by its opening phrase, *Sha naqba imuru*, "He who saw into the depths"—a phrase that refers to deep water and metaphorically signifies profound understanding, since Ea, god of the waters under the earth, was the god of wisdom. Ashurbanipal probably inherited some copies of the epic, while others were made for him by his scribes, as can be seen from their colophons, scribal notations identifying a tablet and its contents: "Tablet X, 'He who saw the Deep,' series of Gilgamesh. Palace of Ashurbanipal, king of the world, king of Assyria." Sometimes a colophon takes the opportunity to praise the king: "Palace of Ashurbanipal, king of the world, king of Assyria, who trusts in Ashur and Ninlil. May he who trusts in you not come to shame, O Ashur, king of the gods!" In one colophon, an ambitious young scribe inserted a little advertisement for himself: "Tablet VI, 'He who saw the Deeps,' series of Gilgamesh. Written and checked according to its original. Document of Ashur-ra'im-napishti, junior apprentice, whose ears are attuned to [the gods] Nabu and Tashmetu." No mere toilers in humble anonymity, the court's scribes were—or hoped to become—powerful public figures.

Ashurbanipal grew up in a court pervaded by writings. The court bureaucracy lived to write memos, and there was no limit to the matters they deemed necessary to bring to the attention of Ashurbanipal's father, Esarhaddon. "To my lord the king . . . Idri-aha'u came and brought the shoes in the evening of the 16th." Almost anything could provoke a dispute between rival officials, and the rivals regularly appealed to the king. When a new shipment of wine arrived at a time when the wine cellars were already full, the wine steward wrote that the king should command that "storage rooms be shown to us, so that we may proceed. There is much wine for the king—where should we put it?" Or again: the king must approve the design for a new statue of himself ("Let the king pay attention to the hands, the chin, and the hair"). Even in selecting his own portrait, Esarhaddon couldn't simply follow his personal inclination, for he had to decide whether to side with the designers or the sculptor: "As for the royal image which they are making, the scepter is lying across his arm and his arm is resting on his thighs. I myself do not agree with this and I will not fashion it so."

The avalanche of querulous correspondence was not created only by the bureaucracy. Any parent of a careless teenage driver can readily imagine Esarhaddon's feelings on receiving the following plea—or demand—from one of his many sons: "Yesterday, when I was coming after the king, I entered the center of Nineveh. There were bricks at the king's guard. The wheel of the chariot hit them and broke instantly! Now let my lord the king give an order, so that they may do the work on it." Then again, the young prince may not have been entirely at fault. Nineveh was one of the largest cities in the world, with as many as 120,000 inhabitants thronging its mostly narrow and always dusty streets. These conditions often led to frictions that the king had to sort out. In one letter, a group of donkey sellers demanded a bodyguard to protect them from Nineveh's governor, who had barred them from their accustomed spot by the palace, shouting at them, "If I see you at the palace I shall crush your skulls!"

Almost as crowded as the streets, Nineveh's palaces and temples were staffed with status-conscious scribes, priests, and officials, both "bearded ones" and eunuchs. (Like the Ottomans after them, the Assyrian kings favored eunuchs as civil servants, with the idea that their loyalty to the throne would not be undercut by a desire to amass wealth and power for children of their own.) Disparities of wealth and prestige were keenly felt within the court, and neglected officials constantly appealed for better treatment. One forlorn scholar complained that younger scholars were always riding past his house, while he had to walk to the palace; he had begun taking roundabout routes so that people wouldn't notice his lack of transportation. Considering his many services to the king, he wrote, surely his lord could grant him a pair of donkeys: "May the king['s . . . heart] soften, and may he at least send

me the two beasts . . . and a spare suit of clothes!"* But giving
gifts to one person would inevitably breed resentment in another. Ashurbanipal learned this lesson while he was still
crown prince, as another letter reveals: "Now my lord the
crown prince has added to my misery by dressing another diviner in purple robes; as for my heart, my lord the crown
prince has broken it."

The problem was not just that there were never enough
donkeys and purple robes to go around. In the barrage of
pleas and reports, the trick was to determine which were sig-
naling a real threat. Which disaffected petitioners would find
a few like-minded friends and begin to assuage their heart-
break by plotting against the throne? The donkey sellers could
easily be kept away from the governor's precious gate, but
what of Qurdi, a chariot driver who spoke insultingly of the
governor? Was this just another traffic dispute, or was it
something more? Certainly the situation looked alarming to
the informant who reported Qurdi's blasphemous outburst in
the temple of Ishtar: "Qurdi, the chariot driver of the treasury horses, is treading on the authority of the [Pa]lace. He
has laid his hands on the [cone] of Ishtar, saying: 'Let her
strike me! Let's see what happens! Bring me an iron knife, so
I can cut it off and stick it in the [gov]ernor's ass!' "

Esarhaddon had every reason to be concerned by such reports, for Assyrian kings often died violently. His grandfather

---

*Most of the clay tablets recovered from Nineveh are damaged. Words and syllables
in brackets represent the editor's educated guess as to probable restorations; ellipses
are used when no likely restoration can be determined. Translations from letters are
taken from the twenty-five-volume State Archives of Assyria series, now being completed by an international team of scholars centered in Helsinki. I have sometimes
modified their translations on the basis of the Akkadian originals and occasionally
dispense with the editors' brackets when supplied phrases are obviously correct, either from the context or from parallel passages in other letters.

Sargon II had come to power by usurping the throne in 721 BCE, overthrowing a short-lived king whose own father had seized the throne in a revolution. A commanding figure who greatly extended the empire, Sargon ruled for twenty years but was killed in a humiliating battle defeat—a shocking sign of rejection by his gods. Sargon's son, Sennacherib, seldom mentioned his father again. He abandoned the capital his father had constructed and established a new one of his own at Nineveh, an old settlement that soon grew into a true metropolis. There he built his huge "Palace Without Rival," as he proudly named it, a physical manifestation of absolute power and security—only to be murdered inside its walls in 681 by two of his own sons, who were jealous that Sennacherib had appointed their younger brother Esarhaddon as crown prince. Still more violence lay behind these events, for the entire issue of succession had been thrown open by the death of their oldest brother, who had been kidnapped during an uprising in Babylon and deported to Elam in southern Persia, where he was killed.

Esarhaddon managed to emerge as king after his father's murder, but he always felt the insecurity of his position. During his twelve-year reign, from 681 to 669, he was forced to make a treaty with the Elamites—his older brother's murderers—and went to great lengths to pacify and rebuild Babylon after his father laid it to waste following his son's death. Esarhaddon paid close attention to the steady stream of reports of plots both within and beyond Assyria that came to him.

Knowledge is supposed to be power, yet it may only breed uncertainty when the course of action is unclear. Take as an example a striking letter written to the king in 671 by a diviner named Kudurru, who revealed a simmering palace revolt. One day, according to Kudurru, he was invited to dinner by the chief tailor (a high administrative official, whose duties included distributing the elaborate robes that were prime status symbols at court). Kudurru was shown into a private upper room in the chief tailor's house, where he found himself alone with a handful of important men. "They tossed me a seat and I sat down, drinking wine until the sun set." Having softened Kudurru up, the chief tailor got down to business: "Moving my seat closer, he started speaking to me . . . saying: 'You are an expert in divination?'" He went on to ask Kudurru to perform a divination before Shamash, seeking the sun god's answer to a pointed question: "Will the chief eunuch take over the kingship?"

Kudurru did as he was asked: "I washed myself with water in another upper room, donned clean garments and, the chief tailor having brought up for me two skins of oil, I performed it and told him: 'He will take over the kingship.'" Kudurru and the conspirators then spent the next day drinking in celebration. After sobering up, however, Kudurru wrote to Esarhaddon to tell him the whole story and assure the king of his own loyalty. The letter's vivid details seem to be intended to lend the account an air of strict accuracy and reliability. Yet Kudurru could demonstrate his sincerity only by insisting he had been lying about the god's decree—a major breach of priestly duty: "[By the gods of my lord the king]: The divination which I performed was nothing but windy and empty words! [I was only th]inking: 'May he not kill me.' [Now th]en, I am writing to the king, lest [my lord the king] hear about it and kill me!"

So Kudurru was giving Esarhaddon timely warning of a plot against his life. Imagine the king thinking things through after receiving this alarming letter, perhaps reclining at night on a lion-footed couch in his harem, having dismissed his wives so he could think in peace, torches flickering as he pondered the clay tablet in his hand, the broken halves of its clay casing littering the floor. The warning was well and good, but a question remained: Just who should he kill? The obvious question to ask, but not so easy to answer. Esarhaddon had commanded his advisers to report any such rumors directly to him, but Kudurru was implicating some of those very advisers. This question must have haunted the king, since months went by as he weighed his options. Should he believe Kudurru and kill the chief eunuch and the other accused plotters? Or should he decide that Kudurru—an admitted liar—was lying again and kill him instead? Or should he take no chances and kill them all?

Esarhaddon knew that Kudurru was hardly a person of proven loyalty. The son of a rebellious Babylonian chieftain who had been executed three years earlier, Kudurru had been brought to Nineveh and kept under house arrest, a common Assyrian strategy to train and indoctrinate young men of prominent families from restless areas prior to sending them home to help govern their homelands. In his letter, Kudurru had let slip that the chief tailor had approached him not only for his skills in divination but also to recruit him on behalf of the chief eunuch: "From that day on [he has been telling me]: 'He will take you back into your father's [house . . .] and give you the kingship of all Babylonia.' "

All in all, Kudurru's word alone could not be decisive, but Esarhaddon was also receiving warnings from one of his regular informants. Nothing is known of this shadowy figure apart from his name, Nabu-rehtu-usur, but he wrote a series of letters late in 671, urgently advising the indecisive king to take swift action: "Hear me, O my lord king! . . . Let [these people] die! [Save] your life and the life of your family!" So

Esarhaddon had independent confirmation of a plot. Yet his second source only increased his perplexity, for Nabu-rehtu-usur believed that the ringleader wasn't the chief eunuch but a man named Sasî, the city overseer. What was Esarhaddon supposed to do—kill every possible conspirator and live in an empty palace? Even then, a hundred echoing rooms would not offer much protection on their own. He would still need some-one to guard the gates, but who would guard the guards? It was evidently at this time that Esarhaddon commissioned an oracle concerning an almost endless series of possible plotters, including the keepers of Nineveh's inner and outer gates:

> Shamash, great lord, give me a definite answer
> to what I ask you! . . . Will any of the eunuchs
> and the bearded officials, the king's entourage,
> or any of his brothers and uncles, or junior
> members of the royal line, or any relative of
> the king whatever, or the prefects, or the re-
> cruitment officers, or his personal guard, or
> the king's chariot men, or the keepers of the in-
> ner gates, or the keepers of the outer gates, or
> the attendants and lackeys of the stables, or the
> cooks, confectioners, and bakers, the entire
> body of craftsmen . . . or their brothers, or
> their sons, or their nephews, or their friends, or
> their guests, or their accomplices . . . make an
> uprising and rebellion against Esarhaddon,
> king of Assyria? . . . Will they act in a hostile
> manner against him and kill him?

The god's reply is not recorded.

Esarhaddon held off for several months before acting, and

then finally instituted a major purge. It is unknown whether
Kudurru survived it, though the overseer Sasî is still listed
several years later as holding an important post. One recent
analyst of this conspiracy has speculated that "in reality Sasî
was there as a fink, keeping the king informed about their actions," in which event informers were informing on informers.

However he arrived at his decisions, Esarhaddon had to execute a number of once-trusted palace officials. In the ancient
equivalent of a security clearance check, a series of oracle requests in 670 asked Shamash if people being promoted into the
newly vacant positions could be trusted not to rebel in turn.
These requests urged the sun god to consider the full range of
possibilities: "While he is in the entourage of Esarhaddon,
king of Assyria, will he plan something bad, an evil plan of
sedition, rebellion, and insurrection, against Esarhaddon, king
of Assyria? Will he instigate it, or cause others to instigate it?
Will he plot it, or cause others to plot or undertake it, or will he
turn to his enemy? Does your great divinity know it?"

Plots and rebellions were so common that many kings must
have accepted them as disagreeable facts of royal life, but
Esarhaddon took these disturbances deeply to heart. A letter
to the king from his chief physician, Urad-Nanaya, offered a
diagnosis of the lingering psychological effects of the 671 conspiracy: "Ashur and the great gods bound and handed over to
the king these criminals who plotted against his goodness. . . .
The goodness of the king caught them up. However, they
made all other people hateful in the eyes of the king, smearing
them like a tanner with fish oil."

In principle, the king's anxieties should have been allayed
by his inquiries to the gods, enabling him to know who to trust.

Esarhaddon didn't rely on the ambiguous reports of his human intelligence agents alone; he could write letters to Shamash, the all-seeing sun god, as well as to Assyria's patron god Ashur, and to Nineveh's protective goddess Ishtar, all of whom had his kingdom's interests deeply at heart. Ashurbanipal's libraries housed dozens (perhaps hundreds) of these letters, commissioned first by Esarhaddon and then by Ashurbanipal. Many of the letters from the Assyrian state archives may make a modern reader feel relatively at home in the court at Nineveh, whether through their everyday concerns with shoe deliveries and broken wheels, or through the familiar workings of a major bureaucracy. The kings' oracle requests have a different effect, for there is no modern equivalent to the elaborate ancient methods the Assyrians used for communicating with the gods.

Building on older Babylonian and Egyptian practices, the Assyrian kings employed five different kinds of specialists in human-divine communication: astrologers, diviners, exorcists, physicians, and lamentation chanters. Ashurbanipal had forty-five of these specialists at his palace in Nineveh, as well as others stationed around the country. In different ways, these positions all involved appealing to the gods, discerning their will, and creating favorable outcomes in times of trouble. Exorcists and physicians worked to cure physical and mental illness, either of which could be caused by a demonic spirit or hostile god. Patients were often treated with a combination of remedies, the physician prescribing herbal drugs and the exorcist performing rituals to drive out the evil spirit infesting the body. If their ministrations failed and the patient died, the lamentation chanters would perform rituals to send the departed soul safely on its way to the underworld. Whereas these specialists dealt with existing conditions, astrologers and diviners sought to read the future, determining favorable days for political and religious events, and advising on major decisions facing the king, such as whether to go to war.

The basis of all these disciplines was advanced training in reading and writing cuneiform script, and these specialists were the elite of the scribal class. By Esarhaddon and Ashurbanipal's day, most people were no longer speaking Akkadian, the classical language used by the scribes. Akkadian was being displaced by the language that would one day be Hormuzd Rassam's native tongue, Aramaic, written in an easy-to-learn phonetic alphabet, precursor of the Phoenician, Greek, and Roman alphabets. Despite its convenience, the scholarly specialists clung to the Akkadian language and its cuneiform script, in which their traditions had developed over the centuries; the common language was not for them. Scribal training was arduous, all the more so as students were made to learn both Akkadian and the even more obscure Sumerian, originally spoken by the inventors of cuneiform. As one student lamented, in Sumerian, in a Babylonian school text:

> The door monitor said, "Why did you go
> out without my say-so?" and he beat me.
> The water monitor said, "Why did you help
> yourself to water without my say-so?" and he
> beat me.
> The Sumerian monitor said, "You spoke in
> Akkadian!" and he beat me.
> My teacher said, "Your handwriting is not
> at all good!" and *he* beat me.

In between beatings, the teachers tried to instill a love of learning in their unhappy pupils. This was a struggle throughout the ancient Near East. "Your heart is denser than an obelisk," one Egyptian instructor complained to his pupil. "Though I beat you with every kind of stick, you do not listen. . . . Though I spend the day telling you 'Write,' it seems like a plague to you. Writing"—the teacher sternly concluded— "is very pleasant!"

Like Egyptian hieroglyphics, the cuneiform system had an aura of hidden knowledge and sacred mystery. The cuneiform symbols, originally derived from natural objects, showed a family relationship to the lines and patterns that astrologers would trace in the sky and diviners would seek in earthly sources. As the French scholar Jean Bottéro has observed, "In the view of the ancient Mesopotamians, the whole of creation was presented as an immense page of divine scripture. When everything was normal and routine, with nothing special to attract the attention, the divine 'writers' therefore had nothing to point out to human beings, their readers. If they had to pass on some particular decision that had been taken, they would arrange to produce some unusual, singular, or monstrous phenomenon." Bottéro's comparison of creation to a divine text had already been made by the Assyrians themselves. According to a hymn to Shamash, the sun god could read the world by the light of his own solar radiance:

> Lofty judge, creator of the above and below,
>   you scan all lands in your light like a graven sign.
> You who never weary of divination,
>   you render daily verdicts for heaven and earth.

Many forms of divination were employed to read these verdicts, such as observing the flight of birds and studying the patterns made by smoke in the sky or by oil dripped onto water. The most common mode of divination in Esarhaddon's time, however, was to sacrifice a sheep. Before performing his sacrifice, the diviner would appeal to an appropriate god, asking for specific information: "Shamash, great lord, give me a definite answer to what I ask you! Should Esarhaddon, king of Assyria, strive and plan, and take the road with his army and camp, and go to the [dis]trict of Egypt, as he wishes? . . . Be present in this ram, place in it a definite answer, favorable designs, favorable, propitious omens by the oracular command of your great divinity, and may I see them." The priest would perform an autopsy on the sacrificed animal, looking at its internal organs for significant markings or abnormalities; these would be interpreted as the gods' reply. Such analyses were widely practiced around the ancient world; this sort of diviner was known in ancient Rome as the haruspex, or "innards inspector."

George Smith and the other early Assyriologists often regretted that the Assyrians were steeped in superstition, yet in many ways the Assyrians were remarkably systematic, even scientific. Far from being pious frauds or fearful guessers at the gods' inscrutable will, the astrologers and diviners were highly trained professionals, confident in their skill and contemptuous of shoddy work. As an astrologer named Nabu-ahhe-eriba wrote in dismissing another astrologer's report, "He who wrote to the king that Venus is visible in the month of Adar is despicable, a fool and a liar. . . . If he does not know, he should shut up."

The astrologers became so skilled at following the movements of the moon and planets that they could predict eclipses in advance. Their colleagues the diviners were equally systematic in studying phenomena on Earth. They worked out elaborate analyses of sheep's lungs and livers, dividing them into many component parts, including the Station, the Path, the Crucible, the Strength, the Palace Gate, the Well-Being, the Gall Bladder, the Base of the Throne, the Finger, the Increment, and the Yoke. They then inspected these features to see what message the god had written in answer to their prayer, and would advise the king accordingly.

Kings would sometimes try to improve the results by commissioning a series of a dozen or more divinations, either to reach a desired outcome or simply to widen the database and decrease what we would now call the sampling error. In a message to Esarhaddon, his father, Sennacherib, recommended a further and highly scientific refinement: "In order for me to set straight the divination, I divided the diviners into four groups to make a divination for me. May you do as I did. . . . I have made known to you my clever procedures that previously none among kings had done." This may be the earliest known instance of a blind study, cross-checked among four independent groups.

These elaborate means of divining the divine will reflect an admirable scientific impulse, and yet it may seem surprising that intelligent people would persist in using such methods. For century after century, did no one ever realize that sheep's livers could not tell when an enemy would attack? Why didn't the randomness of the results lead to the abandonment of these methods early on?

In part, the priests' conclusions were accepted because they often provided a set of parameters and probabilities rather than an absolute judgment. Their analyses often listed a mixture of favorable and unfavorable signs, and several priests might consult to determine whether on balance the oracle was favorable, unfavorable, or ambiguous. If the omens were unfavorable for an attack, a king might call it off—with no way to know whether the oracle had mistakenly predicted defeat—but he also might choose to go ahead. If so, he could reinforce his troops to counter the added danger suggested by the omens, and so the ominous prediction would actually result in greater likelihood of success. As for predictions of victory, the Assyrian armies were nearly unstoppable, so those predictions usually came true. In any case, when a belief system is deeply entrenched, it is powerfully assisted by the mechanism known today as cognitive dissonance—people tend to notice evidence that shows what they expect to find, while they minimize or even miss contrary evidence. Predictions about the future are particularly open to this tendency, as subsequent events can be selectively related to the prophecy, emphasized or disregarded as needed.

Echoes of ancient methods can be found even now, though relatively few people consult horoscopes seriously today, or send around chain letters of the form "Jonathan W. passed this letter on and won the lottery the next month; Mary P. ignored it and died." But such logic was accepted wisdom in antiquity, when divine intervention was observed everywhere. As one priest assured Esarhaddon, who was worried that a solar eclipse might portend his death, "The Series itself [of astrological omens] has said as follows in connection with this new-year's eclipse: 'If during the eclipse, Jupiter stands there: well-being for the king, a famous noble will die in his stead.' Has the king observed? A full month had not yet passed before his minister of justice was dead."

Esarhaddon's scholar-priests were confident in their ability to discern the gods' will; their greatest problem lay with the king's consuming doubts. Few kings in ancient Mesopotamia ever displayed anything approaching Esarhaddon's hesitations and insecurities, shading at times into outright paranoia. Given his father's murder and the ever-present threat of a palace coup, he did have reason to feel that people were out to get him. Matters were no better at the borders of his empire. Assyria's restless Egyptian vassals took the opportunity to rebel when his father was murdered, forcing Esarhaddon to march west to Egypt to retake the lands his grandfather and father had conquered. The Medes were massing to the east, and the power of a hostile group to the north called the Urartu was growing. South of Assyria, the situation with Babylonia was particularly dicey. Babylonia was the heartland of Mesopotamia and the fountainhead of its civilization: in earlier eras it had often dominated the region, but had now been reluctantly brought under the Assyrian yoke. Some Babylonian cities were securely loyal, but Babylon was a seedbed of conspiracies, often seconded by hard-to-control nomadic groups in the open countryside, such as the tribe of Kudurru's executed father.

Esarhaddon never forgot the insecurity of his empire's position, and he made many oracle requests trying to determine which enemies—or allies—would attack him next. His father and grandfather had extended the empire's boundaries well beyond what they could effectively control. But conquest had to continue, since the empire needed ever more external wealth to sustain itself. "The chief occupation of the Assyrian king and state," as the historian A. K. Grayson has remarked, "was warfare." Mesopotamia had fertile land but few other valuable resources, since crude oil had no known uses. The empire's internal economy was also weakened by large tax exemptions given to major cities to buy their loyalty. With the

wealthy paying few taxes, the residents of smaller cities and the peasants in the countryside could not yield enough revenue to support lavish building programs and the heavy costs of the world's largest army. Esarhaddon's annals did their best to paper over these problems, showing the king as an almost hysterically confident master of his world: "I am powerful, I am all powerful, I am a hero, I am gigantic, I am colossal, I am honored, I am magnified, I am without an equal among all kings." Behind the gigantic facade was a deeply troubled man.

Esarhaddon's spirits were further lowered by a chro· ic illness, one that his physicians could never cure or even diagnose. Letters between the king and his doctors discussed symptoms including persistent fever, aching joints, eye pain, and lassitude. Some scholars believe that the disease may have been lupus, incurable even today; one serious side effect of lupus is often depression. Whatever the causes of the king's depression, it was deeply disconcerting to his advisers. When Esarhaddon was in dark moods, no omen was ever favorable enough, no ritual powerful enough. As one priest wrote him in frustration: "[As to what my lord the king] wrote to me: 'Have I been purified with the help of Urad-Ea [. . .]'? . . . Truly, [my lord the king] has been purified ten times over!" Another baffled adviser wrote: "Why is the king like this?"

In one letter, a pair of scholar-priests named Balasi and Nabu-ahhe-eriba joined forces to stop the king from prolonging a fast beyond its normal term: "Our lord the king will pardon us. Is one day not enough for the king to mope and to eat nothing? For how long? This is already the third day the king does not eat anything. The king, a beggar! Surely when the moon appears in the beginning of the month, one says: 'I will not fast any more!' . . . The king can ask for a whole year's worth of food! We became worried and were afraid, and that is why we are writing to the king."

Esarhaddon's advisers were only human, and their views might be mistaken, but the king seems not to have found relief even when the gods tried to reassure him. For, in addition to standard forms of divination, he commissioned dozens of oracles from ecstatic priests and priestesses. Like the sibyls of the classical world, the ecstatics could put themselves into trance states and convey direct messages from the gods. Many of these oracular responses survive, often communicated by the goddess Ishtar. She consistently comforted and encouraged the king, usually in beautifully poetic language: "[Esarh]addon, king of the lands, fear [not]! What wind has risen against you whose wing I have not broken? Your enemies will roll before your feet like ripe apples." Or again:

"Like a winged bird ov[er its young] I will twitter over you and go in circles around you. Like a beautiful [lion] cub I will run about in your palace and sniff out your enemies."

Even the gracious Ishtar, though, sometimes grew impatient with Esarhaddon's constant need for reassurance: "What words have I spoken to you that you could not rely upon?" she asked. "Did I not vanquish your enemy? Did I not collect your haters and foes [like but]terflies?" In one oracle, she explicitly addressed his state of mind: "I will keep you safe in your palace; I will make you overcome anxiety and trembling." The great goddess may have had the power to keep Esarhaddon safe, but his anxiety was beyond her reach.

Lightning couldn't strike a distant town without Esarhaddon taking it personally, as can be seen in a letter from his adviser Balasi: "As to what my lord the king wrote to me: 'At the town of Harihumba lightning struck and ravaged the fields of the Assyrians'—why does the king look for trouble, and why does he look for it in a peasant's [hut]? There is no evil inside the palace, and when has the king ever visited Harihumba?" Even this direct rebuke failed to do the trick; the king wrote to Balasi's colleague Nabu-ahhe-eriba, seeking a second opinion. Nabu-ahhe-eriba patiently replied that the lightning had struck only because the local farmers had weakened in their devotion to Adad, the storm god; the king should order an exorcist to perform the ritual "Purification of the Field," though just to be on the safe side he could also commission the ritual "Evil of a Lightning Strike."

This calming second opinion may have quelled the king's anxieties on one point, but there were always others. When a minor earthquake took place—a fairly common event in Assyria—the king convinced himself that it was a warning that his courtiers were about to turn against him. Now Balasi replied in tones of complete exasperation: "Was there no earthquake in the times of the king's fathers and grandfathers? Did I not see earthquakes when I was small? The god has only wanted to open the king's ears; he should pray to the god, perform the ritual, and be on his guard."

Esarhaddon's letters are amusing to read today, but his mental state must have inspired near panic among the two dozen or so members of his inner circle. The king was the supreme ruler, the army's commander in chief, and the head of the state religion, all rolled into one, and everything depended on his spiritual and mental well-being. At the first sign of weakness, allies would fall away and the empire's many enemies would attack. Access to the king was always restricted in the Assyrian court, and Esarhaddon's advisers must have gone to great lengths to keep news of his depression and anxiety from becoming widely known. Yet there is one person beyond the palace walls who certainly learned of it: his son and crown prince, Ashurbanipal.

Ashurbanipal may have sensed his father's problems from finding how difficult it was to see him. It was customary for crown princes to be raised away from the royal residence, in a separate palace across town called the Bit Reduti or "House of Succession." There the young prince was tutored in all the skills required of a king, learning the fundamentals of statecraft, administration, and the art of war, and was instructed in his many religious duties by the priests of Ashur and Ishtar. The House of Succession also served as a backup administrative center; once old enough, a crown prince could manage the day-to-day governance of the country during the king's almost annual battle campaigns.

The crown prince lived away from his parents from an early age. In a fictional dialogue between Ashurbanipal and the god Nabu, patron of writing, Nabu remarks, "You were young, O Ashurbanipal, when I left you to [Ishtar] the Queen of Nineveh, you were a baby, O Ashurbanipal, when you sat on the knee of the Queen of Nineveh. Her four teats were set in your mouth, with two you were suckled and with two you drew milk for yourself." Nothing should have kept Ashurbanipal from regular visits to his parents' palace, but royal movements were subject to astrological advice concerning auspicious days to go out. Given Esarhaddon's many anxieties, it comes as no surprise that they came into play here, too.

The king's worries prevented his son from seeing him for weeks at a time. As in other cases, Esarhaddon's adviser Balasi struggled against his lord's tendency to seize on the gloomiest forecast he received: "Concerning the crown prince about whom my lord the king wrote to me that '[I have been told that he should not go out]doors on the first day of the month.' . . . The planet Mercury signifies the crown prince, and it is bright, clothed with brilliance. So in view of what sh[ould he] not [come]?" On another occasion, Balasi had to plead with the king not to invent danger signs where none existed to begin with: "Concerning the crown prince about whom my lord the king wrote to me that 'The planet Mars is bright' . . . When is it that he can come into the king's presence? When Mars is bright, have we got no profit from it? . . . What is wrong? If it does not suit the king this month . . . let him come into the king's presence next month!"

With Ashurbanipal's life colored early on by his father's exaggerated worries, it seems likely that Balasi gave the prince a fairly clear picture of the problems he continually encountered with the king. For Balasi was not only one of

Esarhaddon's most worried advisers, he was also Ashurbanipal's principal tutor. Ashurbanipal was as notable for his devotion to reading and writing as Esarhaddon was for his psychological difficulties. Ashurbanipal's scholarly interests were in part an outgrowth of his father's problems, which formed the backdrop or even a direct impetus to his unusual literary training.

Esarhaddon took an almost obsessive interest in two kinds of texts: omen interpretations and confidential reports from spies. Yet the king faced one difficulty in studying these reports: he couldn't actually read. If he pondered Kudurru's alarming letter in his darkened palace at night, the tablet in his hand would have been frustratingly opaque to him. Under ordinary circumstances, this situation would present no problem. Ancient monarchs rarely troubled to master the intricacies of writing, leaving that task to their scribes. When one correspondent complained that Esarhaddon hadn't read his last letter, the king replied impatiently that he had people to do that for him: "When a letter which [you send me comes] to my reporter, he [opens it and I hear] what it says. Why [should I read] a letter? I take care of myself. When I see a letter, I do not open it or read it!" Esarhaddon was mocking his correspondent here by stating the obvious, the implication being that he found nothing worth responding to when the letter was read to him. Knowing that his letter would be read by an intermediary, one out-of-favor official ended his plea to the king with a direct message to the king's reader: "Whoever you are, O scribe, who are reading this, do not hide it from your lord the king! Speak for me before the king, so Bel and Nabu may speak for you before the king."

Near Eastern monarchs were no more expected to read and write letters than modern presidents are expected to write their own speeches. As a result, princely education rarely included training in literacy. Ashurbanipal is an exception to this rule, and he is the only Assyrian monarch who boasted that he could read both Akkadian and Sumerian. His abilities in this sphere have usually been interpreted as a reflection of personal interest and inclination, which might partly be the case, yet it is unlikely that as an adult he took up the arduous work of learning two archaic languages—one dying, the other already dead—and their exceptionally difficult script. The only plausible time for him to have acquired these skills was as an adolescent in the House of Succession, under the tutoring of Balasi and Nabu-ahhe-eriba, who was also one of his teachers. These men reported directly to the king on the prince's well-being, and they taught what the king wanted his son to learn.

But why would the illiterate Esarhaddon have had his heir undertake a long program of literary training? Here is where the king's paranoia comes into play, for in his more troubled periods Esarhaddon believed that people were keeping things from him. At one point he berated Balasi for standing silently near him; apparently he thought Balasi had been refusing to reveal something important. In another letter, the long-suffering Balasi insisted he had not concealed an ominous sign from the king: "Concerning what my lord the king wrote to me: 'You must certainly have observed something in the sky'— I keep a close eye on it but I must say, I have seen nobody and nothing. . . . My lord the king must have given up on me!" Even the chief scribe Issar-shumu-eresh—the firm interpreter of the meaning of the mongoose's appearance beneath the royal chariot—came under suspicion. In one letter, he called on the gods to witness that he hadn't been hiding the truth: "Concerning what my lord the king wrote to me: '[Why] have you never told me [the truth]? [When] will you tell me all there is to it?' May [Ashur, Sin, Shamash], Bel, Nabu . . . be my witnesses that I have never [spoken] untruly."

The king's fears probably had some basis in reality. As his faithful retainers struggled to reassure him, they may indeed have concealed bad news, particularly regarding unfavorable omens that would set off Esarhaddon's fears. This claim was made to the king by an out-of-favor astrologer named Belushezib, who was trying to persuade him to fire his advisers and take him back: "Now [portents] have occurred in my lord the king's reign, bearing upon [a demon]. They have set aside whatever [. . .]; but where are they? They are looking for a pleasant sign [. . . , saying]: 'Keep evil [omens] to yourselves.' " A correspondent wrote in from the provinces to report that a local official had taken direct action to suppress news of a cow giving birth to a lion: "Now then Sin-eresh has struck down the lion which the cow gave birth to and eaten it. None of his associates [knows about it]; he has killed the farmer and the scribe."

These circumstances help to explain Esarhaddon's interest in giving his son the training in literacy he never had himself. If people outside the king's inner circle worried that the royal scribes might not read their letters to the king, the paranoid king must have had the same concern. Fearing that his advisers were hiding things from him, he must have doubly worried that he had to take their word on messages that actually reached him from outside the palace. It was too late for Esarhaddon—fully occupied in governing, and suffering from eye trouble to boot—to take up the difficult study of cuneiform, but his son would be better prepared. Ashurbanipal would never be at the mercy of his scribes; he would be able to read his gods' omens and his spies' reports for himself.

Thus the initiative for Ashurbanipal's literary training might have come down as an order from Esarhaddon or it might have come from below, as a precocious early interest on Ashurbanipal's part, welcomed with pleased surprise by his tutors and then approved by his father. In either event, as one historian recently noted, Ashurbanipal began collecting tablets concerning omens "during the reign of his father Esarhaddon, who was, doubtless, behind it." Later on, Ashurbanipal's library grew substantially through his efforts to deal with his father's ambiguous political legacy. When all is said and done, we may owe the preservation of *The Epic of Gilgamesh* as much to Esarhaddon's paranoid depression as to his son's love of learning.

Though Ashurbanipal evidently began his ambitious program of acquisition for political purposes, he expanded his library to include a wide range of literary texts to read for his personal instruction and pleasure. He detailed his literary training in the longest of his surviving annals, known as the Rassam Cylinder in honor of its finder:

> Marduk, master of the gods, granted me as a gift a receptive mind and ample power of thought. Nabu, the universal scribe, made me a present of his wisdom. . . . I acquired the skill of the Master Adapa—the hidden treasure of all scribal knowledge, the signs of heaven and earth. I was brave, I was exceedingly industrious, in the assembly of the artisans I received orders; and I have studied the heavens with the learned masters of oil divination,

I have solved the laborious problems of division and multiplication, which were not clear,
I have read the artistic script of Sumer and
the obscure Akkadian, which is hard to master,
taking pleasure in reading from the stones
from before the flood, now being upset because
I was stupid and confused by the beautiful
script.

Ashurbanipal mastered the divinations that so obsessed his father, but he also broadened his interests to include stories
"from before the flood." These were mythic tales and epic poems, prominently including *Gilgamesh*, whose hero "saw what
was secret, discovered what was hidden," and "brought back a
tale of before the Deluge."

Even in the case of epics such as *Gilgamesh*, the Assyrians'
interests were not purely literary. *Gilgamesh* was regarded as
a source of ancient wisdom, and this wisdom could be applied
to current concerns. Well digging, for instance. On a long
journey through desert wastelands early in the epic, Gilgamesh finds water by digging a series of wells, apparently
inventing the practice. It is easy for a modern reader to miss
this feature of Gilgamesh's story, as it receives only a couple
of lines at each stage of his journey with his companion
Enkidu: "Facing the sun they dug a well, / they put [fresh wa-
ter] in [their waterskins]." Though it is only described in passing, this accomplishment deeply impressed the epic's early
audiences, for the invention of wells marked a crucial advance in people's ability to survive in harsh conditions far
from Mesopotamia's few rivers.

The ancient listeners derived direct benefits from the
knowledge of Gilgamesh's success with his wells. Not that

they needed the epic for instructions on well digging, a practice they knew intimately. Rather, and much more powerfully, Gilgamesh could help them find water. Digging wells in the wilderness was a chancy enterprise, and a life-and-death affair for travelers whose supplies were running low. It was only reasonable, then, to improve the odds by invoking the aid of powerful beings, notably Ea, god of fresh water, and Gilgamesh himself. As a Babylonian tablet instructs well diggers upon starting to dig, "You say, 'Well of Gilgamesh!' " This phrase was probably the first line of an incantation designed to enlist Gilgamesh's assistance in repeating his archetypal feat.

If the Assyrians often appreciated literature for its practical applications, the converse was true as well: sober chronicles of events were regularly enlivened with bursts of poetic language. Assyrian chronicles are typically fairly dry records of the year's major events (wars waged, festivals observed, canals repaired), but the annalists sometimes infused their battle accounts with bloody lyricism. In one narrative of Ashurbanipal's grandfather Sennacherib, for example: "I filled the plain with the bodies of their warriors, like grass. Their testicles I cut off, and tore out their privates like the seeds of summer cucumbers." In a polemical text that was probably written during Esarhaddon's reign, a scribe insulted a rebel leader in passing as a "shit bucket," and then had a happy thought for a way to enrich this image: he went on to call the rebel "the shit bucket of a farter." Under Ashurbanipal, motives as well as metaphors were developed in new detail, with dream visions and vivid speeches fleshing out incisive accounts of shifting alliances and the fortunes of battle.

Ashurbanipal did more than set a general tone for the court's writing; he took a direct editorial role. According to one letter, he sent back a draft report and asked his scribes to tighten it up: "The talk was better than this [. . .]; there is much space, there is much [. . .]. Assign some ten sentences and send them to me, I shall have a look." Responding to these instructions, his scribe fawningly declared that the king's editorial guidance "is as perfect as that of a sage. . . . Does it not inspire awe? Is this not the very acme of the scribal craft?"

In addition to editing his scribes' work, Ashurbanipal tried his hand at writing himself. In one letter, a scribe praised the king's handwriting, even remarking how envious another scribe would be: "Concerning the writing of my lord the king, Keni will die of envy when he sees it: Bel and Nabu have given a fine hand to my lord the king." Even allowing for the inflation that usually occurs when someone compliments the king of the universe, Ashurbanipal's handwriting must have at least been decent, and it was an extraordinary thing that a king could write at all.

And what was Ashurbanipal interested in writing? Several hymns and poems survive in his name, either written directly or commissioned personally by him. Poetry always served kings for ceremonial purposes on feast days and great occasions, but for Ashurbanipal it also gave public voice to personal fears in difficult times. No Assyrian king ever expressed a moment of self-doubt in the royal annals, but in several of Ashurbanipal's poems the king directly alludes to the difficulties of his reign. His anguished outbursts can be compared to the "penitential psalms" attributed to Israel's King David. In the biblical case, there is no way to know which if any psalms date from David's time and which were attributed to him long afterward, but Ashurbanipal's poems definitely were composed during his reign, and several are likely to be

his own work. These poems clearly reflect Ashurbanipal's
situation, or at least his situation as he wished to present it in
poetic form for sympathetic public hearing.

In one remarkable poem, Ashurbanipal makes an appeal to
Nabu, patron of writing. He begins by recalling his happy
childhood days as a budding scholar: "In my childhood, I
longed for the Assembly, to sit in the tablet house." Yet now,
he says, his enemies surround him, and he cries out to the distant gods for aid. As the poem continues, the poet confesses to
suicidal impulses:

> Often I go up to the roof in order to plunge down,
> but my life is too precious, it turns me back.
> I would hearten myself, but what heart do I have to give?
> I would make up my mind, but what mind do I have to
>   make up?   ·
> O Nabu, where is your forgiveness,
> O son of Bel, where is your guidance?

In a companion poem, Nabu sends Ashurbanipal a dream vision in reply:

> Your ill-wishers, Ashurbanipal, will fly away
>   like [pollen] on the surface of the water.
> They will be squashed before your feet
>   like [mayflies] in the spring!
> You, Ashurbanipal, you will stand before the great gods
>   and praise Nabu!

One long hymn in praise of the god Marduk and his wife is
composed as an acrostic: the opening syllables of each stanza

identify the poet and spell out a personal message, *Anaku
Aššurbaniapli ša ilsuka bulitanima Marduk dalilika ludlul*—
"I am Ashurbanipal, who has called out to you: Give me life,
Marduk, and I will praise you!"

None of these poems is a literary masterpiece, though some
of the verses are quite good. Ashurbanipal's poems can be
compared to the verses of the Roman emperor Hadrian or,
much later, England's Queen Elizabeth I and China's Chairman Mao, all of whom wrote some excellent stanzas amid a
larger output of lesser quality. All four leaders can best be described as talented amateurs, and more specifically as talented amateurs whose audience was not going to risk offering
much in the way of constructive criticism.

Ashurbanipal created his great library in part from a love
of writing, but he had practical purposes as well, for he
wanted to assemble written resources that could help him manage the mess he had inherited from his father. Having ascended the throne after his father's murder, Esarhaddon had
found that his own succession was going to be a serious problem. His oldest son died, and he was forced to choose a new successor. Next in line was a son named Shamash-shumu-ukin, yet
Esarhaddon preferred to anoint his younger son, Ashurbanipal. Too little is known about Shamash-shumu-ukin to assess
the wisdom of Esarhaddon's choice, but the crucial fact is that
Esarhaddon, all too typically, doubted his decision as well.

A striking letter from Esarhaddon's chief exorcist, Adad-
shumu-usur, reveals how conflicted the king was following ·
the eldest son's early death: "As to what my lord the king
wrote to me: 'I am feeling very sad; how did we act that I have
become so low-spirited for this little one of mine?'—had it

been curable, you would have given away half your kingdom
to have it cured! But what can we do? O my lord king, it is
something that cannot be done. And as to what my lord the
king said to me about the lords your sons: 'The burning question of "who" is eating me up'—in the third month I wrote to
my lord the king: 'Take hold of yourself, prepare for everything!' "

Eventually Esarhaddon made a compromise decision, hoping to avoid the all-or-nothing choice that had led to his own
brothers' murder of their father. Unfortunately, the compromise proved disastrous. Esarhaddon tried to have things both
ways: to give the kingdom to his preferred son Ashurbanipal
and yet pacify Shamash-shumu-ukin by making him a sub-
sidiary king in Babylon. Sending him south would keep him
away from his half brother and ease tensions between them,
and giving Babylonia its own king might soften the resentment the southerners continued to feel toward Assyria.

Once Esarhaddon had settled on this problematic solution,
his advisers had to make the best of it. His chief exorcist,
Adad-shumu-usur, wrote him a rather perturbed letter of con-
gratulation: "What has not been done in heaven, my lord the
king has done upon earth and shown us: you have girded a son
of yours with a headband and entrusted to him the kingship
of Assyria; your eldest son you have set to the kingship in
Babylon. You have placed the first on your right, the second
on your left side!" This unheard-of choice must have seemed
dubious to many, but Adad-shumu-usur tried to look on the
bright side: "Seeing this," he continued, "we blessed our lord
the king, and our hearts were delighted." Yet most of all, the
exorcist hoped that the king's depression would lift now that
he had finally made a choice: "Look upon these fine sons of
yours and your heart will rejoice. My lord the king should

banish unpleasant thoughts from his mind; such thoughts make
you weak."

Esarhaddon died in 669 BCE on the way to quell a rebellion
in Egypt—perhaps the mongoose had a point after all—and
Ashurbanipal inherited the throne as planned while his half
brother went to Babylon, with the title of king but still subordinate to Ashurbanipal. The arrangement held up for sixteen
years, and Ashurbanipal occupied himself with lion hunting
and poetry when he could take time away from the endless effort to hold the empire together. He led campaigns in Egypt
to reassert Assyrian rule, recapturing Memphis in 667 and
Thebes in 663, successfully installing a loyal puppet king.
Within a few years, however, Assyrian control over Egypt began to weaken once again. Meanwhile, the ever-scheming
Elamites broke the treaty they had made with Esarhaddon,
and under their new king, Teumman, they invaded Assyria.

Ashurbanipal crushed this force and adorned his garden
with Teumman's severed head. He was always inventive in displaying his defeated enemies as object lessons for would-be
rebels. When one defeated former ally threw himself on
Ashurbanipal's mercy, he said, "I took pity on him, and spared
his life," according to the royal annals. Yet few could wish to
experience such pity: "I laid on him a heavy penalty.... I
passed a rope through his jaw, put a dog chain upon him, and
set him in a kennel to guard Nineveh's east gate, which is
named Entrance of the Thronging Nations." A bas-relief from
his palace shows the sons of another rebel kneeling at one of
Nineveh's gates, doing something with rolling pins. A caption
explains that they are being made to grind up their father's
bones so that Ashurbanipal could scatter the dust of his enemy's bones in the gateway.

All in all, by Assyrian standards, it was a good time for
the empire. Ashurbanipal claimed that the storm god Adad
favored his dry country with so much rain that his only trouble was flood control, and animals grew so fertile that lions
became a serious threat to cattle. This was not the worst of
problems for a king who loved to hunt lions. People would assemble to watch staged hunts, in which the beasts were released for the king to kill with spear or bow and arrow.

The situation took a drastic turn for the worse in 652, when
Shamash-shumu-ukin finally tired of playing second fiddle to
his half brother. He formed a secret alliance with neighboring
Elam and made a surprise attack on Assyria. In his annals,
Ashurbanipal recorded his outrage at this betrayal: "In these
days Shamash-shumu-ukin, my faithless brother, whom I had
treated well and had set up as king of Babylon . . . forgot this
kindness I had shown him and planned evil. Outwardly, with
his lips, he was speaking good words while inwardly in his
heart he was designing murder." The civil war culminated
with a two-year siege of Babylon; by the end, the annals say,
the people were so famished that they ate their children and
the leather of their sandals.

Esarhaddon's uneasy compromise had led to exactly the
fratricidal warfare he had most hoped to avoid, and the empire was fatally weakened by this long internal conflict.
Ashurbanipal saw his brother's rebellion as a repetition of his
uncles' murder of their grandfather. In an act of intergenera-
tional revenge, he brought some of the rebels up to Nineveh
and executed them in the very spot where Sennacherib had
been murdered in his palace thirty-three years before: "By the
colossi, between which they had cut down Sennacherib, the
father of the father who begot me—at that time, I cut down

those people there, as an offering to his shade. Their dismembered flesh I fed to the dogs, swine, wolves, and eagles, to the birds of heaven and the fish of the deep."

In the aftermath of this traumatic struggle, Ashurbanipal pursued two policies: to exterminate his enemies and to build up his library. He carried out the extermination with grim intensity, visiting particular devastation upon Elam. Resolving to remove it forever as a threat, he invaded in 647, the year after he finally subdued Babylon. He pressed his attack further in 646, and finally overran the capital, Susa, in 645. Once there, Ashurbanipal went far beyond the usual plundering of treasure: he attacked the dead as well as the living. He dismembered one enemy leader's corpse, and as he succinctly put it, "I made him more dead than he was before." He then hung the severed head around the neck of the man's surviving brother. Not content with destroying the current generation, he attacked their ancestors as well: "The sepulchers of their earlier and later kings . . . I destroyed, I devastated, I exposed to the sight of Shamash. Their bones I carried off to Assyria. I laid restlessness upon their shades." Still unsatisfied, he vented his fury on the Elamites' gods, leveling their temples and desecrating their sacred precincts, "reduc[ing] their gods and goddesses to phantoms." Finally he attacked the land itself, sowing it with salt and thorns, so that nothing should ever grow there again.

At home, he repaired Nineveh's walls and ordered a survey to be made of libraries throughout Mesopotamia, seeking copies of any texts that would be useful to him in ruling his empire. "We shall not neglect the king's command," his scribes in Babylon assured him. "Day and night we shall strive and toil to execute the instruction of our lord the king!" Other tablets were copied in Nineveh by prisoners of war working in chains. One copy of *The Epic of Gilgamesh* was acquired in 647, evidently among the texts expropriated from Babylon.

In addition to assembling existing texts, Ashurbanipal commissioned an epic poem on his conquest of Elam. Several of his predecessors had commanded laudatory poems to be composed about their exploits, and now his own story of resilience and conquest could take its place next to *Gilgamesh* and the other Babylonian epics, immortalizing his achievements for his own pleasure and the greater glory of Assyria. During the final years of his forty-year reign, measured stanzas celebrating wise rule and heroic valor resonated against the walls of his palace as enemy forces massed on his borders.

But it couldn't last. The empire was seriously overextended, an ever more restive Babylonia was growing in strength, and hostile powers were biding their time all over the empire. Nineveh went into outright decline during Ashurbanipal's later years—one sign being that few annals were written. The most voluble of courts was falling silent, and nothing is known about Ashurbanipal's final decline. Even the date of his death is uncertain, though 627 BCE is most likely. Several years of instability followed, including a brief takeover in 623 by a eunuch who had been the prime adviser to Ashurbanipal's short-lived heir, Ashur-etel-ilani. Soon the eunuch was ousted by another of Ashurbanipal's sons, and amid these upheavals Assyria's enemies saw their chance. The governor of Babylon declared independence and soon regained control of most of Babylonia. He forged an alliance with the Medes in northern Persia, joined by various smaller tribes and groups, and the combined forces began attacking Assyria from the south and east in 621. Assyria held on for several years, but gradually its cities fell to the coalition. Finally, in 612, the invaders lay siege to Nineveh, which fell after only three months.

Modern historians propose three factors behind this surprisingly quick defeat. First, Nineveh's great size would have
made it difficult to defend against a large force armed with
the assault machinery that the Assyrians themselves had perfected. Nineveh's high walls would have been hard to scale,
but whereas a typical city had perhaps four gates to protect,
Nineveh had eighteen. The attackers had huge battering
rams—virtual tanks—enclosed in heavy wheeled housings,
with turrets on top for archers to repel defenders. Archaeologists have discovered a pile of skeletons in the ruins of one of
the city's gates, their bones riddled with arrows, evidence of a
desperate last stand.

The second likely force behind Nineveh's fall was, appropriately, a flood. Nineveh was settled on the banks of a small
river, the Khosr, which branched off from the Tigris. When
Sennacherib made the city his fortified capital, he diverted
the Khosr to create pleasure gardens north of the city and a
moat around it. By breaking the dams and dikes Sennacherib
had constructed, the invaders were able to flood the center of
the city, eating away at its foundations of clay. After Ashurbanipal, a deluge truly descended on his city.

Lastly, though the Assyrians possessed the world's largest
and best-equipped army, their forces would have been greatly
reduced in numbers. There was a large standing army, but to
mount their full fighting force—said to be as many as 400,000
troops—the commanders had to call up reserves from around
the country. Many of the Assyrian reserves had probably
stayed home in their towns and villages rather than answer a
call from the beleaguered capital. In any case, many soldiers
were Babylonians and were now among the attackers. There
must still have been a strong force inside Nineveh, which contained a large and well-stocked armory, but the Assyrians'

best weapons were offensive ones. For generations, Assyrian military policy had been based on a twofold strategy of peace in the heartland and overwhelming force at the periphery of the empire. The armory's swift chariots and massive battering rams were useless to walled-in defenders, surrounded by 100,000 or more besiegers. It was only a matter of time before the invaders succeeded in breaching the gates and turning the river Khosr against the city it had watered and protected.

A fragmentary Babylonian chronicle offers the sole surviving contemporary account of these events:

> From the month of Simanu to the month of Abu, three times they battled [. . . . . .] a mighty assault [the enemy] made upon the city. In the month of Abu, [the . . . day, the city was taken . . . . . .]. A great slaughter was made of the people and nobles. On that day Sin-sharishkun, king of Assyria, fled from the city [. . . . . .] great quantities of spoil from the city, beyond counting, they carried off. The city [they turned] into a mound and ruin heap [. . . . . .] the army of Assyria deserted the king [. . . . . .] of the king of Akkad [. . . . . .].

After all the blood-and-thunder Assyrian accounts of sacking city after terrified city, it seems somehow appropriate that the only record of Nineveh's downfall should be these few somber lines. Some more broken sentences follow on cleanup operations elsewhere in Assyria, and then the tablet breaks off, with only a final postscript to the reader: "He who loves Nabu and Marduk, let him preserve this tablet, let him not allow it to leave his hand."

Once the invaders took the city, they stripped its temples and palaces of their riches but did not bother to carry off Ashurbanipal's library. Instead, they sacked it, shattering many of the tablets. Tablets that George Smith found hidden away in an inner courtyard suggest an effort by the library's despairing scribes to salvage what they could. But then the invaders burned the royal palaces. The library rooms collapsed in the flaming wreckage, sending some 25,000 tablets plunging into the palaces' foundations. There they would rest unseen for two and a half millennia.

We owe much of our knowledge of Mesopotamian literature to Ashurbanipal's creation of his great library, but it is worth reflecting that we are also indebted to its sudden destruction by his mortal enemies. In the ordinary wear and tear of life, things break, times change, and old books are forgotten and abandoned. Of Aeschylus's ninety tragedies, for instance, only seven survive today. People never ceased speaking Greek, so those seven plays somehow escaped the fate of the rest, but the Akkadian language and its cuneiform script were falling out of usage in Ashurbanipal's day, as the much easier alphabetic script of Aramaic gained in popularity. Even if Nineveh had survived, within another century or two Ashurbanipal's magnificent collections would have been dispersed to the winds, their tablets lost, stolen, or crushed to use as subflooring. Sudden destruction is disastrous for the people who suffer it, but it can be a godsend for archaeologists: no neighborhood of ancient Rome has been preserved with the perfection of Pompeii.

Ashurbanipal's collections guided him on governing his overstretched empire, but many forces pressed against the wisdom they conveyed—from the legacy of Esarhaddon's divisive choices to growing prosperity in Babylonia, to the unsustainability of empire on fear and awe alone. It may be no coincidence that the ruins of Ashurbanipal's library do not preserve the epic of his merciless obliteration of Elam following the crushing of Babylon's rebellion. The invaders had not forgotten their hatred of Ashurbanipal in the fifteen years since his death, and before they burned his palace, they went through the rooms and hacked away at his face wherever they saw it on a relief. In the scene showing Ashurbanipal's garden picnic, King Teumman's dangling head is still sharply etched today, but Ashurbanipal's features are not: he was defaced by the enemies who rampaged through his palace.

Perhaps targeted for particular destruction too, the epic poetry of his reign survives only in half a dozen brief fragments, ranging from seven to forty-six lines long. The tablets are so badly broken that hardly a single line remains complete. One of the better preserved passages in these fragments depicts a tragic scene of a mother mourning her royal son's mortality, a theme also found in *Gilgamesh* and the *Iliad*. Half of each line is missing, but enough remains to suggest that a powerful poem has been lost:

> [. . . . . .] tears rolled down his mother's cheeks:
> [". . . . . .] you, I glance
> [. . . . . .] Who taught you [the . . .] of kingship?"
> [. . . . . .] her beautiful figure, has [taught] me her
>   weeping,
> [. . . . . .] has [put] wailing on my lips
> not to harm [. . . . . .]

Unless some future Hormuzd Rassam has the good fortune to recover more of this poem, we will never know the extent of our loss. Perhaps "The Conquest of Elam" was nothing more than propagandistic hack work. On the other hand, Ashurbanipal loved poetry, and he had amassed the world's greatest treasury of texts; he certainly had the means to foster a vibrant literary culture at his court. There were great poets in Babylonia as recently as the previous century; if Ashurbanipal had one such poet in his service, "The Conquest of Elam" could have been the Assyrian *Iliad*.

Ashurbanipal's epic has been lost, but his library preserved much of Babylon's literature. Spared Nineveh's spectacular end, Babylon decayed more slowly but more completely in the following centuries, and its ruins have yielded no such treasury. In his quest for guidance on governance, Ashurbanipal collected the masterworks of the culture he could never dominate. After Ashurbanipal, seeking to erase his great works from memory, the Babylonian invaders unwittingly preserved their own literature in the ruins of their hated enemy's palace. And then, across Mesopotamia, two thousand years of literary heritage slowly melted away, under later waves of conquest and through the general transience of human attention to the past. The authors of *The Epic of Gilgamesh* would fully appreciate the irony that Ashurbanipal's library preserved their verses for posterity precisely through its cataclysmic destruction.

CHAPTER 6

AT THE LIMITS
OF CULTURE

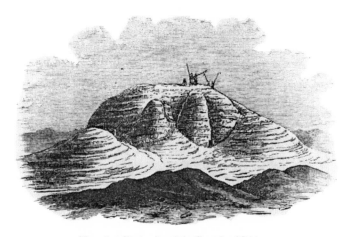

Mound at Uruk, site of the Temple of Ishtar.

THE Epic of Gilgamesh was already ancient in Ashurbanipal's day, copied and recopied for more than a thousand years before the young crown prince studied it in the Temple of Nabu. The epic appealed to audiences in the Assyrian and Babylonian courts both for its poetic power and for its exploration of the difficulties of rulership. A cultured king like Ashurbanipal could certainly enjoy the beauty of the verse and the epic's timeless themes of friendship and the brevity of mortal life, yet he would do so only if he managed to survive long enough to ponder these questions, and the epic itself could help him stay in power. It is no coincidence that

Ashurbanipal added a fresh copy to his library in 647 BCE, as
he sought texts to help him govern his kingdom in the wake of
his brother's disastrous rebellion.

The Gilgamesh epic highlighted a range of problems con-
fronting ancient kings and their subjects. For many centuries
it was known under the title "Surpassing All Other Kings,"
the epic's opening phrase when it was first composed in Babylonia in the eighteenth century BCE. This Old Babylonian version of the epic began by emphasizing Gilgamesh's kingly
magnificence:

> Surpassing all other kings, heroic in stature,
>> brave scion of Uruk, wild bull on the rampage!
> Going at the fore he was the vanguard,
>> going at the rear, one his companions could trust!

Gilgamesh is introduced here as a royal superhero, and by
birth he is actually closer to the gods than to ordinary mortals. He is two-thirds divine and one-third human: his divine
mother Ninsun has had double the genetic influence of his
mortal father Lugalbanda. "Who is there can rival his kingly
standing?" the poet asks. For all his godlike splendor, though,
Gilgamesh is far from a model ruler. The initial verses introduce troubling notes of violence, excess, and lack of control:
Gilgamesh is a "wild bull on the rampage," and a few lines
later he is compared to "a violent flood-wave, smashing a stone
wall." As the poem opens, Gilgamesh is shown abusing his subjects in a variety of ways. "Gilgamesh lets no son go free to his
father," imposing exhausting contests on them for his own
amusement; "by day and night his tyranny grows harsher."
His city's daughters fare even worse than the sons, for Gilgamesh forces himself upon them on their wedding night: "He

will couple with the bride-to-be, / he first of all, the bridegroom after." *Gilgamesh* is often read today as an existential tale of the fear of death and the quest for immortality, but the epic is equally a tale of tyranny and its consequences.

Uruk's violated women complain to the gods, who decide that something needs to be done. On orders from the sky god Anu, the goddess Aruru fashions a formidable opponent for Gilgamesh, "a match for the storm of his heart." She throws clay onto a deserted patch of ground, treating the earth as her potter's wheel, and "in the wild she created Enkidu, the hero, offspring of silence." Enkidu then reaches Uruk by a strangely circuitous route. Instead of simply setting him down at Uruk's gate with a mandate to knock some sense into the king, the gods let him loose in the steppe, where he runs among the animals, naked except for a natural covering of matted hair, with no clue as to his purpose in life. This roundabout setup allows the poet to introduce one of the epic's great themes, an exploration of the limits of culture, here presented in contrast to the world of nature.

Enkidu's early life is an Edenic idyll. "Offspring of silence," he is as happily solitary as Rousseau could wish anyone to be in the state of nature. Enkidu roams about with the animals, drinking at their watering holes and tearing apart the traps that hunters have set to catch them. It is this activity that—again indirectly—leads to his being brought to Uruk. Outraged at the destruction of his traps, a hunter asks his father for advice, and the father tells him to go talk to Gilgamesh, who can send a temple prostitute out to the wilderness to tame the wild man.

Gilgamesh does send a temple prostitute named Shamhat to Enkidu, who until then has been entirely innocent of sexual knowledge. Shamhat wastes no time in freeing him of this regrettable innocence. She strips in front of him and they lie down atop her garments for an epic bout of lovemaking:

> Shamhat unfastened the cloth of her loins,
>> she bared her sex and he took in her charms.
> She did not recoil, she took in his scent:
>> she spread her clothing and he lay upon her.
> She did for the man the work of a woman,
>> his passion caressed and embraced her.
> For six days and seven nights
>> Enkidu was erect, as he coupled with Shamhat.

Enkidu's sexual initiation is a mixed blessing: he gains "knowledge and wide understanding," the poem says, but he is physically weakened. Worse, his animals now flee from him. He can stay in the wild no longer.

This episode shares clear similarities with the biblical story of Adam and Eve, with the knowledge achieved at the price of the earthly Paradise. Indeed, much as the biblical serpent tempts Eve by promising that "your eyes will be opened, and you will be like God," Shamhat praises her lover in a post-coital conversation: "You are handsome, Enkidu, you are just like a god!" Yet nothing is said of sin, and Enkidu's loss of innocence is a prelude to something greater: his entry into civilized life. Whereas the early Hebrews were a seminomadic people profoundly suspicious of city culture, the Mesopotamians were the creators of the world's first great urban societies. For them, as later for the Romans, civilization was epitomized in city life.

A city girl herself, Shamhat cannot see why Enkidu would want to be anywhere else. Having praised his godlike good looks, she declares, "Why with the beasts do you wander in the

fields?/Come, I will take you to Uruk-the-sheepfold." She
goes on to enumerate her city's many virtues. Rather briefly,
she mentions that Uruk holds the sacred temples of the god
Anu and her own employer Ishtar, the goddess of love. She
waxes far more eloquent about the city's social pleasures: people wear lovely clothing in the city, and every day is like a festival: "Drums there rap out the beat,/and there are harlots,
most comely of figure. . . ./Even the aged they rouse from
their beds!" Best of all, Shamhat says, in the city Enkidu will
find a true friend, his only equal on earth: Gilgamesh.

In order to help Enkidu make the transition to civilized
life, Shamhat shares her robes with him and has a barber
comb out his shaggy hair. She introduces him to the pleasures
of fresh-baked bread and beer; after drinking seven cups in a
row, "his mood became free, he started to sing,/his heart grew
merry, his face lit up." Enkidu still lingers in the country,
though, until a seemingly random event moves him to action.
A stranger passes by on his way to a wedding in the city;
pausing to rest a little, he mentions that Gilgamesh will probably intervene in his usual way and insist on sleeping with the
bride before she can go to her husband. Hearing this, Enkidu
becomes furious, perhaps reflecting country dwellers' tradi-
tional suspicion of loose-living ways in the city. He determines to leave for Uruk immediately and put a stop to
Gilgamesh's bad behavior.

Remarkably, none of these characters—Shamhat, the
hunter, the hunter's father, the passing stranger, nor Enkidu
himself—knows that they are all performing roles planned for
them by the gods. Still less does Gilgamesh realize that in
sending Shamhat to pacify the wild man in the countryside,
he is connecting her with the person created to stem his own
disorder in the city. But why should the gods keep everyone

in the dark in this way? Why couldn't Ninsun simply convey the gods' disapproval directly to her son and order him to mend his ways? The gods' behavior is puzzling as a matter of plotting, and differs from the ways gods and kings alike are portrayed in the Mesopotamian royal annals. This difference, however, can illuminate the social role of literature in the ancient Near Eastern world.

The Assyrian and Babylonian chroniclers went to great lengths to portray their kings as all-powerful and all-knowing; they regularly turned military defeats into victories and suppressed unpleasant surprises of all sorts. The omnipotent kings were guided by their even more powerful gods and goddesses, who marched with them into war, watched over the palace at home, and did everything in their formidable power to keep the king secure and the kingdom prosperous. The extensive religious literature of hymns, prayers, and incantations helped guarantee the gods' close and favorable attention to human needs. Yet in *Gilgamesh*, no human actor—least of all the king—knows what is really happening. When the gods grant the anguished petition of Uruk's raped women, their response is unannounced, and to mortal eyes the divine plan would seem to be nothing more than a crescendo of coincidences.

This situation may seem surprising, but it reflects the epic's profound realism. In their elaborate indirection, the gods and goddesses are behaving in a highly realistic way, as the poem's ancient audiences understood the way of the world. People sensed the gods' power everywhere around them but were well aware that the gods were nowhere to be seen. In theory, the gods could speak directly with favored mortals—and Gilgamesh does in fact talk with his divine mother Ninsun—but ordinarily they preferred to communicate through dreams, omens, and unusual natural events, including extraordinary births. Such behavior was not surprising in a world whose kings were sequestered within their palaces, communicating with their subjects through two or three layers of palace bureaucracy, so it was logical that the great gods would also use intermediaries to interact with their servants on earth.

The problem lay in knowing how to read the messages that filtered down from heaven. In principle, such communications were instantly understandable to the king and his sagacious priests, but in practice the gods' messages were often obscure, ambiguous, even contradictory. Esarhaddon's anxious correspondence with his priests reveals a reality that would never have been admitted into the royal annals and hymns. In this context, literature had a privileged role, serving as a rare forum in which these uncertainties could be played out in public. In literature as in life, a king could be seriously flawed as a person or as a ruler, and even a good king could chafe under pronounced limitations in his power and knowledge; listening to the epic's recital, king and courtiers could reflect on the perplexities of their own situations.

Dreams offer a good example of the ambiguities of divine-human communication. Before Enkidu arrives in Uruk, the gods send Gilgamesh advance notice in the form of a pair of prophetic dreams, symbolically introducing him to his friend-to-be. Yet these dreams are bafflingly opaque to the king, who has to ask his mother to explain them. In the first dream, a meteor falls from heaven, and a crowd gathers around, caressing and kissing it; Gilgamesh picks it up and offers it to Ninsun. In the parallel second dream, an ax takes the place of the meteor. Asked to explain these dreams, Ninsun reveals that both the meteor and the ax are images of an intimate

friend: "Like a wife you'll love him, caress and embrace him, /
he will be mighty and often will save you." So the dream's
message has been decoded, yet Gilgamesh has no idea who this
friend will be. Enkidu then appears in Uruk, but Gilgamesh
takes him for an enemy and tries to kill him—perhaps understandably, as Enkidu's first act is to bar the way as Gilgamesh tries to go into the house where a wedding is being
celebrated, to violate the bride. Their struggle is so fierce that
the building's walls and doorway tremble; gradually they
fight to a standstill. Gilgamesh realizes he's finally met his
match, and he and Enkidu become fast friends.

All in all, the god-sent dreams give poor guidance, either
because their symbolic messages are obscure or because the
headstrong Gilgamesh refuses to pay proper attention to
them, seeing in Enkidu a barrier to his pleasures, rather than
realizing that the imposing stranger must be his promised
friend. The epic thus dispels any fiction of total transparency
in communicating with the gods. At the same time, the episode
also provides an opportunity for the poet to add some sugges-
tive hints of his own. Ninsun says that Gilgamesh will "caress
and embrace" Enkidu like a wife, using the same verbs that described Enkidu's lovemaking with Shamhat. In the early
Sumerian poems on which the epic was based, Enkidu was a
faithful servant and trusted adviser, but there was no suggestion of a romantic connection with his master. In the epic, Ninsun's language suggests that Gilgamesh and Enkidu have a
more intimate relationship, and the two dreams slyly insinu te
that they may be outright lovers. This hint is given by the
choice of objects that Gilgamesh starts to love and caress in his
dreams: the words for "meteor" and "ax," *kisru* and *hassinnu*,
strongly suggest two sexually loaded terms: *kezru*, a male
prostitute, and *assinnu*, a eunuch who would take the female

role in sexual rituals at Ishtar's temple. This may be the first known time in world literature when a poet realized that the ambiguity of dreams—a source of profound anxiety in waking life—could be a writer's delight.

Caressing and embracing Enkidu in whichever sense, Gilgamesh abandons his abuse of his subjects, and order is restored in the city. His restless heart, however, cannot stay content for long, and he soon conceives a bold plan to journey to a distant Cedar Forest to acquire trees for his city's temples. The location of this forest shifts over time: in the early Sumerian version of this episode, the Cedar Forest was found to the east in the mountains of western Persia, but in time those slopes became deforested. The Babylonians and Assyrians began to travel westward to Lebanon, whose cedars were famous throughout the Near East. The major action of the first half of *The Epic of Gilgamesh* concerns the friends' journey to Lebanon—digging their wells en route—to reach the Cedar Forest. There they must defeat the terrible ogre Humbaba, whom the god Enlil has set in the forest as its guardian.

With the attack on Humbaba the adventure takes on a double focus, well suited to a Mesopotamian monarch's dual role: military conquest and the control of scarce natural resources. Mesopotamia was a great source for clay and straw, the ingredients used to make brick walls, but good hardwood was difficult to find. Monumental building projects required trees of exceptional height and strength for ceiling beams and doors, and the cedars of Lebanon were ideal for the purpose. The royal architects were not shy about complaining if their monarchs failed to provide such lumber—by trade or by conquest, no matter, they just wanted the goods. As one irritated builder wrote to Sargon II, "The second-rate logs we [have been cutting into shape] here are quite plentiful but, truly, none of them will do for the job. . . . They are of fir and are much too thin. I have tried them out here but have rejected them. Had they been of cedar, I would already have cut them into shape and installed them." The king himself would need to intervene: "Now, what are my lord the king's orders? If the king orders that they should be used, let my lord the king write specifically . . . and I will duly comply and give them over to the accounting of the palace superintendent." The

Clay image of the ogre Humbaba's face, which is shown as though made of a single length of sheep's intestine. According to an inscription on the back, a sheep's intestine resembling Humbaba's face would signify "revolution."

builder wanted the record to be clear: it would be the king's own fault if the palace roof collapsed on his head.

Mesopotamian kings regularly described quests for high-grade lumber as among the greatest exploits of their bold careers. Around 2130 BCE, a chronicler boasted that his king, Gudea of Lagash, "made a path into the Cedar Mountain, which nobody had entered before; he cut its cedars with great axes." Over a thousand years later, the Assyrian king Shalmaneser III erected a stela on Mount Amanus in Lebanon to commemorate seizing timber during a campaign of conquest against the region's Aramean tribes: "I covered the wide plain with the corpses of their fighting men, I dyed the mountains with their blood like red wool.·... I ascended the mountains of the Amanus, I cut there cedar and pine timber." Not surprisingly, these raids on Lebanon's resources aroused fear and hatred around the region. In the Bible, Isaiah shows the trees themselves celebrating the downfall of a Babylonian king, probably Nebuchadnezzar:

> The whole earth is at rest and quiet;
>   they break forth into singing.
> The cypresses exult over you,
>   the cedars of Lebanon, saying,
> "Since you were laid low,
>   no one comes to cut us down."

The Epic of Gilgamesh likewise presents the Cedar Forest expedition as a challenging military adventure. At the outset, Enkidu tries to discourage Gilgamesh from the idea. He says that he had encountered the terrifying Humbaba while roaming around the wilderness in his early days, and it would be foolhardy to go against him: "His voice is the Deluge,/his speech is fire, and his breath is death!.../An unwinnable battle is Humbaba's ambush!" Gilgamesh responds to Enkidu's words of caution with the fearless pride of every true epic hero: "Why, my friend, do you speak like a weakling?" He then elaborates his motives:

> Who is there, my friend, can climb to the sky?
>> Only the gods [dwell] forever in sunlight.
> As for man, his days are numbered,
>> whatever he may do, it is but wind.
> Here are you, afraid of death!
> What has become of your mighty valour?

Gilgamesh's thirst for adventure is fueled by a sense of the brevity and futility of life. This theme is more fully emphasized in this episode's Sumerian source, "Bilgamesh and Huwawa" (the Sumerian versions of the names Gilgamesh and Humbaba). In that poem, Bilgamesh tells Enkidu, "since no man can escape life's end,/I will enter the mountain and set up my name"—he plans to erect a victory stela in the cedar forest, much as Shalmaneser would later do in Lebanon. Bilgamesh then appeals for aid to the sun god Utu (the Sumerian equivalent of Shamash), and here his deep fear of death comes to the surface:

> O Utu, let me speak a word to you, give ear to what I say!
> Let me tell you something, may you give thought to it!
> In my city a man dies, and the heart is stricken,
> a man perishes, and the heart feels pain.
> I raised my head on the rampart,

my gaze fell on a corpse drifting down the river,
      afloat on the water:
I too shall become like that, just so shall I be!

In the epic, Uruk's elders share Enkidu's concern with Gilgamesh's plan: "You are young, Gilgamesh, borne along by emotion," they tell him, "all that you talk of you don't understand." Gilgamesh laughs at their fears but realizes he needs help. As in the old Sumerian poem, the sun god is the logical source of support, but in a reflection of the gods' increasing distance from humanity in the later periods, Gilgamesh no longer tries to speak directly to Shamash the way Bilgamesh was shown talking with Utu. Instead Gilgamesh goes to his mother, who makes the appeal on his behalf. Though she is a minor deity herself, she simply goes to the roof of her palace, where she makes an incense offering and prays to Shamash.

This scene is far more earthbound than the parallel scene in *The Iliad*, when Achilles' divine mother, Thetis, pleads with Zeus to assist her son in battle. To make her appeal, Thetis ascends to "the highest peak of rugged Olympus"—the meeting point of heaven and earth—where she finds Zeus enthroned. There, she grasps his knees with her left hand and takes him by the chin with her right, forcing him to look into her eyes as she makes her appeal. By contrast, in *Gilgamesh* there is no direct contact between Shamash and Ninsun, who acts for all the world just like a human priestess:

She climbed the staircase and went up on the roof,
      on the roof she set up a censer to Shamash.
Scattering incense she lifted her arms in appeal to the
      Sun God:

"Why did you afflict my son Gilgamesh with so restless
     a spirit?
For now you have touched him and he will tread
     the distant path to the home of Humbaba.
He will face a battle he knows not,
     he will ride a road he knows not."

Ninsun asks Shamash to send his thirteen powerful winds to
help Gilgamesh defeat Humbaba. The epic records no direct
reply from Shamash—again, reflecting the conditions of human prayer—but the thirteen winds do come to Gilgamesh's
aid in the decisive battle, incapacitating the ogre so that Gilgamesh and Enkidu can capture him.

Though *Gilgamesh* and *The Iliad* portray their heavenly
encounters differently, they use the goddess's appeal to similar ends. Ninsun's anxiety about her son's safety is paralleled
by the fear that Achilles' mother expresses when he asks her
to secure Zeus's aid in his struggles:

Thetis answered him then, her tears falling:
"Oh, my own child: unhappy in childbirth, why did I
     raise you?
Could you but stay by your ships, without tears or
     sorrow,
since the span of your life will be brief, of no length."

In both epics, the fragility of mortal life is dramatized
through the concern of the hero's immortal mother. In each
case, the mortal hero escapes death for the time being, though
his ultimate mortality shadows the entire story. Within the
epics, the hero's mortality is transferred to the person of
the hero's beloved friend, who does die, tragically, within the

frame of the epic's action. In this respect, Enkidu is a direct ancestor of Patroklos, Achilles' intimate friend and lover.

Such parallels are probably not the result of random chance. *The Epic of Gilgamesh* circulated widely around the Near East; fragments of its tablets have been found at Megiddo in Palestine, a little north of Jerusalem, as well as in Asia Minor, where the epic was translated into Hittite, the language of the powerful Hittite kingdom that bordered the Greek settlements in Troy and elsewhere along the coast of what is now Turkey and Syria. As the classicist M. L. West has argued, poet-singers were likely performing *Gilgamesh* in Syria and Cyprus during the period in which the Homeric epics were first being elaborated.

The early Greek bards were illiterate, and no passages in Homer are direct translations of anything in *Gilgamesh*, but many people in the region were bilingual (indeed, multilingual). Hearing *Gilgamesh* performed, it is likely that the Homeric poets found themes they could adapt to their own purposes. Intensive cultural exchanges went on around the ancient Mediterranean world over the centuries, clearly visible in the profound debt that Greek art owes to Persian and Near Eastern traditions. Writing reached Greece through Phoenician traders who had adapted early West Semitic alphabets used by Syrian and Canaanite groups. Through such means of transmission, Achilles and his restless fellow hero Odysseus came to bear a distinct family resemblance to Gilgamesh, their greatest epic predecessor.

In *The Epic of Gilgamesh* as in *The Iliad*, the hero's adventures lead to the death of his beloved companion. Gilgamesh's victory over Humbaba is a major triumph, yet it is also the first act of Enkidu's tragedy. Having warned Gilgamesh against making the expedition, Enkidu reluctantly goes along, but Gilgamesh has a series of ominous dreams as they journey toward the Cedar Forest. Assorted disasters occur in these dreams: Gilgamesh is buried beneath an avalanche, overwhelmed by a volcano, assaulted by a wild bull and then by a ferocious lion-headed eagle. His flesh frozen with fear by these terrifying dreams, Gilgamesh asks Enkidu to interpret them. This would be the perfect opportunity for Enkidu to renew his good advice against the planned attack, but instead of drawing the obvious conclusion from the dreams, Enkidu falls into the classic temptation of an autocrat's adviser: he tells Gilgamesh what he knows his master wants to hear. In a circular argument, he asserts that the avalanche and volcano must somehow be good omens, as they cannot signify Humbaba, whom they are going to defeat. He asserts they will bind the lion-headed eagle's wings, and he even claims that Gilgamesh must himself be the powerful bull, even though in the dream Gilgamesh is being attacked by the bull.

Once they reach the Cedar Forest, Enkidu becomes increasingly rash in his actions and advice. He mocks Gilgamesh when his master hesitates to attack, and he is ruthless once they have captured Humbaba. The ogre pleads for mercy, saying he will give them lavish gifts and adding that he is protected by the great god Enlil, who had stationed him in the sacred forest to guard its trees. Having procured the desired timber and the glory of the victory, Gilgamesh is inclined to spare Humbaba, but Enkidu intervenes. Rather than releasing their captive, Enkidu says, they should murder him on the spot, since he could be a danger to them if left alive. As for Enlil's anger, that is simply a reason to act quickly. They

should achieve a fait accompli ahead of the news cycle, so to
say, before word of Humbaba's capture gets around:

> finish him, slay him, do away with his power,
>> before Enlil the foremost hears what we do!
> The [great] gods will take against us in anger,
>> Enlil in Nippur, Shamash in [Larsa] . . . ,
> establish forever [a fame] that endures,
>> how Gilgamesh [slew ferocious] Humbaba!

Gilgamesh follows Enkidu's advice and cuts off Humbaba's head, but not before the ogre has delivered a fearsome
curse: "May the pair of them not grow old together!/None
shall bury Enkidu beside Gilgamesh his friend!" In developing the old adventure tale of "Bilgamesh and Huwawa," the
epic poet has fashioned a resonant portrayal of the pressures
facing a willful king's counselors. Enkidu progressively fails
to measure up to the task, and his death will be the result.

Next comes the poem's pivotal event, the midpoint of the
epic's eleven tablets: the attempted seduction of Gilgamesh by
the goddess Ishtar, a confrontation that will end in Enkidu's
death and shift Gilgamesh's thoughts away from earthly glory.
On returning to Uruk with Humbaba's head, Gilgamesh bathes
and then dresses in his royal finery; observing him, Ishtar is
smitten. She abruptly appears and invites him—almost orders
him—to become her husband, promising him fabulous wealth
in return. To her shock and surprise, Gilgamesh spurns her offer, roundly insulting her for promiscuous infidelity:

> You are an oven that [melts] ice,
>> a half-door that keeps out neither breeze nor blast,
> a palace that crushes down valiant warriors,
>> an elephant who devours its own covering,

> pitch that blackens the hands of its bearer,
>> a waterskin that soaks its bearer through, . . .
> limestone that buckles out the stone wall,
>> a battering ram that destroys the enemy,
>> a shoe that bites its owner's foot!

Not content with assailing her character, Gilgamesh gives a sarcastic summary of her erotic history. "Come, let me tell you the tale of your lovers," he says, and lists a series of men—and even a lion and a horse—whom Ishtar has seduced and abandoned. They all lived blighted, wretched lives thereafter. Gilgamesh concludes with a hostile question: "Must you love me also and [deal with me] likewise?" Enraged, Ishtar unleashes the fearsome Bull of Heaven, a monster so powerful that its snorting opens a pit that swallows two hundred men and so huge it can lower a river by seven cubits at a single drink. Yet Gilgamesh and Enkidu succeed in killing the bull, a great deed often represented in Mesopotamian art.

This episode was first recorded in a Sumerian poem, "Bilgamesh and the Bull of Heaven." There, the advances of the goddess of love are also shown to be improper, but in a limited and specific way: she would divert the king from his ritual duties if he became her lover. Unsure what to do, Bilgamesh asks his mother's advice, and when she recommends that he decline the honor, he does so diplomatically, offering gifts in place of himself. In *The Epic of Gilgamesh*, the confrontation is dramatically heightened: Gilgamesh doesn't ask Ninsun's advice but rejects Ishtar out of hand, lambasting her with his insulting account of her promiscuities.

How should Gilgamesh's reaction be understood? Is he standing up for humanity against the archaic order of the often immoral gods, or is he displaying an absurd hubris,

Impression from a cylinder seal, showing Enkidu (on the left) and the royally attired Gilgamesh slaying the Bull of Heaven.

thinking he can insult and reject a great goddess at will? Both may be true. In part, the stark quality of the encounter reflects the growing separation of the human and divine worlds over the course of the second millennium BCE. In contrast to the older Sumerian poem, the epic implies that it is inappropriate, even a little absurd, for a goddess to come to earth to sleep with a mortal, however handsome he may be. In earlier periods, kings regularly engaged in ritual sexual relations with priestesses representing Ishtar and her Sumerian counterpart, Inanna. The king helped in this way to ensure the land's fertility and prosperity, via a "sacred marriage" ceremony, or *hieros gamos*, with the chief priestess of the goddess's temple.

In the twenty-first century BCE, for example, King Shulgi of Ur took his intimacy with the goddess of love as a point of pride: "I am Shulgi," he declared, "who has been chosen by Inanna for his attractiveness." Almost a thousand years later, the standard version of *The Epic of Gilgamesh* does not present such sacred unions as plausible or proper events. The poem is not entirely consistent in this viewpoint, as Gilgamesh's own mother is divine and so he himself must have been the product of a fairly recent union of goddess and mortal. Even so, within the action of the epic, human culture is shown to occupy its own proper realm, poised between the world of nature and the world of the gods.

The epic's audience probably enjoyed the misogynistic comedy of Ishtar's humiliation, and even the gods think Gilgamesh has a point. When the outraged Ishtar returns to heaven and demands vengeance, the god Anu replies, "Ah, but was it not you who provoked King Gilgamesh?" At the same time, it is ironic that in rejecting the immoral goddess, Gilgamesh ignores the fact that he is condemning her for his own chief failing: promiscuously forcing himself on unwilling sexual partners. Ishtar, moreover, is not just one powerful divinity among many; she is the patron goddess of his own city, and her great temple is Uruk's very heart. He ought to be on the best possible terms with her, and even if he is now rejecting women in favor of intimate male bonding with Enkidu, he should at least find a way to flatter Ishtar and appease her. The episode with Ishtar thus doubles the adventure against Humbaba. In love as in war, Gilgamesh hasn't yet accepted his human limits, which necessitate not only a separation of human and divine realms but constant negotiations with imperious overlords who if crossed are capable of vicious retaliation.

Perhaps Ishtar is making a proposition she shouldn't

make, but it is also an offer Gilgamesh shouldn't refuse, or at
least not so bluntly. Gilgamesh is guilty of a failure in royal
judgment, and once again his companion Enkidu only makes
matters worse by not offering the kind of moderating counsel
that might have salvaged the situation. Having been rebuffed
by Gilgamesh, Ishtar doesn't punish him directly; instead she
sends down the Bull of Heaven, contenting herself with acting through an intermediary in the usual way. Yet when Gilgamesh and Enkidu have slain the bull, Enkidu cannot leave
well enough alone. Ishtar has been watching from the top of
Uruk's high wall, and she starts hopping and stamping with
rage when her champion is slain. Hearing her outcry, Enkidu
cuts off one of the bull's haunches and hurls it at her, shouting, "Had I caught you too, I'd have treated you likewise, / I'd
have draped your arms in its guts!" In attacking Ishtar directly, Enkidu is fatally breaching the separation between the
human and divine realms, a separation that Ishtar has already undercut by alighting on Uruk's wall. Ishtar returns to
heaven, and though the gods had not approved of her sending
down the Bull of Heaven, they agree that Enkidu has gone
too far and they decree his death.

Two full tablets out of the epic's eleven are devoted to
Enkidu's lingering death and Gilgamesh's extended mourning for his intimate friend. As Enkidu begins to waste away,
he has a terrifying dream. A grim man with fingers like eagle's talons seizes him by the hair; though Enkidu doesn't
know who this is, his assailant is the angel of death, Humut-
tabal, whose name means "Take Away Quickly." Humut-tabal
drags Enkidu by the hair down to the House of Dust,

> to the house which none who enters ever leaves,
>   on the path that allows no journey back,

to the house whose residents are deprived of light,

where soil is their sustenance and clay their food,

where they are clad like birds in coats of feathers,

and see no light, but dwell in darkness.

As he enters the House of Dust, Enkidu sees a heap of crowns piled just inside the doorway: earthly lordship has no meaning in the underworld, where kings and servants mingle indistinguishably. He approaches Belet-seri, the scribe of the underworld, who looks up from her tablet, annoyed to find him there so soon: "[Who was] it fetched this man here?" she asks. "[Who was it] brought here [this fellow?]"

Another forty lines follow, apparently describing the horrors of the underworld, but in an all too appropriate illustration of the epic's own theme, these lines have not survived in any copy of the tablet yet discovered. When the text resumes, Gilgamesh exclaims over Enkidu's vision, and then Enkidu's strength begins to fail. His death must occur in the tablet's final thirty lines, which are also lost. At present only about two thousand of the poem's three thousand lines are basically complete. An apt proportion: the epic is one-third mortal, two-thirds immortal, like its own hero.

Enkidu, however, is entirely mortal, and the next tablet details Gilgamesh's extreme grief at his companion's death. He sits by the corpse for six days and seven nights—a time that echoes Enkidu's lovemaking with Shamhat—refusing to admit that Enkidu is truly dead, until a maggot crawls out of his friend's nose. Covering Enkidu's face "like a bride," he delivers an eloquent lament for his beloved friend. In his anguish, Gilgamesh in turn takes on feminine qualities: he weeps for Enkidu "like a hired mourning-woman" and paces around the corpse "like a lioness deprived of her cubs." His mourning can be compared to that of another ancient monarch, King David, who delivers a similarly moving lament when his beloved friend Jonathan is slain, comparing him, too, to a bride:

> How the mighty have fallen in the midst of the battle!
> Jonathan lies slain upon your high places.
> I am distressed for you, my brother Jonathan;
> greatly beloved were you to me;
> your love to me was wonderful,
> passing the love of women.

Known to have circulated into Palestine as well as Asia Minor, *Gilgamesh* finds echoes in the Bible as well as in Homer.

Gilgamesh gives Enkidu an elaborate burial and then abandons Uruk, terrified at the prospect of his own death. He determines to seek out the hidden home of his ancestor Uta-napishtim the Faraway, survivor of the Deluge. Unsure where to go, he wanders at random through the wilderness, replacing his disintegrating clothes with skins of lions he kills along the way. He seems to have regressed to Enkidu's primitive state. Looking down from heaven, Shamash is moved to pity, but he cannot offer any encouragement: "O Gilgamesh, where are you wandering?" he asks. "The life that you seek you never will find."

Gilgamesh ventures eastward beyond the known limits of human habitation and finally arrives at the shore of the ocean that encircles the globe. There he encounters Uta-napishtim's boatman, Ur-shanabi, who ferries him across the Waters of Death to the distant island where Uta-napishtim dwells with his wife. Gilgamesh has finally reached his long-sought destination, but he gets a discouraging reception. "Why, Gilgamesh," Uta-napishtim asks, "do you ever [chase] sorrow?" He insists that Gilgamesh is only exhausting himself, shortening the time until he will be taken by "Death so savage, who hacks men down." A mortal, Uta-napishtim continues, is like a mayfly floating for a few days on a river in spring: "On the face of the sun its countenance gazes,/then all of a sudden nothing is there!"

The tenth tablet ends with this sobering speech, but Gilgamesh hasn't come this far to be put off so quickly. As the climactic eleventh tablet opens, he interrogates his ancestor: "How was it you stood with the gods in assembly?/How did you find the life eternal?" Uta-napishtim responds with the long story that made George Smith famous and led to his untimely death: the tale of the Deluge.

A recurrent problem in Mesopotamia, floods were a resonant metaphor for wholesale destruction. Major floods could devastate the mud-brick cities of the southern Mesopotamian floodplain, and royal annals regularly used flood imagery to describe particularly vicious attacks on a city, as in Sennacherib's account of the taking of Babylon in 689 BCE. "Like the oncoming of a storm I broke loose, and overwhelmed it like a hurricane," he declares. "The wall and outer wall, temples and gods, temple towers of brick and earth, as many as there were, I razed and dumped them into the Arahtu Canal. Through the midst of that city I dug canals, I flooded its site with water, and its very foundations I destroyed. I made its destruction more complete than that by a flood." Floods, then, were a point of contact between the mythic past and the imperial present, and every major flood or conquest recalled the great Flood that almost ended life on earth.

The Flood story was added to the epic relatively late in its history. After circulating for several centuries in its Old Babylonian form, the epic achieved its fullest and final form in what is today called the Middle Babylonian period, probably around 1200 BCE. Nothing certain is known about the poet who made these changes, though according to later tradition he was a Babylonian priest named Sin-leqe-unninni. In the original Old Babylonian form of the epic, Gilgamesh traveled to learn the secret of immortality from his ancestor, but from the surviving portions of that version, it appears that Utanapishtim did not tell his life story when they met; instead, he gave Gilgamesh long-lost information on how to conduct rituals that had fallen out of use since the time of the Flood. Sin-leqe-unninni expanded the meeting to include a full account of the Flood, adapting it from an existing poem called *Atrahasis*, "Exceedingly Wise," the name of the Flood's survivor in that version of the story. By adding in this account of universal destruction, Sin-leqe-unninni powerfully expanded the frame of Gilgamesh's tale to encompass the limits of human achievement as a whole.

Forewarned by his patron god Ea to build an ark and escape the coming deluge, Uta-napishtim takes on board as many animals as he can hold. Unlike Noah, he also brings along a full complement of craftsmen: he is intent on reestablishing civilized life as soon as he can. The Flood rages for six days and nights, and when it ends on the seventh day, Utanapishtim finds a scene of total devastation:

I looked at the weather, it was quiet and still,
    but all the people had turned to clay.
The flood plain was flat like the roof of a house.
    . I opened a vent, on my cheeks fell the sunlight.

Down sat I, I knelt and I wept,
down my cheeks the tears were coursing.

The ark comes to rest on a mountaintop, and after waiting a week Uta-napishtim sends out three birds: first a dove and then a swallow, neither of which can find a patch of dry land, and finally a raven, who doesn't return. Uta-napishtim then opens up his ship and begins the arduous process of restoring civilization.

The Babylonian Flood story shows little of the ethical emphasis of its counterpart in the Book of Genesis. When he begins his story, Uta-napishtim doesn't pause to explain why the gods ordained the Flood, but their motivation can be learned from Sin-leqe-unninni's source, *The Atrahasis Epic*. According to *Atrahasis*, the underlying problem was not human iniquity, as in the Bible, but the fact that the human race was multiplying uncontrollably, and people had begun making too much noise. Disturbed in their sleep, the gods appeal to their leader, Enlil, who sends the Flood in response. Enlil's action is violent, but it has a certain ecological logic: the noisiness of the human race is an outgrowth of overpopulation, a serious issue in ancient Mesopotamia, whose large populations often put the region's resources under stress. Even so, there is no indication of any moral failing on the part of humanity.

While the Flood story is not concerned with sin, Sin-leqe-unninni used it to carry on the epic's engagement with issues of good and bad political judgment. As the floodwaters fill the earth and all life begins to perish, the gods realize they have made a terrible mistake, since they love to receive sacrificial offerings from their human servants. They lay the blame squarely at Enlil's feet: he has overreacted, not ordering a remedy proportionate to the problem. The answer to overpopulation should have been to thin out the human race, not to expunge it entirely. Angrily Ea reproves Enlil:

> Instead of your causing the Deluge,
>> a famine could have broken out, and ravaged the land!
> Instead of your causing the Deluge,
>> the Plague God could have arisen, and ravaged the
>> land!

Lions and wolves, he helpfully notes, could have diminished the population quite effectively, without causing wholesale destruction. In short, the king of the gods has been guilty of egregious mismanagement.

What is particularly interesting is the reason behind Enlil's failure. As both Ea and the mother goddess Belet-ili declare, "he did not take counsel and brought on the Deluge." "To take counsel," *malakum*, is the term for a king's policy discussions within the circle of his close advisers. It is the act of kingly deliberation par excellence: *malakum* is related both to "king," *malkum*, and to "royal adviser," *maliktum*. The needless destruction of life on earth repeats on a grand scale the unnecessary slaying of Humbaba when Gilgamesh listens to the ill-judged advice of Enkidu, in the first half of the epic.

It is none other than Uta-napishtim who brings home to Gilgamesh the issue of lack of good judgment. When Gilgamesh presents himself and asks for the secret of immortality, Uta-napishtim curtly asks him, "[Did you] ever, Gilgamesh, [compare your lot] with the fool? / . . . Because he has no [advisers to guide him], / his affairs lack counsel." Gilgamesh promptly rejects Uta-napishtim's counsel that he should learn to accept the limits of human life, insisting that when "I look at you, Uta-napishtim, / your form is no different, you are just like me."

Judging by appearances, Gilgamesh feels that he should be able to receive the same benefit of eternal life.

Uta-napishtim then tells the story of his experience in the Flood, which ended with Enlil repenting his rash decision and coming personally into the hold of Uta-napishtim's ark. He took Uta-napishtim by the hand and led him and his wife up on deck, where he bestowed his blessing upon them: "In the past Uta-napishtim was a mortal man,/but now he and his wife shall become like us gods!" Yet Uta-napishtim concludes that this ancient precedent cannot apply to his descendant. The reason he gives is simple but absolute: times have unalterably changed. "But you now," he says to Gilgamesh, "who will convene for you the gods' assembly, so you can find the life you search for?"

The Assyrians and Babylonians of the second millennium BCE knew they were heirs to an ancient culture, handed down via old monuments that they restored, and recorded in the cuneiform script invented to write the archaic language of Sumerian. They believed that their culture's history stretched back before the time of the Flood, yet they knew that the post-Flood world differed in significant ways from the antediluvian age. A list of kings of Sumer survives, and it extends back to pre-Flood days, demonstrating an important measure of continuity with the early past, yet the Sumerian King List marks a major shift at the time of the Flood. The earlier kings were said to have lived to fantastic ages, of 21,000 or more years, but after the Flood the life span drops precipitously, soon reaching modern-scale life spans.

The antediluvian world, then, was different from the world the Mesopotamian writers saw around them. Those were the days when gods and goddesses walked the earth, took people by the hand, and granted them extraordinary favors. Comparable views can be found in the Bible, where God walked in the evenings with Adam in Eden, figures like Enoch and Methuselah lived for eight or nine hundred years, and "the sons of God saw that the daughters of men were fair; and they took to wife such of them as they chose" (Genesis 6:2). Following the Flood, life spans rapidly decline, and people in the biblical world no longer marry heavenly beings, much as it no longer seemed appropriate for Gilgamesh to marry Ishtar. For the Mesopotamians, the "modern" world—the world as they knew it—dated from the time the Flood waters receded. When Gilgamesh visits Uta-napishtim, then, history visits the world of myth, both to take the measure of the modern world and to measure its distance from the lost era of Uta-napishtim the Faraway.

Resisting human limits as usual, Gilgamesh refuses to accept that times have changed, and so Uta-napishtim stages a test to show him that time will never be on his side. If Gilgamesh thinks he deserves to become immortal, Uta-napishtim says, the least he can do is stay awake for seven nights. Gilgamesh agrees to the test, but he has been exhausted by the effort of getting to Uta-napishtim's island, and he falls asleep the minute he sits down. Waking a week later, he denies that he slept at all, but Uta-napishtim has had his wife bake a loaf of bread every day and set it beside the slumbering hero. Looking at the progressively stale and moldy line of loaves, Gilgamesh finally admits defeat.

A fine poetic irony is at work in this demonstration of Gilgamesh's humanity. When his mother appealed to the sun god, she regretted that Gilgamesh had been born with a "restless heart." That phrase, *libbi la salila* in Akkadian, literally means "a sleepless heart," but now sleeplessness is the very thing he cannot achieve. Gilgamesh will have to live within the parameters of common human life. Uta-napishtim doesn't send Gilgamesh away entirely empty-handed, though: he has Ur-shanabi clean him up and dress him in beautiful robes that will remain unstained throughout his long journey home. Better yet, at his wife's urging, Uta-napishtim also tells Gilgamesh the location of a magical plant of rejuvenation that grows on the seafloor—it will not confer immortality, but it can restore a person's youthful body. Gilgamesh dives to retrieve it, but on his way home with Ur-shanabi he stops to bathe at a swimming hole. A serpent steals into the scene and eats the plant; as the serpent slithers away, its old skin falls off.

In the poem's final lines, Gilgamesh returns to Uruk in tears, his quest a total failure. He can comfort himself only by pointing proudly to his city when it comes in sight:

> O Ur-shanabi, climb Uruk's wall and walk back and forth!
> Survey its foundations, examine the brickwork!
> Were its bricks not fired in an oven?
> Did the Seven Sages not lay its foundations?
> A square mile is city, a square mile date-grove,
> a square mile is clay-pit, half a square mile the temple
> of Ishtar:
> three square miles and a half is Uruk's expanse.

The epic ends abruptly with these lines.

The Roman poet Horace famously praised the Homeric epics for plunging directly *in medias res*, into the middle of things. Sin-leqe-unninni made the opposite decision: not to begin but to end in the middle of things. His audience must have been surprised, because they knew how the story was supposed to end. According to an old Sumerian poem known as "The

Death of Bilgamesh," when it came time for Bilgamesh to die, the gods debated what his fate should be. They discussed his journey in search of immortality and considered finally granting his great wish, but in the end, "despite his mother we cannot show him mercy." Die he must, yet he need not share the shadowy, deprived existence of most shades in the House of Dust; instead, he will be made governor of the Underworld, "chief of the shades." In this capacity, he will have many benefits of life on earth. Torches will light his region of the underworld, and he will be reunited with his family and his "precious friend" Enkidu. Bilgamesh is then buried in state and descends to the underworld to take on his honorable new role.

Sin-leqe-unninni's audience did not regard this special dispensation as mere poetic fiction. On the contrary, from early times people began to make offerings to Bilgamesh/Gilgamesh in his capacity as a judge of the underworld, urging him to look favorably on their deceased loved ones. Yet instead of following his Sumerian sources, Sin-leqe-unninni chose to leave Gilgamesh at Uruk's threshold, torn between grief at his mortality and pride at the greatness of his city. The epic ends as it begins, with its hero unaware of the gods' plans for him. The poem comes full circle as its final lines recall the epic's opening, in a prologue added by Sin-leqe-unninni. This new beginning has a different emphasis than the original stress on Gilgamesh's kingly strength and violence. Instead, he is introduced as a searcher for ancient wisdom, "He who saw the Deep, the country's foundation, /[who] knew . . . was wise in all matters!" Crucially, he preserves this knowledge by writing it down for posterity:

He saw what was secret, discovered what was hidden,
    he brought back a tale of before the Deluge.

He came a far road, was weary, found peace,
and set all his labors on a tablet of stone.

Along with Gilgamesh's wisdom, the prologue emphasizes his role as a builder: "He built the ramparts of Uruk-the-Sheepfold," the poet says. "View its parapet that none could copy. . . . Survey its foundations, examine the brickwork." He then describes Uruk's four regions (houses, date grove, clay pit, and temple precinct), using the very words of Gilgamesh to Ur-shanabi that form the epic's concluding lines.

The poet and his audience knew that Uruk had been established long before Gilgamesh's day, and the foundations of its great wall were laid by "the Seven Sages," primeval wise men who first taught the arts of culture to humanity, long before the Flood. So it is not supposed here that Gilgamesh is the wall's first builder; instead, he has repaired and rebuilt the ancient wall, no doubt enlarging it in the process. This was a major form of royal public works. In emphasizing this activity, Sin-leqe-unninni casts Gilgamesh in the role of a responsible monarch of his own day, custodian of ancient cities and monuments that have to be maintained and repaired.

The Mesopotamian kings loved to boast of conquering new lands and building new palaces of unrivaled splendor, but they also publicized their careful conservation of the great works of their ancestors. Sometimes they even portrayed themselves carrying baskets of bricks, as though they were personally joining in the labor. Royal inscriptions record the kings' awareness that their own monuments would likewise be dependent on future generations' perhaps fickle attention. When Esarhaddon restored one temple, he set up a plaque commemorating his restoration work, with an appeal to his descendants: "In future days among my sons the kings," he implored, "when that temple becomes old and falls to decay, let him restore its ruins. . . . Do thou as I have done. Look upon the memorial with the inscription of my name, anoint it with oil, offer sacrifices, set it up alongside the memorial with the inscription of your own name. Then Ashur and Ishtar will hear your prayers."

The epic's prologue concludes by merging the themes of Gilgamesh as builder and Gilgamesh as acquirer of ancient wisdom, for he engraves his story on a tablet of stone and buries it in the foundation of his renovated city wall. The poet tells his audience to uncover this buried report, much as Hormuzd Rassam would find the "Rassam Cylinder" recording the glories of Ashurbanipal's reign buried within the walls of Ashurbanipal's palace. "[See] the tablet-box of cedar, /[release] its clasp of bronze!" the poet urges his listener. "[Lift] the lid of its secret, /[pick up] the tablet of lapis lazuli and read out /the travails of Gilgamesh, all that he went through."

The epic's audiences in Babylon and Nineveh knew they were not supposed to go and dig cedar chests out of Uruk's foundations, but by reading or hearing the story they could in a way repeat Ur-shanabi's tour of Uruk's sacred precincts. Ur-shanabi had come along on the return to Uruk because Uta-napishtim had banned him from returning to his island, so as to ensure that no mortal would ever again enter his immortal realm. The lapis lazuli tablet, though, could enable the audience to accomplish imaginatively what was no longer possible in reality: to revisit the ancient past, meeting Gilgamesh and even Uta-napishtim the Faraway. In Sin-leqe-unninni's presentation, Gilgamesh emerges not only as the first great hero of world literature but also as a founding writer as well, and Gilgamesh purposely plants his story where future seekers can find it. When Layard and Rassam unearthed his story's

Ashurbanipal as a day laborer.

tablets and George Smith unlocked the secret of their message, they were doing the very thing that Sin-leqe-unninni
had instructed his own audience to do, three thousand years
before their time.

Remarkably, the epic may have played a role in the shift
of Assyria's capital to Nineveh, where Ashurbanipal would
one day create the library in which Layard and Rassam discovered the poem's best-preserved text. The epic ends with

Gilgamesh's return to Uruk at the close of the eleventh tablet, but the full "Series of Gilgamesh" consists of twelve tablets. The final tablet is a direct translation of portions of one of the Sumerian poems about Bilgamesh, known in ancient times by its first line, "In those days, in those distant days," and now often called "Bilgamesh and the Netherworld." Attached to the epic as a kind of appendix, the twelfth tablet came to be read as providing important information about the underworld, and it was consulted at the time the decision was made to establish Nineveh as Assyria's capital.

In the twelfth tablet, Enkidu descends into the underworld to retrieve some wooden implements, apparently a ball and mallet, which Gilgamesh has dropped into a fissure in the ground. Enkidu, here portrayed as Gilgamesh's servant, offers to bring them back. Gilgamesh gives Enkidu detailed instructions about how to behave so as not to arouse the notice and the anger of the beings in the underworld; rashly, Enkidu disobeys all his instructions, drawing attention to himself with his beautiful clothing, perfume, and active behavior not befitting a dead person. Realizing that he is an intruder, the underworld forces seize him.

Weeping, Gilgamesh approaches a series of gods to ask for their aid; turned down by two gods, he is pitied by Enki, god of fresh water and of wisdom. Enki conjures Enkidu in the form of a phantom, so that Gilgamesh can see his friend and learn about life in the underworld. Enkidu informs him that people who die childless fare poorly, while the more sons they have the better off they are, thanks to the offerings their sons make for them on earth. The poem breaks off with the sobering information that unburied corpses find no rest in the netherworld, while "the one whose shade has no one to make funerary offerings . . . eats scrapings from the pot and crusts of bread thrown away in the street."

Sin-leqe-unninni, or another editor in the late second millennium, included a translation of this tale as an appendix to *Gilgamesh*, though it is clearly not a continuation of the epic. Enkidu is alive as the episode begins and is Gilgamesh's servant rather than the wild man and intimate friend shown in the epic. Moreover, Sin-leqe-unninni created the standard version of the epic by expanding the Old Babylonian version, not by direct translation from the still older Sumerian poems. The tablet's readers were surely aware of all these differences, but it was not uncommon for ancient texts to conclude with some miscellaneous matter at the close of the main story.

The tale of Enkidu's underworld descent had a particular utility, moreover, greater even than the association of Gilgamesh with well digging early in the epic, for the story gave important clues as to how to behave and thrive in the underworld. At least for some readers, the twelfth tablet had a usefulness that overshadowed literary interest. On the twenty-seventh day of the fourth month of 705 BCE, a scribe in the Assyrian city of Kalah wrote out a careful copy of the twelfth tablet. He did this soon after his king, Sargon II, had been killed in battle in Anatolia. As the Assyriologist Eckart Frahm has argued, news of Sargon's death had probably just reached Kalah, an important scribal center and former capital of Assyria.

It has long been known that Sargon's son Sennacherib was so shocked by his father's death that he shunned his father's memory, abandoned his father's capital, Dur-Sharrakun, and established a new capital at Nineveh. Yet death in battle was generally regarded as a glorious sacrifice, not as a disgraceful death for a king. It might cause succession conflicts among his heirs, but this appears not to have been an issue for Sennacherib, who quickly and decisively assumed power shortly after his father's death. What was shocking was the manner of Sargon's demise: he had been overwhelmed by the enemy and his army had been routed, unable even to retrieve his body and bring it home for burial. This was a serious matter indeed, for unburied phantoms were likely to haunt their old homes, increasingly restless and malevolent. If not appeased, they could render a home unlivable—a motif that survives to this day in horror movies centered on nightmarish haunted houses.

Nabû-zuqup-kēnu was acting in his official capacity when he copied the twelfth tablet of *Gilgamesh* that day in 705 BCE. He was an interpreter of omens; almost all the other texts in his library, where this tablet was found, are omen texts. He must have been consulting *Gilgamesh* for its information and guidance in this difficult situation, for the twelfth tablet closes with its description of the fate of the unburied and the unattended. As the next to last couplet says: " 'Did you see the one whose corpse was left lying on the plain?' 'I saw him. / His shade is not at rest in the Netherworld.' " Nabû-zuqup-kēnu, then, was studying the tablet in the same way he would study an omen text: to gain insight on what would happen in a situation that could be dangerous not only for the new king but for the entire kingdom. In copying the tablet, he was making it available for consultation by the new king and other priests, no doubt along with other relevant omen texts in his possession. Perhaps the tablets would also be used in rituals designed to appease Sargon's angry shade.

Evidently the prognosis was unfavorable and the rituals were unavailing. Certainly the *Gilgamesh* tablet could not have been reassuring to Nabû-zuqup-kēnu or to Sennacherib, since it speaks of the deprived phantom's restlessness as a permanent condition. In the end, Sennacherib decided to undertake the huge expense and disruption of moving his capital to Nineveh rather than stay in the haunted palace of his doomed and unresting father. The twelfth tablet of *Gilgamesh* is regarded today as an expendable appendix, often not included in translations of the epic; yet its presence may be a prime reason why Sennacherib's grandson Ashurbanipal kept multiple copies of the epic in his library.

Preserved in part through its advice on dealing with the dead, the epic has once again become, as it was for Sin-leqe-unninni, its own best answer to the problem of death and the transience of human life. Kings and heroes die, and even the greatest of cities can become a flood-swept mound; yet the buried book waits, reposing in darkness, for the distant day when it will be recovered, telling a new era's readers about the quest for immortality, the perils of advising headstrong monarchs, and the pleasures of beer and fresh-baked bread.

CHAPTER 7

THE VANISHING POINT

Underground stairway.

In drawing perspective, lines that recede into the distance ultimately converge in what artists call the vanishing point. Pressing beyond the Old Babylonian epic in search of the historical Gilgamesh, it is possible to glimpse his shadowy form at the very edge of vision, on the threshold of history.

Historical records from Gilgamesh's archaic era are few and far between. It is only by chance that inscriptions have been found that name a few individuals from the early centuries of the third millennium BCE, but no records from his lifetime feature Gilgamesh. To reconstruct the outlines of Gilgamesh's life and achievements, it is necessary to project back from the documents that discuss him in the centuries after his death, supplementing these sources with archaeological information about Uruk. Gilgamesh's history is inextricably bound up with his city's rise, for Uruk was the first great city of ancient Sumer, and its founding heroes were remembered long after other cities had come to dominate Mesopotamia. One of Uruk's creators, Gilgamesh is equally a creation of Uruk itself.

An important early record that mentions Gilgamesh is the Sumerian King List, written down nearly four thousand years ago at the command of the king of another city-state, Isin. Because the king of Isin wanted to portray himself as successor to the great dynasties of the past, he commissioned a list of the kings of the dominant Sumerian cities from the very dawn of history, when "kingship descended from heaven." Evidently drawing on earlier court annals, the scribes of Isin created genealogies with the length of the kings' reigns. Archaeological evidence has confirmed the general accuracy of the Sumerian King List, at least back to Gilgamesh's day. Prior to that point, the genealogies recede into the realm of legend and of myth. Before Uruk's rise, a city called Kish was the major Sumerian power, but Kish's kings were said to have each had reigns of a thousand years and more. Apparently uneasy with these figures, the Isin scribes attempted to lend them an aᵣ ra of accuracy by means of an almost manic precision: Kish's twenty-three kings ruled, the scribes claimed, "for 24,510 years, 3 months, and 3½ days."

In Uruk, Gilgamesh's forebears were also credited with long reigns, each averaging five hundred years. Most of these kings may well have been real historical figures, but they had. taken on a largely legendary status. Immediately after Gilgamesh, however, the King List settles into a plausible sequence; his son Ur-Nungal and the dynasty's remaining kings all have reigns between six and thirty-six years in length. Gilgamesh stands on the threshold between his legendary forebears and his historically grounded successors: his reign is given as 126 years. As with his dates, so with the traditions about his life: a core of fact has clearly grown in the telling.

From early times, Gilgamesh was famous for having constructed the imposing wall around Uruk. In 1900 BCE, for example, a king named Anam recorded that he "restored the wall of Uruk, the ancient structure of Gilgamesh." This tradition was probably based on fact; excavations in Uruk have uncovered a major city wall dating to Gilgamesh's day. Over twenty feet high and protected with battlements, it stretched for nearly six miles, encircling the city and the date-palm gardens and clay pits that Gilgamesh proudly shows Ur-shanabi at the end of the epic. It has also been possible to reconstruct the likely reason Gilgamesh built up his city's fortifications: an ongoing struggle against Kish, a hundred miles north. The Sumerian King List cites two kings named Enmebaraggesi and Akka as Kish's final rulers before power shifted over to Uruk. Inscriptions survive from Enmebaraggesi, dated to around 2750 BCE, placing him and Akka as contemporaries of Uruk's Lugalbanda and Gilgamesh.

Two early texts record that either Gilgamesh or his father defeated Enmebaraggesi in combat, and an old Sumerian poem celebrates Gilgamesh's decisive victory over Akka. Interestingly, in view of Gilgamesh's later reputation as the inventor of wells, the poem opens with Gilgamesh rejecting a

Photograph of an excavation of the remains of Uruk's wall, c. 1930.

demand that he perform service to Kish in repairing and maintaining wells—a perfect instance of a grain of historical fact around which later legends could arise:

> There are wells to be finished,
>   many wells of the land yet to be finished;
> there are shallow wells of the land yet to be finished,
> there are wells to deepen and hoisting gear to be
>   completed.
> We should not submit to the house of Kish!
>   Let us smite it with weapons!

Gilgamesh inflicts a crushing defeat on Akka's troops: "Multitudes were smeared with dust/... the land's canal-mouths were filled with silt." A nice case of poetic justice: having tried to force Gilgamesh to maintain his water supplies, Akka is repaid by Gilgamesh ruining his canals. Gilgamesh captures Akka in the midst of his army, but then magnanimously recalls Akka's past favors to him. He releases Akka, declaring, "Before the Sun God, I hereby repay your kindness of old!" Spared but humiliated, Akka returns to Kish, and Uruk is free to become the dominant city of southern Mesopotamia.

Although George Smith was wrong to read *The Epic of Gilgamesh* as dramatizing a Babylonian war of independence against the "foreign tyrant" Humbaba, he was closer to the truth than he knew. Long before the epic was composed Gilgamesh was famous as the hero who secured his city's independence. The epic's account of the defeat of the Cedar Forest's guardian is a distant echo of the protracted struggle of the kings of Uruk against the kings of Kish.

Like George Smith, the right person at the right time to discover Gilgamesh's epic, Gilgamesh was the right person at the
right time to be memorialized in heroic poetry. Most of the
early kings in the Sumerian King List are known today only
through the King List's passing mention of their names and
the length of their reigns, supplemented perhaps by a votive
inscription on a piece of pottery. By contrast, tales and poems
were regularly written about the early kings of Uruk. Gilgamesh had the special good fortune to become the hero of a
poetic masterpiece, but other poems memorialized his father,
Lugalbanda, and his grandfather Enmerkar. Rather like the
House of Atreus in Greece, so important for Greek drama and
epic, the kings of Uruk became models for later Mesopotamian
literature.

Many other Sumerian kings accomplished similar feats—
conquering neighboring cities, improving irrigation, import-
ing cedar trees—but the early kings of Uruk had a unique
advantage in the literary struggle against oblivion: their city
was the world's first great center of writing. This in turn is
not surprising; during the fourth millennium BCE Uruk became the dominant city in Babylonia, with tens of thousands
of inhabitants and monumental public buildings. Earlier
cities such as Kish and the old religious center of Eridu were
more like large towns; in a recent study, Uruk has rightly
been called "the first city in human history."

Writing developed through a long process, beginning with
simple notations of images and numbers, needed by traders to
account for goods exchanged and received. According to one
theory, full-scale writing gradually emerged over the course
of several centuries, as symbols accumulated and people began to use them for their phonetic value. Yet widely scattered

experimentation would have produced a proliferation of mutually incomprehensible systems, each useless to anyone beyond a given scribe and his circle. An increasing number of historians of writing have come to regard this process as marked by punctuated equilibrium, to use a term from evolutionary biology. In this theory, the transition from established methods of accounting via symbols to true writing entailed an intellectual revolution, carried out by a group of scribes working together between about 3300 and 3200 BCE to formulate the basic norms of a workable system. It could represent sounds with a limited set of symbols and convey abstract concepts beyond anything that could be pictured. These scribes would have been located either in Uruk or in one of the neighboring cities, but in any case Uruk was then the region's major city and quickly became Mesopotamia's leading scribal center.

The Sumerians recognized Uruk's pivotal role in the history of writing. An early poem known as "Enmerkar and the Lord of Aratta" describes Gilgamesh's grandfather as inventing the very first clay tablet, which he uses to deliver an ultimatum to the distant ruler of Aratta in western Persia. Taken aback by this new technology, Enmerkar's enemy stares gloomily at the tablet, overwhelmed by the sheer power of writing:

> The Lord of Aratta looked at the kiln-fired clay.
> The words were fierce words.
> Frowning, the Lord of Aratta kept looking at his piece
>   of clay.

Clay tablets were in fact used well before Enmerkar's time, but this legendary accomplishment rightly continued to be associated with Uruk. For several centuries, the Mesopotamians used writing almost exclusively as an aid in their extensive trade and in the management of city-states of growing wealth and reach. It is only between 2600 and 2500 BCE, a century or two after Gilgamesh's death, that texts appear that can be called literature in something like the modern sense— poems employing figurative language to portray imagined events.

So Gilgamesh lived in a propitious time and place, just when scribes began to experiment with writing imaginative works, stretching themselves beyond the everyday business of palace administration and trade. For the balance of the third millennium, their written literary output was modest in scale and scope; storytelling and poetry remained largely oral in nature. This situation began to change around 2100 BCE, when a few Sumerian kings began to take greater interest in literary production, partly as propaganda and partly for entertainment. As far as is known today, the world's first great patron of literature was King Shulgi of Ur, some thirty miles down the Euphrates from Uruk. Shulgi established a small empire during his forty-seven-year reign (2094–47 BCE). In time, he began to have ambitions to preserve his growing fame forever. He started adding the sign for divinity to his name, and he established two scribal schools, one in Ur and one in Nippur to the north. These schools became centers of poetic activity, and Shulgi's poets composed lovely lyrics on all sorts of themes, including a charming lullaby for one of Shulgi's sons:

> Sleep come, sleep come,
> sleep come to my son,
> sleep hasten to my son!

Put to sleep his open eyes,
settle your hand upon his sparkling eyes—
as for his murmuring tongue,
let the murmuring not spoil his sleep.

Shulgi is the first king known to have taken a close personal interest in writing. As he remarks in one text: "I, Shulgi the noble, have been blessed with a favorable destiny right from the womb. When I was small, I was at the academy, where I learned the scribal art from the tablets of Sumer and Akkad. None of the nobles could write on clay as I could." Shulgi commissioned dozens of poems praising his accomplishments and character, and these poems provide a fascinating portrait of an energetic and insatiably curious monarch, deeply in love with learning and, above all, with himself.

Shulgi was an accomplished linguist, fluent in no fewer than five languages: "When I provide justice in the legal cases of Sumer, I give answers in all five languages. In my palace no one in conversation switches to another language as quickly as I do." But then, Shulgi claimed to be good at every intellectual pursuit: he was adept in mathematics, could play the lute better than his court musicians, and even outdid his priests in divination: "As I prepare the sheep with words of prayer, my diviner watches in amazement like an idiot. The prepared sheep is placed at my disposal, and I never confuse a favorable sign with an unfavorable one." It would not be surprising if archaeologists one day uncover a hymn in which Shulgi praises himself as did the multi-talented Major General Stanley in *The Pirates of Penzance*. The major general boasts that among his many scientific and artistic skills, "I can write a washing bill in Babylonic cuneiform," a line reflecting popular interest in Hormuzd Rassam's ongoing excavations in Babylonia at the time Gilbert and Sullivan composed their operetta.

Shulgi's literary patronage cemented Gilgamesh's fame as well as his own, for Shulgi was obsessed with Gilgamesh. In several hymns, Shulgi declares that like Gilgamesh he was the child of the goddess Ninsun, and he often speaks of Gilgamesh as his brother. He compares his military prowess to that of Gilgamesh, using appropriate flood imagery: "Shulgi, roaring like a rising flood against the rebel lands, embraces Gilgamesh, his brother and friend, his comrade." In particular, he associates himself with Gilgamesh's underworld position as a judge, a role that Shulgi plays on earth: "Like my brother and friend Gilgamesh, I can recognize the virtuous and I can recognize the wicked. The virtuous gets justice in my presence, and the wicked and evil person will be carried off. . . . Who like me is able to interpret what is spoken in the heart or is articulated on the tongue?"

Shulgi commissioned the series of Sumerian poems that would later become the basis for the Old Babylonian Gilgamesh epic. There is no way to know to what extent Shulgi's poets were inventing the episodes in these poems, and how much they were building on earlier poems. Sumerian literary culture was generally conservative in its choice of themes, though, and Shulgi certainly claimed to be devoted to conserving old texts: "I am no fool," he declared, "as regards the knowledge acquired since the time that heaven above set mankind on its path: when I have discovered hymns from past days, old ones from ancient times, I have never declared them to be false, and have never contradicted their contents. I have conserved these antiquities, never abandoning them to

oblivion." He ordered the old poems added to his singers'
repertoire, "and thereby I have set the heart of the Land on
fire and aflame."

Most likely, then, Shulgi's poets revised and elaborated
upon older works that had been composed about Gilgamesh in
the previous centuries. In the text just quoted, Shulgi goes on
to describe his literary ambitions in terms that recall Gilgamesh's own obsession with mortality: "Whatever is acquired is destined to be lost. What mortal has ever reached the
heavens? At some time in the distant future, a man of Enlil
may arise, and if he is a just king, like myself, then let my
odes, prayers and learned songs about my heroic courage and
expeditions follow that king in his good palace. He should
take to heart the benefit that has been conferred on him; he
should exalt the power of my odes, absorb the exuberance of
my songs, and value highly my great wisdom."

Shulgi hoped that future kings would admire and preserve
his poems just as he treasured those of Gilgamesh. Indeed,
Shulgi even asserted that he and Gilgamesh had formed a
kind of literary alliance for just this purpose: "On the day
when the destiny of the Land was determined . . . Gilgamesh,
the lord of Kulaba, conversed with Shulgi, the good shepherd
of Sumer, at his shining feet. So that their praise would be
sung forever, so that it would be handed down to distant days,
so that it should be not forgotten in remote years, they looked
at each other favorably in their mighty heroism." Just as in
the standard version of Gilgamesh's epic, literature is a royal
road to immortality.

Shulgi hoped for another sort of immortality as well, an
eternal life after death of the sort achieved by his brother Gil-

gamesh. Deeply aware that "whatever is acquired is destined to be lost," Shulgi was perhaps among the first to sense literature's power to help people face the unthinkable and imagine the unimaginable. One of the poems he commissioned was a somber account of the hero's death and burial. Lying on his deathbed, Bilgamesh has a dream vision in which the chief god Enlil tells him that the time is coming when he must leave his earthly adventures behind:

> The darkest day of mortal man awaits you now,
> the solitary place of mortal man awaits you now,
> the flood-wave that cannot be breasted awaits you now,
> the battle that cannot be fled awaits you now,
> the unequal struggle awaits you now,
> the fight that shows no pity awaits you now!

Enlil urges Bilgamesh not to go down to the underworld with his heart knotted in anger; instead, he should unravel his clenched heart like palm fiber and peel it like an onion. For he will pass judgment and render verdicts in the netherworld, and there he will be reunited with his mother, his siblings, and "your precious friend, your little brother, your friend Enkidu, the young man your companion!" Feeling himself on equal terms with Enkidu, Shulgi must have taken heart at Enlil's words as well.

Over four thousand years old, "The Death of Bilgamesh" presents a fascinating mix of immediacy and distance when it is read today. The immediacy comes partly from the universality of its concerns, but also from the vivid language it uses to explore its theme. To protect his tomb from robbers, Bilgamesh has the course of the Euphrates temporarily diverted so that his tomb can be hidden in the riverbed. His workmen hasten to carry out his orders; once they have diverted the river from the desired stretch of riverbed, "its pebbles gazed on the Sun God in wonder./Then in the bed of the Euphrates the earth cracked dry."

A modern poet could be pleased to have thought of the charming personification of the surprised pebbles, nicely contrasted with the realistic cracking of the riverbed under the sun's unaccustomed heat. Yet only a few lines later, the poem details an archaic burial scene of horrific strangeness, for Bilgamesh has himself interred together with a host of his family and attendants. Some had perhaps predeceased him and were now being buried with him, while others may have been slain for the purpose or else would be buried alive:

> His beloved wife, his beloved child,
> his beloved senior wife and junior wife,
> his beloved minstrel, steward and . . . ,
> his beloved barber, [his beloved] . . . ,
> [his beloved] attendants and servants,
> [his] beloved goods . . . ,
> were laid down in their places,
> as if for a palace-review in the midst of Uruk.

Finally, Bilgamesh enters and lays himself down. His attendants then seal the tomb and release the barriers holding back the Euphrates: "its waters swept over,/his [resting place] the waters removed from view."

Today such a scene is most readily imaginable in the grim terms of a Jonestown massacre, but this was not at all the ancient poet's intention. The sense of cultural distance is only increased by the calm formality with which the Sumerian poet recounts Bilgamesh's funeral preparations. Nor was this

scene a pure literary fiction: mass interments have been uncovered at Shulgi's city, Ur, dating from the twenty-fourth
century BCE. It is not known whether such burials were actually performed in Uruk three centuries earlier, but in describing Bilgamesh's death, Shulgi's poet was imagining it in the
most splendid terms he could.

Even without the wholesale looting and destruction of sites
under way in Iraq today—bulldozers dig indiscriminately into
mounds, and large reliefs are hacked into pieces for easy removal and piecemeal sale—it would be unlikely that Gilgamesh's actual remains could ever be uncovered and
identified. A pity in a way, but whatever the true manner of
his burial, the great king of Uruk certainly wanted his body
to lie forever undisturbed, never to be seen by living eyes.

Yet the epic's ancient audiences did expect to see him
again. By far the greatest number of early references to Gilgamesh concern his god-given role as a judge in the underworld. Votive offerings have been found dating back as early
as 2600 BCE, with inscriptions invoking Gilgamesh's aid and
protection after death. No one today still credits the old
Mesopotamian accounts of the underworld, but not because
they have ever been disproved—how could they have been?
Other accounts have taken their place, inspired by later the-
ologies and changing views of the world. Where devotees of
Enlil and Ishtar once expected Gilgamesh to assign their
places in the underworld, Christians began envisioning Saint
Peter holding the keys to the Pearly Gates.

The Mesopotamian House of Dust is the earliest known
version of the underworld realm that later developed into the
Hebrew Sheol, the Greco-Roman Kingdom of Hades and
Persephone, and the infernos of Satan and Iblis. Unlike most
of their successors, the Mesopotamians believed that the

gloomy underworld is all we get. To them, the Greeks' sunny
Elysian fields, Islam's heavenly gardens, and the New Testament's bejeweled New Jerusalem would have looked like wish-
ful thinking, far less credible than their conception of the
dark realm deep within the earth.

For the Assyrians and Babylonians, Gilgamesh became a
vision of possibility: an earthly human being who had made
the best of the bad situation awaiting everyone in death. He
had found light and fellowship in the netherworld with his
beloved friend Enkidu, and he could share in the infernal
gods' feasts, far better fare than the clay and brackish water
given to the ordinary dead. Shulgi was surely not the only
devotee of Gilgamesh to hope that he might earn a place beside Enkidu in the company of his brother and friend. For
the epic's early audiences, Gilgamesh was both an ancient
hero and a person they fully expected to meet one day.

Having traced Gilgamesh back to the vanishing point of
history, it may be appropriate to take leave of him where his
ancient admirers were sure he would be found—in the House
of Dust. Poems such as "The Descent of Inanna to the Underworld," as well as Enkidu's feverish dream in *Gilgamesh*, paint
a compelling picture of the common final home of all humanity, awaiting everyone on earth.

This is how it would be to enter that realm. Having been
led—or dragged—down the Road of No Return by the clawed
hand of Humut-tabal, you pause, trying to catch the breath
you no longer have, as Humut-tabal opens the massive outer
door to the House of Dust. As he does so, you may see some
odd-looking animals passing by. They are not large, emaciated

dogs, as they first appear, but naked sheep: nothing grows in the underworld, so the sheep bear no wool. Shoved inside the doorway, you notice that the inside bolt is covered with dust. People come in through this door, but they never leave.

Though you are now inside what is called a house, it is really a complex of interlocking spaces, not unlike Sennacherib and Ashurbanipal's hundred-room palaces, though vastly larger. The harried scribe Belet-seri checks you off on her tablet, and then you make your way through a series of seven gates. At each gate, you are stripped of one of your garments; "In accordance with the ancient rules," the gate attendant brusquely tells you when you ask why. Deprived progressively of your breastplate, belt, robe, staff, tunic, armbands, and sandals, you finally arrive naked in a shadowy throne room. Receding into the distance along one end of this enormous room, lines of the dead are seated at long tables, eating. Most have to make do with lumps of clay, stale crusts of bread, and brackish water in place of beer. Some are better provided, since they are lucky enough to have children making proper offerings for them: a lesson that you sincerely hope your own children will not forget.

Enthroned at the far end of this room are Ereshkigal, queen of the Underworld, and her silent consort Nergal. Only Ereshkigal can release anyone from her eternal kingdom, but she spares no mortal man, woman, or child. When her own sister, Inanna, came down from heaven to visit her, Ereshkigal had her stripped naked just like everyone else and hung her rotting corpse from a meat hook on the wall, until the heavenly gods offered a ransom for her release. Perhaps Ereshkigal will be too consumed in her own sorrow to notice you. According to some sources, she lies eternally on the ground, raking her fingers through her hair as if through a bed of leeks, her alabaster breasts exposed because she has torn her royal robe in grief, mourning her dead son Ninazu.

Passing by Ereshkigal, you enter a farther chamber, and at last come into the lordly presence of Gilgamesh. You will want to remember everything you have heard or read about him: the more you know about your judge when your case comes up, the better. The atmosphere is lighter here in the judgment chamber; torches line the earthen walls, giving Gilgamesh's braided beard a ruddy glow. If you have been buried properly with good supplies, you will be able to offer him an appropriate gift (naked though you are, you still have your gifts with you): a richly ornamented dagger, perhaps, or a beautifully embossed shield. Ideally, you will have been making offerings to the semi-divine hero for some years now, and so Gilgamesh will recognize your name with approval. He may even smile. Ereshkigal's sobs may still be heard in the distance, but you suddenly realize that all will be well, or at least as well as can be. The gods cannot change your ultimate destiny, but in their severe mercy, they have appointed as judge the man most famous in history for his hatred of death, his longing for life, and his love of fellowship and beauty wherever they can be found. Like him, you may be granted a measure of life in the very palace of death itself.

EPILOGUE

SADDAM'S GILGAMESH

IN February 2003, as the United States pressured Saddam Hussein to step down and go into exile, Iraq's dictator gave a speech to his generals in which he considered doing just that. Seeking to put the idea in a positive light, he compared himself to Gilgamesh, in his decision to leave his country in search of immortality. "The king gave up the helm," Saddam remarked to his startled commanders, "and left his senate leading the country till his return." Saddam didn't ultimately follow through on this plan, but his comparison was hardly random, for he had a long-standing interest in Gilgamesh and his age. The previous spring, Saddam had announced plans to rebuild Ashurbanipal's library in Nineveh. He intended to fill the library with plaster casts of the tablets it had once held, and had reached an agreement in principle with the British Museum to have casts made of its twenty-five thousand tablets. The reconstructed library was to be the centerpiece of the Saddam Institute of Cuneiform Studies, which would be devoted to research in Iraq's cultural heritage.

Though Gilgamesh had been forgotten for two millennia, his story is read again in his homeland today and circulates beyond Iraq on a global basis, translated into Arabic, Chinese, French, German, Japanese, Persian, Russian, Spanish, and many other languages. It has become a staple text in American

world literature courses and is inspiring writers around the
world, from an avant-garde American theater collective called
"The Gilgamesh Group" to the Australian novelist Joan London, in whose 2001 novel *Gilgamesh* a single mother of the
1930s travels from rural Australia to Soviet Armenia in search
of her vanished lover. Today as in antiquity, Gilgamesh's story
underwrites explorations of issues of tyranny and justice, love
and death, and art and immortality.

One fascinating use of the ancient material can be found
in Philip Roth's *The Great American Novel* (1973). Centered
on a baseball team in the fictional Patriot League, the novel
features an ace pitcher named Gil Gamesh, of Babylonian
parentage. If Sin-leqe-unninni saw Gilgamesh as the inventor
of well digging, Philip Roth regards Gilgamesh as the ultimate ancestor of baseball, since the ancient poems show Gilgamesh and Enkidu playing a game involving a ball and a
mallet or bat. In Roth's novel, the modern Gil Gamesh becomes the star pitcher of the Patriot League's 1933 season. He
believes he can never lose: "Because I'm Gil Gamesh! I'm an
immortal!" Yet Gil is subject to uncontrollable rage when calls
go against him, and when an umpire named Mike the Mouth
calls a decisive pitch a ball instead of a strike, Gil tries to kill
him with his next pitch, and is banished from baseball. He turns
on America as a result, and immigrates to the Soviet Union to
train as a spy. He reappears late in the novel, sent back to the
United States by Stalin as a secret agent.

On his return, Gil claims that he missed baseball too m ʒh
to stay away. He then gives an eerily casual description of his
interrogation training in Soviet Russia:

> Summers off in the country, in slave labor
> camps, administering beatings and conducting

interrogations while the regular torturers are
on vacation—occasionally driving a prisoner
insane or tormenting an intractable suspect
into a confession, but by and large the usual
student stuff, cleaning up after suicides, seeing that the bread is stale and there's nothing
nourishing in the soup, and so on. And the
talk, General. The unending lectures. The study
groups. And then the murders, of course. Three
roommates murdered in their beds during my
senior year.

Gil becomes the manager of his old team and inspires his
players by inciting them to hate their opponents and America
itself. In his first speech to his bottom-ranked team, he sounds
oddly like Saddam Hussein inveighing against America: "You
are the scum of baseball and the slaves of your league. And
why? Because you finished last by fifty games? Hardly. *You
are scum because you do not hate your oppressors. You are
slaves and fools and jellyfish because you do not loathe your
enemies.*" In a second speech, on "How to hate, and Whom,"
he declares, "And you ask me, 'But what's there to hate about,
Gil?' *They robbed you of your home! They drove you out like
dogs!*" Gil brings about a congressional witch hunt against
accused Communists in the league, then slips quietly back to
Russia. He is later photographed next to Stalin and then
Brezhnev before finally being denounced as a double agent in
a purge and killed.

The Great American Novel is an uneven effort, but it
works brilliantly as satire of McCarthy-era witch-hunting. In
Roth's alternative history, the Soviets send Gil as a lone agent
specifically in order to stir up a witch hunt against dozens of

falsely accused Communists. This is Stalin's ploy to undermine America from within, by destroying the national pastime and inducing America to subvert its own democratic values while in the grip of paranoia and conspiracy theories. Roth's novel provides an interesting point of comparison to a recent Iraqi work, a novel by a less accomplished writer but a more experienced politician: Saddam Hussein himself. In the wake of his humiliation in the first Gulf War of 1992, Saddam evidently decided that, like Gilgamesh, he could best achieve immortality through literary means, and he embarked on an improbable second career as a writer of political romances. This career was thrown off in 2004 by the onset of the second Gulf War, which interrupted the large print run of his fourth effort, a sparkling fiction called *Be Gone Demons!* As the American-led coalition made its preparations for invasion, Saddam reportedly left most of the defense planning to his sons, spending much of his time working on his novel. After his capture, he started in on another, writing at a card table in prison.

It is Saddam's first novel that is relevant here, for it blended elements from *Gilgamesh* and *The Thousand and One Nights* into an allegory of the first Gulf War. Appearing anonymously in 2000 under the title *Zabibah wal-Malik* (Zabibah and the King), the story is set in ancient Assyria. It tells of an unnamed king's love for Zabibah, a young woman of the people, who comes to the palace and instructs him in the principles of just rule. As of 2006 it had yet to be translated into English, but it appeared in 2004 in a German translation, *Zabibah und der König*, subtitled *Eine Liebesgeschichte* (a love story). This version provides a fascinating case of literary circulation between the Middle East and Europe. A publisher's foreword quotes an anonymous CIA agent, part of a

team that spent three months studying the novel for clues to
Saddam's psyche: "Every time I've read the book, I sympa-
thized with the king. And that's clearly what Saddam wanted
to achieve, among other things, with his novel: for his people to sympathize with him. An elegantly written, intelligent
book, that holds you right to the last page." This quote also
appears as a blurb on the back cover. It is ironically appropriate that the verb I have translated as "holds you," *fesseln*
in German, literally means "to chain" or "handcuff."

The original edition shows a picture of a lush, dark-eyed
beauty on the cover. The cover is not original art, however,
nor is it even Middle Eastern in origin. Instead, it is a Cana-
dian artist's painting called *The Awakening,* representing a
symbolic "Goddess of Spring and Dawn," drawing on imagery
from Asia and the Americas as well as the Middle East. On
his Web site the artist Jonathon Earl Bowser describes his
horror and bemusement upon discovering that Saddam's publisher had stolen his copyrighted image. In an interesting re-
versal, the Iraqi edition of the novel uses a North American
image but the European edition now shows an authentic Iraqi
image: Saddam Hussein, head in hand, darkly contemplating
love and death.

Saddam had long been obsessed with Iraqi history and his
place in it: "Let us go back to our history," he told an inter-
viewer in 1980, "because it is continually before my eyes."
Saddam admired the medieval anti-Crusader Saladin (a Tikrit
native like himself), and he was particularly drawn to Iraq's
pre-Islamic history; he liked to compare himself variously to
Nebuchadnezzar, Sennacherib, or Gilgamesh. This emphasis
reflected his Baathist Party's search for a basis for pan-Arab
nationalism deeper than the ethnic and sectarian divisions
so prominent in Iraq and elsewhere in the Middle East. As

Saddam wrote in a 1978 essay, "On Writing History," he believes that "the history of the Arab nation extends to the ancient ages, and that all the major civilizations which were born in the Arab world are expressions of the characteristics of [its] inhabitants."

In keeping with this emphasis, *Zabibah and the King* opens with a prologue that outlines Iraq's glorious history as home to the Tower of Babel and the birthplace of Adam, Eve, Abraham, and Noah: "Is not Iraq with its mountains and its Najaf Range also the homeland of Noah, who built the Ark at God's command and thereby introduced mankind's second chapter?" This ancient history is still alive today: "In view of so great a past, can it be surprising that in Mesopotamia many marvels still occur today? Has not the spirit of the Arab Nation, provided with the Prophet's blessing, once again been reborn in this land? . . . Here the doors of heaven stand wide open for the righteous—but also the gates of hell. Iraq: it is Sumer, Akkad, Babylon, Assyria, Baghdad, Samarra. Iraq— it is the homeland of proud falcons and of noble beauty, the cradle of writing and of the art of storytelling."

The first chapter of Saddam's novel relates that a prominent citizen has a young wife of common origins, Zabibah. The haughty and unpopular Assyrian king falls in love with Zabibah at first sight when the couple visits him. The king hides his feelings, as "he couldn't let her sense that he felt himself so deeply bound to a mere woman of the people. He found himself his own prisoner." Witty repartee is exchanged about the deliciousness of raisins (the meaning of *zabibah* in Arabic), and the king invites her to come to his palace and tell him about conditions in the country. She proves to be exceedingly direct and frank, urging him to mend his ways as ruler and serve his people rather than tyrannizing them. He finds

Jacket cover of Saddam Hussein's *Zabibah wal-Malik* (Baghdad, 2000).

that she cares for him personally, and not for his power as most people do, and she alone will speak without flattering him or seeking to advance some private agenda.

The Assyrian king is like Gilgamesh, a brash ruler who is abusing his power and causing discontent among his subjects. In the novel as in the epic, the agent of the king's moral and political transformation is an intimate friend, the outsider who restrains him and helps him become a more just ruler. Zabibah comes to the palace much as the natural man

Jacket cover of Saddam Hussein's *Zabibah und der König* (Germany, 2004).

Enkidu does, becoming the king's conscience, muse, and romantic partner. The novel is surprisingly open in its portrayal of a paranoid, entrapped ruler. As Zabibah says, "Just look at your palace: thick walls, hardly any windows, darkness, stale air, twisted corridors. This is just the place for demons to feel at home and romp around to their hearts' content. And where demons are dwelling, there sprouts the seed of conspiracies."

The king's fortress has become his prison: "Just as the thick walls keep you from hearing what's going on outside, just as you can hardly get any daylight or fresh air, so too your cry for help will never be heard, if wicked conspirators fall upon you. Your escape route is blocked, and there's no one around who can help you." The king replies that he can't possibly leave his castle, as he learned in adolescence: "Back then, my brothers and the sons of my father's concubines conspired against me, and they turned my father the King against me, so that he didn't want to see me anymore and banned me—that's when I learned about life outside." There are autobiographical resonances in this. Born into deep poverty, Saddam was denied education and support by his harsh stepfather. After participating in an unsuccessful attempt to assassinate Iraq's military leader, he fled to Egypt and returned to Iraq several years later to become a professional assassin.

In the novel, listening to the bitter story of the king's troubled youth, "Zabibah tenderly stroked the King's hair and cheeks. More than that she wouldn't allow herself. Even so she did feel at times a wish to kiss him—above all because she saw how much he suffered from his bitter memories. But she forbade herself the fulfilling of her wishes, because she did not want to distract the King and wanted to hear the end of his father's story." Here, she is becoming Shahryar to the king's Scheherazade, restraining herself in order to hear more of her beloved's compelling stories.

Partly, this is pure propaganda, seemingly directed at the women of Iraq, showing a kinder, gentler tyrant whom they should love and support: Saddam the feminist. "It is always important to respect women's wishes," the king declares. "Are not women half of humanity? If one abandons this half, then life's boat loses its rudder. How can one leave women out of consideration, as they have so great an influence on society?" Yet the focus on Zabibah goes far beyond a merely propagandistic purpose. In many ways, the author seems to identify more with the sharp-eyed village woman than with the haughty, palace-bound king. It is Zabibah who most directly resembles Saddam, as the commoner who makes it from village to palace by her wits and the force of her personality, and she becomes the guide and mother of her country at the novel's end.

For some time, Zabibah and the king are just good friends. They have long philosophical and political discussions in the darkened palace at night, after which she calls for her horse and rides home to her husband. But then their relationship takes a decisive turn, in the raciest scene in the book. "Instead of trusting your relatives for protection," Zabibah says one night, "you should win over the People to you." Skeptical, the king asks, "Well, but who is 'the People'?" She replies:

> "They are the folk of your land, your Majesty. You should only have native-born soldiers serve in your army and not hired foreigners, as you have far too many these days."
>
> "True, that wouldn't be impossible," the King said reflectively.
>
> "Of course it's possible, you just have to want to do it. If the King serves the People, the People will be his best protection." Zabibah smiled and took his head in both hands. Tenderly she kissed the King's mouth.

"The most beautiful love for a king," she
said softly, "is the love of his people for him.
And I am one of the People."

That night the guards at the palace gate
waited in vain for Zabibah's departure. Finally
she appeared in the grey dawn, radiantly beautiful, and called for her horse so she could ride
home.

Zabibah finds herself increasingly uncomfortable living at
home with her husband, but she feels it is her duty to stay
with him and submit to his sexual demands. As she tells the
king on a later visit: "You have to believe me, it makes me unhappy; I feel like I'm being whipped. But what can I do? Just
imagine you were in my place." Astonished, the king replies:
"How can I do that? Am I a woman?" Her answer makes the
novel's allegory clear: "Is it then so different if a foreign intruder were to lay your land low, shaming and humbling you,
and you had to submit to everything, not having an army at
your disposal with which you could oppose the foreign power?
If you look around, isn't this the case with many kings? They
can't avenge the theft of their honor or their land. Women experience this all the more."

Then things get worse. As Zabibah rides home one night
through a forest, three men attack her; two bind her arms, and
the third rapes her. The rapist proves to be none other than
her jealous husband. As she reflects on her rape, Zabibah
links the personal and the political. She says to herself: "To
have to let oneself be overpowered is always the most horrible
thing, whether only one woman has to endure it or an entire
people. . . . The one thing . . . that eases my inner torment a

little, is that I defended myself until I lost consciousness. Will the shame of the rape last until death? Does the shame last forever for a people who have no helping hand to defend them? No, a people covers itself in shame only when it humiliates itself."

The "blue-eyed" evildoers attack the palace on January 17—the day the Desert Storm invasion was launched in 1992. Helping to defend the palace, Zabibah is struck in her breast with an arrow. She writes a farewell letter, which ends: "I die, but the People lives. I die, but my beloved Arab lives." The people decide to keep the day of her death as a national festival. At a public debate, held beneath her picture, an assembly forms and the people decide to abolish the monarchy, though all agree that a strong leader will always be needed. Meanwhile, the king is devastated by Zabibah's death and dies of a broken heart. The people take this event as a ratification of their decision, ending the assembly with a rousing cry: "Long live Zabibah! Long live the People!"

Zabibah and the King is not a great work of literature. One commentator has dubbed it a leading work in a new genre, "dic-lit"—writing by dictators—including the poems of Chairman Mao and the stories of Muammar al-Gadhafi. Even so, *Zabibah* is a fascinating index of the ongoing afterlife of a true masterpiece. It is only one of many reuses of *The Epic of Gilgamesh*, but if Saddam's novel builds on resemblances between Saddam's protagonist and King Gilgamesh, others have read the analogy differently. In January 2003, the Egyptian weekly newspaper *Al-Ahram* ran an opinion piece by Sharif Elmusa, a political scientist at the American University in Cairo, comparing Saddam not to Gilgamesh but to Humbaba, the Cedar Forest's guardian demon. In Elmusa's allegory, it is George W. Bush who could be compared to the tyrant

Gilgamesh while, like Humbaba, Saddam is attacked by foreigners who want to seize his country's natural resources.
"Timber in antiquity was the most coveted natural resource,"
Elmusa writes. "It was used for building temples and palaces
and houses, for making furniture, for the construction of boats
and for making fuel. Now it is oil that is the lifeline of modern
technological civilization. The U.S. is an addicted guzzler of
cheap oil and . . . oil is at the heart of the U.S. campaign."

As for the Cedar Forest's guardian, according to Elmusa,
"Humbaba might have been a tribal chief, as ruthless as Saddam. But we never hear the story from Humbaba himself or
his tribe—how they perceived themselves or the distant in-
vader who had come to chop down their forest." Aided by the
Iraqi opposition, as Gilgamesh was by Enkidu, Bush mounted
his attack, much as in the epic, where "the subjugation of
Humbaba required the use of raw power. . . . Gilgamesh did
not relent. Only after unforeseen tragedies and soul-searching
in the wilderness did he come to appreciate the cost of hubris
and accept the limits of human reach." In such readings, *The
Epic of Gilgamesh* finds new applications in the contemporary world, though it resonates differently for differently situated interpreters, who may have radically opposing views as
to who is the tyrant, who the aggressor, who the victim.

Beyond its metaphoric applications, *The Epic of Gilgamesh*
illustrates the interconnectedness of contemporary cultures
as it moves freely across boundaries that so often seem to separate "us" from "them," "the Arab World" from "the West,"
Philip Roth from Saddam Hussein. Writing in the early 1970s,
Philip Roth was thinking back to the McCarthy era, but he
clearly chose his theme out of concern that renewed versions
of anti-Communist paranoia were afoot in the years of the
Nixon administration and the bloody winding down of the

Vietnam War. Reading Saddam's novel next to Roth's, it is worth noting that when the young Saddam fled his native land for Egypt, he had extensive contacts with the CIA, which was seeking to stir up Iraqi opposition to Iraq's Soviet-leaning leader at the time, General Abdul Karim Qassem. Returning to Iraq after three years in Cairo, Saddam helped liquidate Iraqi Communists following Qassem's overthrow in 1963 in a CIA-supported coup. Sometimes Saddam personally tortured his prisoners before killing them. So he may bear a closer resemblance to Roth's Gil Gamesh than to the ancient Gilgamesh to whom he has compared himself.

Even as *Gilgamesh* has attained a global presence beyond its homeland, the fact that Saddam turned to writing novels illustrates how deeply Western culture in turn is infusing the Middle East. Poetry has traditionally been the favored literary form in Arab cultures, and novels were an imported genre until relatively recently. So Saddam chose a Western form for his literary debut, and even drew on some of the same models that have been important to Philip Roth. Roth's novel begins with a fifty-page prologue, narrated by a sportswriter called Smitty, who describes his love-hate relationship with Ernest Hemingway—a key father figure for an author writing *The Great American Novel*. In the prologue, Smitty and Hemingway have an argument in which Hemingway insists that there has never yet been a great American novel, and then berates Smitty for trying to imitate him. For years afterward, Smitty says, "Every once in a while I would get a Christmas card from Hem, sometimes from Africa, sometimes from Switzerland or Idaho, written in his cups obviously, saying more or less the same thing each time: use my style one more time . . . and I'll kill you. But of course in the end the guy Hem killed for using his style was himself."

Sending his threatening Christmas cards from Idaho, Hemingway may seem to be worlds apart from Saddam Hussein in Iraq, yet it turns out that Saddam's literary role model was none other than Ernest Hemingway as well. As reported in the London *Daily Telegraph* in December 2003, "Sa'ad Hadi, a journalist involved with the production of his novels, said Saddam's favorite novelist was Ernest Hemingway, in particular *The Old Man and the Sea*, whose style he tried to emulate: 'He'd sit in his state room and recount simple tales, while his aides recorded his words.'" A plot twist worthy of Philip Roth: that a classic American novelist would inspire an aspiring author-dictator.

The process of composition was enjoyable for Saddam, but it wasn't so pleasant for his aides:

> In the beginning, distinguished writers were asked to improve Saddam's stories. Mujiba al-Azizi, whose husband, Sami, contributed to his first novel, *Zabibah and the King*, recalled how he was summoned from his job one morning and told he had three days to produce a book from the president's notes.
>
> "Sami normally came home and kissed his children goodnight," recalled Ms. Azizi. "But that evening he just stood in the hallway sweating. He said 'our uncle' had given him a special task."
>
> Two months later, as 250,000 copies of *Zabibah and the King* were being anonymously distributed, Mr. Azizi came home, walked into the kitchen, drank a jug of water and fell down dead. His widow believes he was killed on the

president's orders to hush up his role in the
book.

In Philip Roth's novel, Ernest Hemingway keeps sending
cards to Smitty "saying more or less the same thing each time:
use my style one more time . . . and I'll kill you." If Sami al-
Azizi's widow is correct, life has imitated art all too well: Saddam killed the writer who imitated Hemingway's style on his
behalf.

In 1996, in the aftermath of the first Gulf War, the political scientist Samuel Huntington published an influential
book called *The Clash of Civilizations and the Remaking of
World Order*. In it, Huntington asserts that America cannot
simply export its values abroad because the world is made up
of a set of several distinct cultures, based on different reli-
gions and social systems. Huntington argues that "every civilization sees itself as the center of the world and writes its
history as the central drama of human history. This has been
perhaps even more true of the West than of other cultures.
Such monocivilizational viewpoints, however, have decreas-
ing relevance and usefulness in a multicivilizational world."
Further, he writes, "Spurred by modernization, global politics is being reconfigured along cultural lines. Peoples and
countries with similar cultures are coming together. Peoples
and countries with different cultures are coming apart. . . .
and the fault lines lie between civilizations."

These incisive comments deserved more attention than they
received; unfortunately, Huntington's book was often read not
for its chastening of American jingoism but for its grim portrayal of the conflict of cultures, an aspect of his thesis that

came into renewed prominence after 9/11. Huntington claims
that all of the world's major cultures are inherently hostile to
one another: "Civilizations are the ultimate human tribes, and
the clash of civilizations is tribal conflict on a global scale. . . .
Relations between groups from different civilizations however
will be almost never close, usually cool, and often hostile."
Huntington held out little hope for sympathetic understanding across cultural lines: "Emerging intercivilizational relations will normally vary from distant to violent, with most
falling somewhere in between." Or, as he most succinctly put
it: "It is human to hate."

Though Huntington casts *The Clash of Civilizations* in
global terms, his specific concern, even obsession, is with Islam versus the West. "Islam has bloody borders," he states, invoking history to support his vision of an endless cultural
clash: "Some Westerners . . . have argued that the West does
not have problems with Islam but only with violent Islamist
extremists. Fourteen hundred years of history demonstrate
otherwise. The relations between Islam and Christianity, both
Orthodox and Western, have often been stormy. Each has
been the other's Other."

Do all those centuries of history really tell only a single
story? And why should we go back fourteen hundred years
only to stop there? The historical record extends much further back, to the era when the patriarch Abraham is said to
have left Ur of the Chaldees—King Shulgi's city, thirty miles
downriver from Gilgamesh's Uruk—to journey westward and
found the monotheistic faith from which Christianity and Islam alike derive. Huntington portrays civilizations, as Hobbes
earlier saw nations, as essentially at odds; in his grim view,
civilizations are mutually suspicious at best and violently com-
petitive at worst, showing none of the ties that bind people

within a civilization into what he calls "an extended family."
Yet the Bible and the Qur'an agree in seeing Jews and Arabs
as Abraham's children, descended from his sons, the half
brothers Isaac and Ishmael. The Qur'an declares: "We believe
in Allah, and in what has been revealed to us and what was
revealed to Abraham, Ishmael, Isaac, Jacob and the Tribes. . . .
We make no distinction between one and another among them,
and to Allah do we bow our will."

The Epic of Gilgamesh powerfully illustrates the underlying unity of the extended family that the historian Richard
Bulliet calls "Islamo-Christian civilization." *Gilgamesh* and
The Iliad, the Bible and the Qur'an were not products of iso-
lated, eternally opposed civilizations; they are mutually related outgrowths of the rich cultural matrix of western Asia
and the eastern Mediterranean world. Isaac and Ishmael are
half brothers, and Uta-napishtim and Noah are closer still:
they are two versions of one and the same character.

Rather than speak of "Islamic culture" and "Western civilization" as sharply separate entities, it is historically more
accurate to speak—as Goethe had—of "West-eastern" culture.
This common matrix was more and more elaborated upon
over the centuries, and distinct cultures grew from this
shared civilizational base. But now, in an increasingly inter-
linked world, those cultures are meeting once again. Almost
five thousand years after his death, the restless king Gilgamesh finds his immortality confirmed by the varied uses of
his story. His distant image is refracted today by authors as
disparate—and as interconnected—as Philip Roth and Saddam Hussein, both children of Abraham, and both heirs of
their common literary father, the globe-trotting Papa Hemingway.

If he sits today at Gilgamesh's side in the House of Dust,

Hemingway's great predecessor Sin-leqe-unninni must be pleased to see how many people are carrying out his ancient instructions: to open the lid of the cedar chest and take out the tablet of lapis lazuli—or its digitized equivalent—and read the story of that heroic youth, borne along by emotion, who scoured the world looking for life, then returned home to his city, weary but at peace, to set down his labors on a tablet of stone.

NOTES

INTRODUCTION: WHEN HISTORIES COLLIDE

PAGE

2 *He is now at a loss* Austen Henry Layard, *Nineveh and Its Remains* (John Murray, 1849), 1: 6–7.

3 *Why did you afflict my son* The Epic of Gilgamesh: A New Translation, ed. and trans. Andrew George (New York: Penguin, 1999), 24.

4 *not of an age, but for all time* Ben Jonson, "To the Memory of My Beloved, the Author Mr William Shakespeare: And What He Hath Left Us," in *The Complete Poems*, ed. George Parfitt (Penguin, 1975), 264.

5 *For the present the orthodox people* "Noah's Log," *New York Times*, 22 December 1872, 1.

8 *the dark backward and abysm of time* William Shakespeare, *The Tempest* 1.2.50, ed. Northrop Frye (Penguin, 1970), 34.

1: THE BROKEN TABLETS

11 *A thousand types are gone* Alfred, Lord Tennyson, "In Memoriam A. H. H." (1850), verse 56, stanzas 1 and 4, in *The Longman Anthology of British Literature*, ed. David Damrosch et al. (Pearson Longman, 3rd ed., 2006), 2:1275.
Smith took the tablet E. A. Wallis Budge, *The Rise and Progress of Assyriology* (Martin Hopkinson, 1925), 152–53.

13 *Sir—I have read your letter* Thomas Hardy, *Jude the Obscure* (New American Library, 1980), 119–20.

15 *an act of pure folly* Budge, *The Rise and Progress of Assyriology*, 106.

18 *unless things alter* George Smith's letters to Mary Smith are preserved (in photocopies donated by a descendant) at the British Museum,

Department of Near Eastern Antiquities, in a file titled "Smith Personalia." Letters from this file will be identified by date; this letter is dated simply "Oct. 14," with no year given.

21 *the best polo player in India* Lesley Adkins, *Empires of the Plain: Henry Rawlinson and the Lost Languages of Babylon* (HarperCollins, 2003), 355.

22 *Even with ladders* Quoted in Budge, *The Rise and Progress of Assyriology*, 34.

24 *the vertical pressure* Ibid., 35.
   a wild Kurdish boy Ibid., 36.

29 *Exit Gištubar!* *Babylonian and Oriental Record* 4 (1888–90), 264.

30 *worked for some years* Budge, *The Rise and Progress of Assyriology*, 129.

31 *Thus, in the beginning of 1867* George Smith, *Assyrian Discoveries: An Account of Explorations and Discoveries on the Site of Nineveh, During 1873 and 1874* (New York: Scribner, Armstrong, 1875), 11.

32 *It is very bad art* Parliamentary Papers 1852–53, 31:9050f.; quoted in Frederick Nathaniel Bohrer, *A New Antiquity: The English Reception of Assyria* (UMI, 1998), 259.
   If I cannot raise the money Smith to Layard, 5 January 1872, British Library Add. Mss. (hereafter BL) 39,000, folio 123.
   Government will not assist Smith to Layard, 11 February 1872, BL 39,000, f. 196.

33 *This must be the only occasion* Andrew George, *The Epic of Gilgamesh: A New Translation* (Penguin, 1999), xxiii.
   breath left in my body *Times* (London), 4 December 1872, 7.

34 *the vulgar expedient* Ibid.

35 *the Great Game in the Middle East* Steven Holloway, "Biblical Assyria and Other Anxieties in the British Empire," *Journal of Religion and Society* 3 (2001), 1–21.
   I look on 'prestige' in politics Ibid., 20.

36 *Affairs in the East* *Times*, 4 December 1875, 4.

37 *which I think is useless* Smith to Layard, 11 February 1872, BL 39,000, f. 196.

38 *His name has become a household word* *Times*, 13 September 1876, 10.

39 *Difficulty of work* Smith, *Assyrian Discoveries*, xiv.
   Service was then going on Ibid., 19–20.

40 *Here and there were Eastern refreshment houses* Ibid., 23.
   we took on board a number of Asiatics Ibid., 23–24.
   people of both sexes bathe Ibid., 96.

41 *I was able to retire to my couch* Ibid., 129–31.
   Yakub, the proprietor Ibid., 26–28.
42 *thousands of years in the East* Ibid., 37.
   a tough fowl Ibid., 27.
   Some of the scenery Ibid., 51–52.
43 *The river was now rapidly rising* Ibid., 52.
44 *I started before sunrise* Ibid., 45.
45 *a miserable-looking town* Ibid., 52.
46 *It is hardly possible to conceive* "Journalism and Archaeology," *New York Times*, 14 May 1873, 6.
   On the 14th of May Smith, *Assyrian Discoveries*, 97.
47 *the great Mr. Smith* A. H. Sayce, "George Smith," *Nature* (1876), 125.
   half of a curious tablet Smith, *Assyrian Discoveries*, 97.
48 *from some error unknown to me* Ibid., 100.
49 *The hand of the wandering Arab* Ibid., 109.
   I used to see this work Ibid., 62.
   the Turkish officials Ibid., 427.
50 *The Turkish officers laughed* Ibid., 115–17.

2: EARLY FAME AND SUDDEN DEATH

51 *"The Daily Telegraph" Assyrian Expedition* *Daily Telegraph*, 21 May 1873, 7.
52 *I have all sorts of treasures* British Museum, "Smith Personalia," George Smith to Mary Smith, 30 March 1874.
   I do not come by Paris Ibid., 10 May 1874.
   I remembered your taste Ibid., 6 May 1874.
53 *I have wished you were with me* Ibid., 11 January 1874.
   I have kept no end of pets Ibid., 3 March 1874.
55 *in a raw English February* Ibid., 8 February 1874.
   Except that I have not you with me Ibid., 1 February1874.
   No salary had been paid him E. A. Wallis Budge, *The Rise and Progress of Assyriology* (Martin Hopkinson, 1925), 115.
56 *Rassam had been disappointed* Rassam discusses Arnold's overture in *Asshur and the Land of Nimrod*, 53.
   The Pacha is determined British Museum, "Smith Personalia," George Smith to Mary Smith, 3 March 1874.
57 *The incaution of Joseph* Ibid., 17 March 1874.
58 *I was told that Rajid Pacha* George Smith, *Assyrian Discoveries* (Scribner, Armstrong, 1875), 136–38.
   At this reasoning the Turks laughed Ibid., 138.

58 *I have had a hard fight here* British Museum, "Smith Personalia," George Smith to Mary Smith, 1 February 1874.

59 *I have not the smallest doubt* Smith, *Assyrian Discoveries*, vii–viii.

60 *a national poem* George Smith, *The Chaldean Account of the Deluge, from Terra Cotta Tablets Found at Nineveh* (Sampson Low, 1874), 204.

It appears that Izdubar George Smith, *The Chaldean Account of Genesis: Containing the Description of the Creation, the Fall of Man, the Deluge, the Tower of Babel, the Times of the Patriarchs, and Nimrod; Babylonian Fables, and Legends of the Gods; from the Cuneiform Inscriptions* (London: Sampson Low, 1875; New York: Scribner, 1876), 185, 216.

61 *I have had considerable difficulty* Ibid., 207.

62 *Humbaba . . . he did not come* Ibid., 215–16.

63 *I sat down and wept* Smith, *Assyrian Discoveries*, 190.

I have changed my own opinions Ibid., 301.

64 *that unity without which* Ibid., 294.

The truth is that no two men Budge, *The Rise and Progress of Assyriology*, 117.

65 *not a favorite with the Ottoman authorities* *Times* (London), 5 September 1876, 4.

Firman . . . ask aid Smith field notebooks, British Library Add. Mss. 30,425, 4–5.

66 *Weary and disappointed* Budge, *The Rise and Progress of Assyriology*, 118.

Smith never understood Ibid., 115.

67 *This region is so shut in* Smith, *Assyrian Discoveries*, 112.

The road here Ibid., 109.

The weather is so hot British Museum, "Smith Personalia," George Smith to Mary Smith, 16 July 1876.

68 *dysentery is a dangerous illness* I owe this information to Dr. Robert V. Tauxe, an old friend who is now an epidemiologist at the Centers for Disease Control in Atlanta, to whom I described Smith's symptoms.

Cross river mules Smith field notebooks, BL 30,425, entry from April 1876.

69 *The plague is sweeping* British Museum, "Smith Personalia," George Smith to Mary Smith, 20 March 1876.

70 *our little pet's stone* Ibid., 16 December 1875.

71 *a small tin etna* John Parsons, *Travels in Persia and Turkey in Asia*, BL 39,300, p. 345.

72 *Mr. M was not an Englishman* Ibid., 348.

   I consider he was sacrificed Ibid., 350.

   the cook at the consulate Ibid., 343.

73 *I do not enjoy my stay here* British Museum, "Smith Personalia," George Smith to Mary Smith, 5 March 1876.

   This the Trustees consider British Museum, "Smith Personalia," S. McAllister Jones to Smith, 10 April 1876.

74 *Do not say anything* British Museum, "Smith Personalia," George Smith to Mary Smith, 14 June 1876.

75 *Smith . . . died on August 19* Budge, *The Rise and Progress of Assyriology*, 119.

   Scholars can be reared A. H. Sayce, "George Smith," *Nature* 14 (1876), 421-22.

76 *In passing the end of Crogsland-road* *Times*, 11 September 1876.

77 *The Queen, sympathizing with you* British Museum, "Smith Personalia," letter from Benjamin Disraeli to Mary Clifton Smith, 20 October 1876.

78 *Night 9-10 from Biradjik* BL 30,425, 28-29.

3: THE LOST LIBRARY

83 *My difficulty was how to do this* Rassam, *Asshur and the Land of Nimrod* (Eaton and Mains, 1897), 23-24.

84 *our most tried and faithful Arabs* Ibid., 25.

   The delight of the workmen Ibid., 26.

86 *an incomplete picture* An exception is the discussion of Rassam by Mogens Trolle Larsen in *The Conquest of Assyria: Excavations in an Antique Land 1840-1860* (Routledge, 1994), the best scholarly account of the early years of Mesopotamian archaeology.

89 *at least seventy years of age* Rassam, *Asshur*, 261.

   a strong hand to rule him Matilda Rassam to Layard, 21 August 1848; British Library, Add. Mss. 38,978, folio 158.

   I think I see a possibility Layard to Henry Ross, 25 August 1847, BL 38,941, f. 11.

   as obstinate as usual Layard to Ross, 31 December 1874, BL 38,941, f. 23.

   I only wish he would apply his mind Layard to Ross, 6 February 1848, BL 38,941, f. 24.

90 *He no longer listens to me* Layard to Ross, 27 March 1848, BL 38,941, f. 26.

90 *About a month ago* Rassam to Layard, 25 February 1849, BL 38,978, f. 269ff.

94 *all she can to instruct me* Rassam to Layard, 17 December 1848; BL 38,978, f. 223.

We were nearly dying from laughter Rassam to Layard, 25 February 1849, BL 38,978, f. 269ff.

95 *There is a report* Rassam to Layard, 25 May 1849; BL 38,978, f. 350.

No doubt you will think me Ibid.

97 *the kind demeanor* Rassam, *Asshur*, 4.

her jealous & vindictive temper Layard to Ross, 2 September 1850, BL 38,979, f. 289.

As for my oldest brother Rassam to Layard, 26 December 1971; BL 39,000 f. 82.

98 *I was very much pleased* Rassam to Layard, 18 November 1851; BL 38,980, f. 166.

100 *a Moslem butcher of the town* Rassam, *Asshur*, 4.

I was sometimes told Ibid., 44–45.

101 *small, but extremely luscious* Ibid., 68.

a supply of Baghdad cakes Ibid., 323.

buffaloes in the place Ibid., 154–55.

horrid irritators Ibid., 418.

102 *The great discomfort* Ibid., 133.

They are generally ankle-deep Ibid., 2–3.

All of a sudden I felt Ibid., 39.

103 *seized with inexpressible frenzy* Ibid., 15.

104 *a European Doctor had insulted us* Rassam to Layard, 20 December 1852; BL 38,981, f. 187.

105 *it is a known fact* Rassam, *Asshur*, 12.

The Mohammedans of this country Rassam to Layard, 24 December 1860; BL 38,987, f. 15.

106 *the most extraordinary assemblage of animals* William Kennett Loftus, *Travels and Researches in Chaldea and Susiana* (Nisbet, 1857), 359; quoted in Larsen, *The Conquest of Assyria*, 282.

The chief of Durnak George Smith, *Assyrian Discoveries* (Scribner, Armstrong, 1875), 155.

107 *the Moslems more easy to pacify* Rassam, *Asshur*, 123.

the system is rotten to the core Ibid., 192.

In describing fully my travels Ibid., ix.

108 *With all the minor annoyances* Ibid., 424.

109 *spending Sunday quietly at Mossul* Ibid., 208–9. Rassam's spelling of
the name of his hometown was not an error; in the nineteenth century
there was no standard system for transcribing Arabic into English, and
the town's name could be rendered as Mosul, Môsul, Mossul, or Mosoul.
those who were adverse to digging Ibid., 219.

110 *Rawlinson had no power* Ibid., 27.

111 *The suffering of one lioness* Ibid., 30.

112 *In the center of the same saloon* Ibid., 31.
At that time I was quite skeptical Ibid., 32–33.

113 *It must be not a little gratifying* Ibid., 40.

114 *no amount of energy* Ibid., 41.
one of the honestest Layard to Sir William Gregory, 8 December
1888, BL 38,950, f. 162; quoted in Gordon Waterfield, *Layard of Nineveh* (John Murray, 1963), 478.

4: THE FORTRESS AND THE MUSEUM

116 *His highness does every thing I recommend* Rassam to Layard, 24
December 1860, British Library, Add. Mss. 38,987, folio 15.
We are grieved at the prospect Quoted by Rassam in a letter to La-
yard, 5 September 1892, BL 39,099, f. 87.

117 *His Savage Majesty* Quoted in Rassam, *Narrative of the British Mis-
sion to Theodore, King of Abyssinia* (John Murray, 2 vols., 1869),
1:301–2.
I was doubled up Quoted in Henry Morton Stanley, *Coomassie and
Magdala: The Story of Two British Campaigns in Africa* (Harper &
Brothers, 1874), 281.

120 *A mere suspicion* Rassam, *Narrative*, 2:79.
The expression of his dark eyes Henry Blanc, *A Narrative of Captiv-
ity in Abyssinia: With Some Account of the Late Emperor Theodore,
His Country and People* (Smith, Elder, & Co., 1868, repr. Frank Cass
& Co., 1970), 10.

121 *For God's sake, don't think of coming* Rassam, *Narrative*, 1:76.

122 *an Asiatic* Many of these speeches are quoted in Percy Arnold, *Prelude to Magdala: Emperor Theodore of Ethiopia and British Diplomacy* (Bellew, 1992), especially on 175–76 and 221–23.
Rassam's "grovelling" approach G. A. Henty, *The March to Magdala*
(Tinsley Brothers, 1868), 182–83.

123 *like a Christian and a gentleman* Henry Stern, *The Captive Missionary: Being an Account of the Country and People of Abyssinia,*

Embracing a Narrative of King Theodore's Life, and his Treatment of Political and Religious Missions (Cassell, Petter, and Galpin, 1869), 360.

123 *Humble were his salaams* H. M. Stanley, *Coomassie and Magdala*, 431.

very able indeed Alan Moorehead, *The Blue Nile* (Harper Perennial, 1962), 237, 280.

124 *at the whim of the royal gamester* Rassam, *Narrative*, 2:41.

Never mind your Government Ibid., 2:154.

125 *to withdraw as much as possible* Clements R. Markham, *A History of the Abyssinian Expedition* (Macmillan, 1869), 78.

the English masters Rassam, *Narrative*, 2:157.

Oh! My beloved, send to me Ibid., 2:240.

I was called a madman Ibid., 2:156.

126 *forty thousand men* Statistics from Stanley, *Coomassie and Magdala*, 507–10.

wearing the ship round Henty, *The March to Magdala*, 356.

127 *the wires were often snapped by baboons* Ibid., 296. "I am assured that this is an absolute fact," Henty adds, which suggests he had his doubts about this report.

An ascent of 1,500 feet Stanley, *Coomassie and Magdala*, 367.

128 *I have seen some rum drunk* Henty, *The March to Magdala*, 283.

The literal truth was never told Stanley, *Coomassie and Magdala*, 357–58.

129 *a major British blunder* Appropriately, Napier's invasion serves as the backdrop for *Flashman on the March* (2005), the twelfth "Flashman" novel by the Scottish writer George MacDonald Fraser, who builds his books around Victorian military disasters. A coward, braggart, and poltroon, Flashman always seeks to avoid danger, only to find himself thrust into a leading role in some imperial fiasco. Flashman invariably emerges unscathed, with an entirely undeserved reputation for heroism. Hormuzd Rassam appears as a minor character in *Flashman on the March*, portrayed as over his head but struggling to do his best, while Flashman must engage King Theodore in desperate duels of wits. In actual fact, some of Flashman's best lines are taken from Rassam.

The whole of the baggage was therefore open Henty, *The March to Magdala*, 375.

Onward, still onward they came Stanley, *Coomassie and Magdala*, 415, 421.

130 *With my glass I could distinguish* Henty, *The March to Magdala*, 379–81.

131 *Some had died instantaneously* Ibid., 382–83.

132 *an engraved plaque* Quoted in Stanley, *Coomassie and Magdala*, 449.
God has given you the power Quoted in Captain Henry M. Hozier, *The British Expedition to Abyssinia: Compiled from Authentic Documents* (Macmillan, 1869), 206–7; also quoted, with typos, in Rassam, *Narrative*, 2:320–21.

133 *On my replying in the affirmative* Rassam, *Narrative*, 2:250.

134 *Proud of having been judged worthy* Ibid., 2:350.
The Saviour was indeed with me Henry Stern, *The Captive Missionary*, 87.

135 *fast fading away* Rassam, *Narrative*, 2:349.

137 *Rassam regretted that he never had time* Rassam expresses this regret in *Asshur and the Land of Nimrod* (Eaton and Mains, 1897), 363.
a Jackal of the Desert Akbal al Ozalik (?)—the signature is unclear—to Henry Layard, 23 June 1880, BL 39,036, f. 108.

140 *we got all the rubbish* Rassam included the full text of Budge's apology in a letter to Layard, 9 December 1891, BL 38,098, f. 130.

141 *unduly sensitive* Thompson to Layard, 26 November 1891, British Museum Central Archive, "Rassam v. Budge, 1893," f. 20.
Budge has certainly been most indiscreet Thompson to Layard, 1 December 1891, ibid., f. 24.
no more of these storms Quoted in a summary by Rassam of his complaints, BL 39,099, f. 97.
the passage referred to Maunde Thompson, letter to the *Times* (London) 29 July 1892; ibid., f. 43.
The first time that I began to suspect From Rassam's summary of his complaints, BL 39,099, ff. 91–92.

142 *without even charging for traveling expenses* Ibid., f. 91.

143 *I cannot place the least confidence* Christian Rassam to Layard, 21 May 1851, BL 38,980, f. 56.
If I followed my own inclinations Matilda Rassam to Layard, 24 November 1851, ibid., f. 169.

144 *a sort of antiquarian festival* British Museum, "Rassam v. Budge, 1893," f. 5.
atmosphere of monastic tranquility *Times* editorial, 4 July 1893, British Museum "Rassam v. Budge, 1893," f. 4.
Gentlemen of the Jury Ibid., ff. 28–32.

145 *an apology which one gentleman ought to write* I disagree here with Mogens Trolle Larsen, who has argued that Rassam "was undoubtedly a clever and competent man and fully lived up to the requirements of

the time for a good excavator, but he was no gentleman and there was no way he could become one. They knew it, he knew it, and he decided to define his own set of rules" (*The Conquest of Assyria*, 330). On the contrary, Rassam fully understood himself as living by the norms expected of Victorian gentlemen, and he was demanding to be recognized as such.

145 *a very unfavourable impression* Eduard Sachau to Maunde Thompson, 26 March 1893, "Rassam v. Budge, 1893," f. 54.

There is something in Rassam's conduct Seton Lloyd, *Foundations in the Dust: A Story of Mesopotamian Exploration* (Oxford University Press, 1947), 151.

148 *the pioneer of Assyrian explorers* Rassam, *Asshur and the Land of Nimrod*, iii.

the most quaint resemblance Rassam, *Babylonian Cities: Being a Paper Read Before the Victorian Institute, or Philosophical Society of Great Britain* (E. Stanford, 1883), 18.

149 *newspaper articles about the trial* E. A. Wallis Budge, *By Nile and Tigris* (John Murray, 1920), 2:300–18.

great 'find' of tablets in 1854 Ibid., 1:23.

150 *must have unearthed them elsewhere* Budge, *The Rise and Progress of Assyriology*, 131–32.

5: AFTER ASHURBANIPAL, THE DELUGE

154 *As to what my lord the king wrote* Simo Parpola, ed., *Letters from Assyrian and Babylonian Scholars*, State Archives of Assyria 10 (University of Helsinki Press, 1993), letter no. 33, 24–25.

155 *a distant country* From the "Rassam Cylinder," in D. D. Luckenbill, *Ancient Records of Assyria and Babylonia* (University of Chicago, 1926–27, repr. 1989), 2:297.

156 *The first organized collections of texts* The classic account of the Sumerian invention of writing and of libraries is Samuel Noah Kramer, *History Begins at Sumer* (Doubleday, 1956).

the Horse Department Klaas R. Veenhof, *Cuneiform Archives and Libraries* (Brill, 1986); especially useful are Veenhof's introductory essay and Simo Parpola's contribution, "The Royal Archives of Nineveh," 223–36.

158 *He who saw the Deeps* This and the two dozen other surviving colophons to *Gilgamesh* tablets are given in A. R. George, *The Babylonian Gilgamesh Epic* (Oxford University Press, 2003), 1:736–41.

158 *Idri-aha'u came and brought the shoes* Mikko Luukko and Greta Van Buylaere, *The Political Correspondence of Esarhaddon*, SAA 16 (Helsinki, 2002), no. 140, 124.

There is much wine for the king Ibid., no. 117, 102.

As for the royal image Steven W. Cole and Peter Machinist, *Letters from Priests to the Kings Esarhaddon and Assurbanipal*, SAA 13 (Helsinki, 1998), no. 34, 36–37.

159 *Yesterday, when I was coming* Luukko and Van Buylaere, *The Political Correspondence of Esarhaddon*, no. 25, 20.

If I see you at the palace Ibid., no. 88, 82.

May the king['s . . . heart] soften Parpola, *Letters from Assyrian and Babylonian Scholars*, no. 294, 234.

160 *purple robes* Ibid., no. 182, 146

Qurdi, the chariot driver Luukko and Van Buylaere, *The Political Correspondence of Esarhaddon*, no. 63, 60.

161 *Sargon II had come to power* This is the likeliest scenario, though the details about Sargon's accession are murky; see A. K. Grayson, "Assyria: Tiglath-Pileser III to Sargon II," in *The Cambridge Ancient History*, ed. John Boardman et al. (Cambridge University Press, 1991), III.2: 71–102, 87. The obscurity of the records supports the idea that Sargon achieved power by suspect means, because the Assyrian annals regularly proclaim the orderly carrying out of the gods' will.

162 *They tossed me a seat* Parpola, *Letters from Assyrian and Babylonian Scholars*, no. 179, 142–44. Simo Parpola believes that "chief tailor" (*ka-sir*) is a slip for "cohort commander" (*ki-sir*), since the chief tailor was a high official who would not have been performing mundane chores for Kudurru like bringing him oil. The letter always uses the term *ka-sir*, however, and I see no reason to alter it; presumably the conspirators were conferring away from the prying ears of as many people as possible, including their own servants. The fact that the chief tailor brought Kudurru oil is one indication of this wish for secrecy: Kudurru performed his divination by studying the pattern of oil in water, the most convenient method to use indoors and in private.

163 *a common Assyrian strategy* This identification of Kudurru's background is made by Martti Nissinen, *References to Prophecy in Neo-Assyrian Sources*, SAA 7 (Helsinki, 1998), 137.

Hear me, O my lord king Luukko and Van Buylaere, *The Political Correspondence of Esarhaddon*, no. 59, 52.

164 *Shamash, great lord* Ivan Starr, *Queries to the Sungod: Divination and Politics in Sargonid Assyria*, SAA 4 (Helsinki, 1990), no. 139,

148–50, with some broken phrases restored from a parallel text, no. 142, 152.

165 *Sasî was there as a fink* Nissinen, *References to Prophecy*, 146.

While he is in the entourage Starr, *Queries to the Sungod*, no. 154, 165, with several phrases restored from parallel texts, nos. 155–66, 166–78.

Ashur and the great gods Parpola, *Letters from Assyrian and Babylonian Scholars*, no. 316, 256.

166 *forty-five of these specialists* Ibid., xiv.

167 *The door monitor said* Quoted in Andrew George, *The Epic of Gilgamesh* (Penguin, 1999), xviii.

Your heart is denser than an obelisk Papyrus Lansing, in Miriam Lichtheim, *Ancient Egyptian Literature* (University of California Press, 3 vols., 1973–80), 2:168–69.

168 *an immense page of divine scripture* Jean Bottéro et al., *Everyday Life in Ancient Mesopotamia*, trans. Antonia Nevill (Edinburgh University Press, 2001), 188–89.

Lofty judge, creator of the above Hymn to Shamash, in Benjamin R. Foster, *Before the Muses: An Anthology of Akkadian Literature* (CDL Press, 3rd ed., 2005), 827.

169 *Shamash, great lord* Starr, *Queries to the Sungod*, no. 84, 101, with some phrases restored from parallel texts, nos. 85–87, 100–102.169

He who wrote Ibid., xxxi.

170 *to set straight the divination* Tremper Longman III, *Fictional Akkadian Autobiography: A Generic and Comparative Study* (Eisenbrauns, 1991), 232.

171 *The Series itself* Parpola, *Letters from Assyrian and Babylonian Scholars*, no. 90, 68.

172 *The chief occupation of the Assyrian king* A. K. Grayson, "Assyrian Civilization," in Boardman, *The Cambridge Ancient History* III.2, 194–218, 217.

173 *I am powerful, I am all powerful* Luckenbill, *Ancient Records of Assyria and Babylonia*, 226.

the disease may have been lupus Grant Frame, *Babylonia 689–627 B.C.: A Political History* (Nederlands Historisch-Archaeologisch Instituut te Istanbul, 1992), 92.

174 *Have I been purified* Parpola, *Letters from Assyrian and Babylonian Scholars*, no. 29, 22.

Why is the king like this? Ibid., no. 265, 208.

Is one day not enough Ibid., no. 43, 33.

174 *king of the lands, fear [not]* Simo Parpola, *Assyrian Prophecies,* SAA 9 (Helsinki, 1997), no. 1.1, 4.

175 *Like a winged bird* Ibid., no. 2.3, 15.

What words have I spoken to you Ibid., no. 1.1, 4, and no. 3.6, 26.

I will keep you safe Ibid., no. 2.3, 15–16.

lightning struck Parpola, *Letters from Assyrian and Babylonian Scholars,* no. 42, 32.

Purification of the Field Ibid., no. 69, 51–52.

176 *Was there no earthquake* Ibid., no. 56, 41.

Esarhaddon's . . . inner circle Simo Parpola puts the number of Esarhaddon's inner circle at seventeen men, who were his principal governors and religious advisers and the heads of the government's major departments (*Letters from Assyrian and Babylonian Scholars,* xxv). Parpola notes that these men constituted almost all of the regular letter writers to the king; even deputy heads of departments rarely wrote the king directly. Of course, Esarhaddon probably also had close advisers who were always at his side and never wrote letters to him.

177 *You were young, O Ashurbanipal* Text in Foster, *Before the Muses,* 829–30.

Concerning the crown prince Parpola, *Letters from Assyrian and Babylonian Scholars,* no. 52, 39.

The planet Mars is bright Ibid., no. 48, 36.

178 *When I see a letter* Luukko and Van Buylaere, *The Political Correspondence of Esarhaddon,* no. 6, 8.

Whoever you are, O scribe Ibid., no. 32, 31.

179 *he berated Balasi* Parpola, *Letters from Assyrian and Babylonian Scholars,* no. 39, 30.

You must certainly have observed Ibid., no. 45, 34–35.

[Why] have you never told me Ibid., no. 8, 8–9.

180 *Now [portents] have occurred* Ibid., no. 109, 87.

Sin-eresh has struck down the lion Ibid., no. 120, 100.

181 *during the reign of his father* Stephen J. Lieberman, "Canonical and Official Cuneiform Texts: Towards an Understanding of Assurbanipal's Personal Tablet Collection," in *Lingering Over Words: Studies in Ancient Near Eastern Literature in Honor of William L. Moran,* ed. Tzvi Abusch et al. (Scholars Press, 1990), 305–36, 328. An alternative theory concerning Ashurbanipal's literacy is that, as a younger son, he may have originally been destined for the priesthood and learned to read and write during that time. Even if this were true, it

remains the case that as crown prince Ashurbanipal used his literacy in his father's mode, commissioning oracles of the sort that his father particularly favored. Whether Ashurbanipal learned his skills as a priest in training or from his own initiative, I believe that this skill was likely a factor in his father's choice of him over his other brothers once the firstborn son had died.

181   *Marduk, master of the gods*   Luckenbill, *Ancient Records of Assyria and Babylonia*, 379.

182   *saw what was secret*   *The Epic of Gilgamesh*, trans. Andrew George, 1.
     Facing the sun they dug a well   Ibid., 31.

183   *You say, 'Well of Gilgamesh!'*   A. R. George, *The Babylonian Gilgamesh Epic*, 1:95.
     I filled the plain   Luckenbill, *Ancient Records of Assyria and Babylonia*, 152.
     the shit bucket of a farter   Alasdair Livingstone, *Court Poetry and Literary Miscellanea*, SAA 3 (Helsinki: 1989), no. 29, 64, no. 30, 66.

184   *The talk was better than this*   Parpola, *Letters from Assyrian and Babylonian Scholars*, no. 30, 23.
     Keni will die of envy   Ibid., no. 235, 188.

185   *In my childhood*   Ibid., no. 12, 30–32.
     Your ill-wishers, Ashurbanipal   Ibid., no. 13, 33–35. In *Before the Muses*, 829–30, Benjamin Foster gives a prose translation of this poem; unfortunately he doesn't include the first poem to which this one replies.

186   *I am Ashurbanipal*   Livingstone, *Court Poetry*, no. 2, 6–10.
     None of these poems is a literary masterpiece   Even so, Foster is a little too severe in dismissing Ashurbanipal's style outright as "turgid," "verbose," and "ponderous" (*Before the Muses*, 815, 821).
     I am feeling very sad   Parpola, *Letters from Assyrian and Babylonian Scholars*, no. 187, 154.

187   *What has not been done in heaven*   Ibid., no. 185, 152–53.

188   *I took pity on him*   Luckenbill, *Ancient Records of Assyria and Babylonia*, 319, with some phrasing adopted from the parallel text of Prism A in Rykle Borger, *Beiträge zum Inschriftenwerk Assurbanipals* (Harrassowitz, 1996), 249.

189   *the storm god Adad favored his dry country*   Ibid., 345, 363.
     In these days Shamash-shumu-ukin   Ibid., 301.
     the people were so famished   Ibid., 303.
     By the colossi   Ibid., 304.

190   *I made him more dead*   Ibid., 310–12, with some phrasing adopted from Borger, *Beiträge zum Inschriftenwerk Assurbanipals*, 241.

190 *We shall not neglect the king's command* Quoted by George, *The Epic of Gilgamesh*, xxiii.

191 *Several of his predecessors* Extensive passages survive from an epic concerning Tukulti-Ninurta, an important thirteenth-century Assyrian king (translated in Foster, *Before the Muses*, 298–317). Peter Machinist has argued that Tukulti-Ninurta intended his poem to demonstrate that Assyria was Babylonia's cultural as well as military equal ("Literature as Politics: The Tukulti-Ninurta Epic and the Bible," *Catholic Bible Quarterly* 38 [1976], 455–82). Ashurbanipal's epic would likely have been meant to convey a similar message.

192 *a pile of skeletons* Gwendolyn Leick, *Mesopotamia: The Invention of the City* (Penguin, 2002), 241–42.

the invaders were able to flood Oates, "The Fall of Assyria," 180.

193 *From the month of Simanu* Luckenbill, *Ancient Records of Assyria and Babylonia*, 419–20.

He who loves Nabu and Marduk Ibid., p. 421.

196 *tears rolled down his mother's cheeks* Ibid., no. 23, 53.

6: AT THE LIMITS OF CULTURE

199 *Surpassing all other kings* Andrew George, trans., *The Epic of Gilgamesh: A New Translation* (Penguin, 1999), 2.

a violent flood-wave Ibid., 3.

200 *will couple with the bride-to-be* Ibid., 15.

in the wild she created Enkidu Ibid., 5.

201 *Shamhat unfastened the cloth* Ibid., 8.

your eyes will be opened Genesis 3:5.

You are handsome, Enkidu George, *Epic of Gilgamesh*, 8.

Why with the beasts Ibid., 9.

202 *his mood became free* Ibid., 14.

205 *Like a wife you'll love him* Ibid., 10.

meteor and ax A. D. Kilmer, "A Note on an Overlooked Word-play in the Akkadian *Gilgamesh*," in *Zikir Šumim: Assyriological Studies Presented to F. R. Kraus*, ed. G. van Driel et al. (Brill, 1982), 128–29. Andrew George adds further evidence supporting this interpretation in *The Babylonian Gilgamesh Epic* (Oxford, 2003), 1:452–54.

207 *The second-rate logs* Giovanni B. Lanfranchi and Simo Parpola, eds., *The Correspondence of Sargon II: Part II, Letters from the Northern and Northeastern Provinces* (Helsinki, 1990), no. 295, 209.

208 *a path into the Cedar Mountain* James Pritchard, ed., *Ancient Near Eastern Texts Relating to the Old Testament* (Princeton University Press, 3rd ed., 1969), 268.

I covered the wide plain with the corpses Ibid., 277–78.

The whole earth is at rest: Isaiah 14:7–8 (New Revised Standard Version).

209 *His voice is the Deluge* George, *Epic of Gilgamesh*, 18.

Why, my friend, do you speak Ibid., 19.

Who is there, my friend Ibid., 110–11, quoted from the Old Babylonian version of the epic. The standard version of the epic has a similar speech at this point, though it is preserved only in fragmentary form.

since no man can escape Ibid., 151.

O Utu, let me speak a word Ibid., 151.

210 *You are young, Gilgamesh* Ibid., 22.

the highest peak of rugged Olympus Homer, *The Iliad*, trans. Richmond Lattimore (University of Chicago Press, 1951), 72.

She climbed the staircase George, *Epic of Gilgamesh*, 24.

211 *Thetis answered him then* *Iliad*, 70.

212 *M. L. West has argued* See West, *The East Face of Helicon* (Oxford University Press, 1997).

214 *finish him, slay him* George, *Epic of Gilgamesh*, 43.

May the pair of them not grow old Ibid., 44, slightly modified.

You are an oven Ibid, 49, adopting several readings from the translation by Maureen Gallery Kovacs, *The Epic of Gilgamesh* (Stanford University Press, 1989).

215 *Come, let me tell you the tale* Ibid., 49.

"Bilgamesh and the Bull of Heaven" In George, *The Epic of Gilgamesh*, 166–75.

217 *I am Shulgi* "Šulgi A," Electronic Text Corpus of Sumerian Literature, http://etcsl.orinst.ox.ac.uk., text 2.4.2.01, l. 15.

Ah, but was it not you George, *Epic of Gilgamesh*, 50.

218 *Had I caught you too* Ibid., 52.

to the house which none who enters Ibid., 61.

219 *[Who was] it fetched this man* Ibid., 61.

like a bride Ibid., 65.

like a lioness Ibid., 64–65.

220 *How the mighty have fallen* 2 Samuel 1:25–26 (New Revised Standard Version). Hans-Peter Müller perceptively discusses parallels between David's lament for Jonathan and Gilgamesh's lament for Enkidu in "Gilgameschs Trauergesang von Enkidu und die Gattung der Toten-

klage," *Zeitschrift für Assyriologie und vorderasiatische Archäologie* 68 (1978): 233–50.

220 *O Gilgamesh, where are you wandering?* George, *Epic of Gilgamesh*, 71.

221 *Why, Gilgamesh* Ibid., 85.

On the face of the sun Ibid., 87.

How was it you stood Ibid., 88.

Like the oncoming of a storm Daniel D. Luckenbill, *Ancient Records of Assyria and Babylonia*, 2 vols. (University of Chicago Press, 1926–27, repr. 1989), 2:152.

222 *I looked at the weather* George, *Epic of Gilgamesh*, 93.

224 *Instead of your causing the Deluge* Ibid., 95, slightly modified.

he did not take counsel Ibid., 94, slightly modified.

[Did you] ever, Gilgamesh Ibid., 85.

I look at you, Uta-napishtim Ibid., 88.

225 *Uta-napishtim was a mortal man* Ibid., 95.

the Sumerian King List A current translation is available online in the Electronic Text Corpus of Sumerian Literature, cited above, text 2.1.1. An older translation can be found in Pritchard, *Ancient Near Eastern Texts*, 265–66.

226 *Uta-napishtim the Faraway* George, *Epic of Gilgamesh*, 88.

227 *O Ur-shanabi, climb Uruk's wall* Ibid., 99.

228 *we cannot show him mercy* Ibid., 199.

his "precious friend" Enkidu Ibid., 204.

He who saw the Deep Ibid., 1.

229 *In future days among my sons* Luckenbill, *Ancient Records of Assyria and Babylonia*, 2:267.

230 *[See] the tablet-box of cedar* George, *Epic of Gilgamesh*, 2.

232 *the one whose shade has no one* "Bilgames and the Netherworld," in George, *Epic of Gilgamesh*, 175–95.

233 *Eckart Frahm has argued* "Nabû-zuqup-kēnu, das Gilgameš-Epos und der Tod Sargons II," *Journal of Cuneiform Studies* 51 (1999): 73–90.

234 *Did you see the one* "Bilgames and the Netherworld," in George, *Epic of Gilgamesh*, 195.

7: THE VANISHING POINT

237 *kingship descended from heaven* The Sumerian King List, Electronic Text Corpus of Sumerian Literature (ETCSL), http://etcsl.orinst.ox.ac.uk, text 2.1.1., line 1.

24,510 years, 3 months, and 3½ days Ibid., l. 132.

238 *restored the wall of Uruk* Quoted in Andrew George, *The Babylonian Gilgamesh Epic* (Oxford, 2003), 1:92, from Douglas Frayne, *Royal Inscriptions of Mesopotamia 4: The Old Babylonian Period* (University of Toronto Press, 1990), 474–75.

240 *There are wells to be finished* "Gilgameš and Aga," ETCSL text 1.8.1.1, ll. 5–8.

Multitudes were smeared with dust Ibid., ll. 95–97.

Before the Sun God Ibid., l. 111, adopting phrasing from the translation of "Bilgamés and Akka" by Andrew George in *The Epic of Gilgamesh: A New Translation* (London: Penguin, 1999), 143–48.

241 *the first city in human history* Marc Van De Mieroop, *A History of the Ancient Near East, ca. 3000-323 BC* (Blackwell, 2004), 23. For more on Uruk, see Gwendolyn Leick, *Mesopotamia: The Invention of the City* (Penguin, 2002), 30–60. Leick has excellent discussions of Uruk, Ur, Nineveh, and other major cities.

242 *punctuated equilibrium* See Jean-Jacques Glassner, *The Invention of Cuneiform: Writing in Sumer*, trans. and ed. Zainab Bahrani and Marc Van De Mieroop (Johns Hopkins University Press, 2003); and Jean Bottéro, *Mesopotamia: Writing, Reasoning, and the Gods*, trans. Zainab Bahrani and Marc Van De Mieroop (University of Chicago Press, 1992).

The Lord of Aratta In Thorkild Jacobsen, *The Harps that Once. . . : Sumerian Poetry in Translation* (Yale University Press, 1987), 275–319, 314, with some phrasing adapted from the ETCSL prose translation, text 1.8.2.3, ll. 537–39.

243 *Sleep come, sleep come* "Šulgi N," ETCSL text 2.4.2.02, ll. 12–18.

244 *I, Shulgi* "Šulgi B," ETCSL text 2.4.2.02, ll. 12–15.

When I provide justice Ibid., ll. 219–20.

As I prepare the sheep Ibid., ll. 142–45.

I can write a washing bill from Major General Stanley's opening patter song in *The Pirates of Penzance*, in *The Complete Plays of Gilbert and Sullivan* (W. W. Norton, 1976), 132–34.

245 *Shulgi, roaring like a rising flood* "Šulgi D," ETCSL text 2.4.2.04, ll. 291–92.

Like my brother and friend Gilgamesh "Šulgi C," ETCSL text 2.4.2.03, ll. 107–11.

I am no fool "Šulgi B," ETCSL text 2.4.2.02, ll. 270–80.

246 *Whatever is acquired* Ibid., ll. 281–90.

On the day when the destiny "Šulgi O," ETCSL text 2.4.2.15, ll. 38–48.

247 *The darkest day of mortal man* "The Death of Bilgames," in Andrew George, *The Epic of Gilgamesh*, 195–208, 203. I have adopted some

phrasings from the translation in the ETCSL database, text 1.8.1.3, ll. 19–24.

247 *your precious friend* Ibid., 204.

248 *its pebbles gazed* Ibid., 206.
   His beloved wife Ibid.
   its waters swept over Ibid., 207.

250 *"The Descent of Inanna to the Underworld"* In Jacobsen, *The Harps that Once*, 205–32; later Akkadian versions of the underworld descent are "The Descent of Ishtar" and "Nergal and Ereshkigal," in Benjamin Foster, *Before the Muses* (CDL Press, 2005), 498–524; also translated by Stephanie Dalley in *Myths from Mesopotamia* (Oxford University Press, 1989), 154–81. For scholarly discussions, see Bendt Alster, ed., *Death in Mesopotamia* (Akademisk Forlag, 1980), and Thorkild Jacobsen, *The Treasures of Darkness: A History of Mesopotamian Religion* (Yale University Press, 1976).

EPILOGUE: SADDAM'S GILGAMESH

254 *The king gave up the helm* As reported by William Ury, "A Last, Best Hope Against War Still Exists," *Christian Science Monitor*, 17 March 2003, www.christiansciencemonitor.com/2003/0318/p09s02-coop.html.
   the Saddam Institute of Cuneiform Studies As reported in *Science*, 3 May 2002, 834–35.

255 *a game involving a ball* In the Sumerian poem known as "Bilgamesh and the Netherworld," Enkidu descends to the netherworld in order to retrieve Gilgamesh's *pukku* and *mekku*, apparently a mallet and ball, which have fallen into a fissure in the earth. Scholars are uncertain as to the nature of the game that was played with these implements; it may have been an early form of polo.
   Because I'm Gil Gamesh Philip Roth, *The Great American Novel* (Holt, Rinehart and Winston, 1973), 62.
   Summers off in the country Ibid., 327.

256 *You are the scum of baseball* Ibid., 342.
   "How to hate, and Whom" Ibid., 344.

258 *Every time I've read the book* Saddam Hussein, *Zabibah und der König: Eine Liebesgeschichte*, trans. Doris Kilias (Thomas Bauer Verlag, 2004), 6.
   the artist Jonathon Earl Bowser As described on Bowser's Web site, www.jonathonart.com. A second German edition has since appeared (Editio de Facto, 2004), with a different subtitle, *Das verborgene Buch* (the suppressed book). In place of a portrait of Saddam, this ver-

sion features an Aladdin's lamp, from which the subtitle emerges like a puff of smoke.

258 *Let us go back to our history* Quoted by Fuad Matar in "The Young President: An Interview with Saddam Hussein in 1980," repr. in *The Saddam Hussein Reader*, ed. Turi Munthe (Thunder's Mouth Press, 2002), 3–35, 8.

259 *Saddam wrote in a 1978 essay* As quoted in Adeed Dawisha, " 'Identity' and Political Survival in Saddam's Iraq," *Middle East Journal* 53:4 (1999): 553–67, 560.

   Is not Iraq with its mountains Saddam Hussein, *Zabibah*, 8 (my translation from the German edition).

   he couldn't let her sense Ibid., 15.

261 *Just look at your palace* Ibid., 34.

262 *Back then, my brothers* Ibid., 35.

   Zabibah tenderly stroked Ibid., 51.

   It is always important Ibid., 114.

263 *Instead of trusting your relatives* Ibid., 57–58.

264 *You have to believe me* Ibid., 63.

   To have to let oneself be overpowered Ibid., 144.

265 *I die, but the People lives* Ibid., 152.

   Long live Zabibah! Ibid., 192.

   a new genre, "dic-lit" Jo Tatchell, "Heroes and Villains," *The Guardian*, 6 July 2004, http://www.guardian.co.uk/Iraq/Story/0,2763,1254859,00.html.

266 *Timber in antiquity* Sharif Elmusa, "In Search of the Epic: Gilgamesh as Bush, Humbaba as Saddam," *Al-Ahram*, 2–8 January 2003, http://weekly.ahram.org.eg/2003/619/op12.html.

267 *a CIA-supported coup* See Con Coughlin, *Saddam: His Rise and Fall* (Harper Perennial, 2005), chap. 2, "The Assassin," 23–51.

   I would get a Christmas card from Hem Roth, *The Great American Novel*, 35–36.

268 *Saddam's favorite novelist was Ernest Hemingway* Jack Fairweather, "Dictator Found Refuge in Fiction—Much of It Bad," London *Daily Telegraph*, 17 December 2003, http://www.theage.com.au/articles/2003/12/17/1071337033784.html.

   distinguished writers were asked Ibid. Sami al-Azizi may of course have died of natural causes, though if the cause was a heart attack brought on by anxiety and overwork, Saddam would still be indirectly responsible. It is also possible that the culprit was not Saddam but one of his sons, Uday or Qusay. In the novel Zabibah advises the king that his sons should never succeed him in power: "Why do we suppose that a prince is something better than a young man of the people? Why should he rule, just because he's a king's son?" (89). She persuades the king to "break with the old custom of naming a king's successor from his own dynasty, so that everyone can strive for this position through his faithfulness and ability" (91). When Saddam put this theme into his story, he was no doubt thinking of himself and how the Baathist Party supplanted the monarchy installed by the British in the 1920s. Since his sons would have received copies of *Zabibah* as soon as it came out, one of them could have read this passage, taken it as a veiled attack, and ordered the writer's execution.

269 *every civilization sees itself* Samuel L. Huntington, *The Clash of Civilizations and the Remaking of World Order* (Simon & Schuster, 1996), 54–55.

Spurred by modernization Ibid., 125.

270 *the ultimate human tribes* Ibid., 207.

It is human to hate Ibid., 130.

Islam has bloody borders Ibid., 258.

Some Westerners . . . have argued Ibid., 209.

271 *an extended family* Ibid., 156.

We believe in Allah The Meaning of the Holy Qur'ān, ed. 'Abdullah Yūsuf Ali (Amana Publishers, 1420 AH; 1999 AC), Surah 3:84.

Islamo-Christian civilization Richard Bulliet, *The Case for Islamo-Christian Civilization* (Columbia University Press, 2005).

as Goethe had Inspired by the Persian poet Hafiz and other Middle Eastern poets, Goethe wrote a sequence in 1819 that he called *West-östlicher Divan*, the "West-eastern Divan," or poetry collection.

SOURCES

Short of years of study at one of the handful of universities
that have programs in Assyrian and Babylonian studies, how
can a nonspecialist gain a better acquaintance with this fascinating body of material from the dawn of recorded history?
Readers interested in exploring *The Epic of Gilgamesh* and
its ancient cultural context may want to know where to look,
as well as what they can expect to encounter when they do.

Long scattered about in hard-to-find scholarly publications
in several languages, the major Mesopotamian literary texts
are now readily available in high-quality English translations.
For *Gilgamesh*, the starting point is Andrew George's *The
Epic of Gilgamesh: A New Translation*, published as a Penguin Classic in 1999. This is the best and most complete translation of the epic ever published, including newly discovered
passages not included in any other translation. George's eloquent translation allows the reader to see the epic in its historical development, presenting Sin-leqe-unninni's standard
version followed by surviving fragments of the earlier Old
Babylonian epic, and then the major Sumerian poems that
served as sources.

Those who want to go more deeply into the epic's history
should consult Andrew George's monumental scholarly edition, *The Babylonian Gilgamesh Epic: Introduction, Critical*

Edition and Cuneiform Texts, published in two volumes by Oxford University Press in 2003. This splendid edition gives the Akkadian text (in alphabetic transcription), with a literal line-by-line translation on facing pages, a useful supplement to the somewhat freer rendering in George's Penguin translation. The Oxford edition begins with an almost book-length introduction on the text, its history, and Gilgamesh and his times. The second volume includes detailed philological notes and a comprehensive bibliography, as well as plates showing the cuneiform texts. In addition to this work, an important earlier study is Jeffrey Tigay, *The Evolution of the Gilgamesh Epic* (University of Pennsylvania Press, 1982). John Maier's *Gilgamesh: A Reader* (Bolchazy-Carducci, 1997) gives a wide-ranging collection of interpretive essays.

Three other very good translations of *Gilgamesh* are John Gardner and John Maier's *Gilgamesh, Translated from the Sin-leqi-unninni Version* (Vintage, 1985); Benjamin R. Foster et al., *The Epic of Gilgamesh: A New Translation, Analogues, and Criticism* (W. W. Norton, 2001); and Maureen Gallery Kovacs's *The Epic of Gilgamesh* (Stanford University Press, 1989), reprinted in David Damrosch et al., eds., *The Longman Anthology of World Literature* (Pearson Longman, 2004), volume A, 88–129. A good recent version, though a more novelistic adaptation than a translation, is Stephen Mitchell's *Gilgamesh: A New English Version* (Free Press, 2004).

For further reading in Akkadian literature, Stephanie Dalley's *Myths from Mesopotamia* (Oxford World's Classics, 1989) is a good collection of the major texts. The most comprehensive and up-to-date Akkadian anthology is Benjamin R. Foster's thousand-page *Before the Muses: An Anthology of Akkadian Literature* (CDL Press, 2005). Still useful is James Pritchard's classic *Ancient Near Eastern Texts Relating to the*

Old Testament (Princeton University Press, 3rd edition, 1969), which has extensive selections from Assyrian and Babylonian literary, religious, and historical texts, as well as important texts from neighboring Hittite and Canaanite cultures—chosen most often, as the book's title indicates, for their relevance to biblical history and religion.

The ancient corpus of Sumerian literature is now available in the most modern of forms, on the Internet. An international team has assembled the Electronic Text Corpus of Sumerian Literature, a database of transcribed original texts with English prose translations, which can be found at http://www. etcsl.orient.ox.ac.uk. A selection of the best known of these texts can be found in a companion printed volume, *The Literature of Ancient Sumer*, ed. Jeremy Black et al. (Oxford University Press, 2004), but the Web site collection is more extensive and also more current, as the texts and translations are updated whenever new discoveries are made or new readings established.

Marc Van De Mieroop's *A History of the Ancient Near East, ca. 3000-323 BC* (Blackwell, 2004) gives a lucid overview of Mesopotamian history; a wider survey of Near Eastern history including Egypt is William W. Hallo and William K. Simpson's *The Ancient Near East: A History* (Harcourt, Brace, 2nd edition, 1998). Simpson is also the lead editor of a comprehensive anthology, *The Literature of Ancient Egypt* (Yale University Press, 3rd edition, 2003). Another good historical survey is Georges Roux's *Ancient Iraq* (Penguin, 3rd edition, 1992). Gwendolyn Leick's *Mesopotamia: The Invention of the City* (Penguin, 2002) is an excellent work on urban culture. Informative historical maps and illustrations can be found in Michael Roaf's *Cultural Atlas of Mesopotamia and the Ancient Near East* (Equinox, 1990).

Turning to the archaeologist-explorers of the Victorian era, their works have almost all been out of print for the past century or more, though Austen Henry Layard's *Nineveh and Its Remains* is occasionally reprinted. His delightful *Early Adventures in Persia and Susiana* has not been reprinted in many years, but early editions, and *Nineveh and Its Remains* and other books by Layard, can readily be found on Internet used book sites such as www.abe.com (a particularly good site for used books from England). George Smith's *Assyrian Adventures* and *The Chaldean Account of Genesis* can also be bought online at reasonable prices. It is much harder to find Hormuzd Rassam's books *Asshur and the Land of Nimrod* and *The Mission to Theodore, King of Abyssinia*. They were published in small quantities and never reprinted; when they can be found at all, they sell for several hundred dollars each.

There is a massive scholarly literature on Victorian views of the Middle East and on the history of the Ottoman Empire in the nineteenth century. Particularly noteworthy are Edward W. Said's pathbreaking *Orientalism* (Viking, 1978) and Mogens Trolle Larsen's *The Conquest of Assyria: Excavations in an Antique Land* (Routledge, 1994). The best recent survey of Middle Eastern history during the "long nineteenth century" is Efraim and Inari Karsh's *Empires of the Sand: The Struggle for Mastery in the Middle East 1789–1923* (Harvard University Press, 1999). Their book gives a refreshingly revisionist reading of Ottoman history, showing the Ottoman rulers and diplomats not as static figures of corruption and decay but as often resourceful players in the unequal "Great Game" being waged by the colonial European powers.

ACKNOWLEDGMENTS

In a world torn by violence and polemical strife, it is a particular pleasure to acknowledge the collaborative work of the international community of scholars who have devoted their lives to recovering Mesopotamia's long-lost history and the great literary works produced in this formative area of the world. The present work is profoundly indebted to all of the books listed in the preceding section on sources, and in the notes for each chapter. I am equally indebted to conversation with friends in the field of Assyriology, particularly Andrew George at the University of London and Marc Van De Mieroop at Oxford, and with Sherif Elmusa in Cairo; Lamia al Gailani in London, and Eckart Frahm at Yale.

At the British Museum, I am grateful for the advice and assistance of Near Eastern curators Susan Collins and Irving Finkel, and the museum's archivist, Gary Thorn. At the British Library, the Manuscript Reading Room's staff made the library an exceptionally pleasant as well as productive place to work, as did the staff of the Columbia University Library, which fortunately continues to maintain a comprehensive collection of actual books even in this digital age. I was also lucky at Columbia to have had skilled research assistance from Felicity Palmer and Adela Ramos.

In writing a book designed to be read mostly by nonspecialists, I have benefited enormously from thoughtful readings and constructive comments from a variety of friends and colleagues. My thanks go to Wiebke Denecke and Hal Freedman, who read every chapter of this book with care, and to Jonathan Arac, Svetlana Boym, Vybarr Cregan-Reid, my brother Tom Damrosch, Mark Getlein, David Kastan, Margaret Popper, Martin Puchner, Bruce Robbins, Haun Saussy, Jim Shapiro, Maura Spiegel, and Robert Tauxe for further feedback and stimulating conversation on the project. As a colleague, scholar, and public intellectual, the late Edward Said had an enormous impact on me over many years; this book certainly would never have been conceived without his fundamental work in nineteenth-century Orientalism, and it wouldn't have been written in the way it has without the inspiration of Said's exceptional ability to write on scholarly issues with passion and clarity.

A first version of some of the discussion of George Smith and Hormuzd Rassam appeared in the opening chapter of my book *What Is World Literature?* (Princeton University Press, 2003). At that time, I was relying on Wallis Budge's misleading portrayals and the limited picture that Smith and Rassam themselves presented in their own published works, so those portions of that chapter are superseded in these pages.

Colleagues at various universities have given me the opportunity to present parts of this book in lecture form and to receive valuable responses; my thanks go to David Sweet at the American University in Cairo, Zhang Longxi at City University in Hong Kong, Stephen Owen at Harvard, Ilana Pardes at Hebrew University, Jerusalem, John Pizer at Louisiana State University, Bruce Mazlish at MIT, Dudley Marchi at North Carolina State University, Hana Wirth-Nescher at Tel

Aviv University, Robert Hegel at Washington University, and David Quint at Yale.

It has been a pleasure to work closely with my editor at Henry Holt, Jennifer Barth, whose advice shaped the developing manuscript in important ways. At Holt, Raquel Jaramillo and Meryl Levavi gave the book its beautiful cover and design, while Christopher O'Connell treated the prose to a thorough and lucid review. I am grateful too for the advice and support of my agent, Eric Simonoff, who early on saw the potential of an unusual project.

Other debts stretch further back in time. My parents, Elizabeth and the Reverend Leopold Damrosch, inculcated a permanent interest in the Bible and its world, which first led me to study biblical Hebrew and Egyptian hieroglyphics in college and graduate school, prior to my more recent work in Akkadian. All along, I have been inspired by the example and the work of my brother Leo Damrosch, who was completing his luminous biography of Rousseau as I began this project, and who gave me a generous blend of wisdom and strategic advice throughout, including incisive readings of the manuscript's draft chapters.

My deepest thanks are closest to home. My wife, Lori Fisler Damrosch, has helped me think about this book from its inception; she has been wonderfully supportive, in both moral and practical terms, of this engrossing and at times obsessive project. Finally, I come to the people to whom this book is dedicated. Probably like many scholars, I suppose I wrote my first book for my teachers; I then wrote the next few books for my colleagues and my graduate students. This book I have written for my children, now moving into and through their college years. For once—as they have pointed out to me—I've written a book they may actually enjoy reading. In dedicating it to them, I hope they will find it useful in thinking about the wider world they are now entering: both its conflicts and also the possibilities for resisting the forces of social division and cultural destruction so visible today. The remarkable cross-cultural group of people who recovered Gilgamesh's story offers us hope from the past; Diana, Eva, and Peter give me hope for the future.

ILLUSTRATION CREDITS

The cuneiform text on the cover is part of a trilingual inscription of Darius the Great, inscribed on gold leaf; courtesy of the Oriental Institute, Chicago. The image on the title page (a portrait of Ashur, patron god of Assyria) is taken from the title page of Austen Henry Layard's *Nineveh and Its Remains* (John Murray, 2 vols., 1849). Except as otherwise noted, the vignettes at the start of each chapter are taken from *Nineveh and Its Remains* or from Layard's lavishly illustrated sequel, *Discoveries in the Ruins of Nineveh and Babylon; with Travels in Armenia, Kurdistan, and the Desert: Being the Result of a Second Expedition Undertaken for the Trustees of the British Museum* (John Murray, 1853). The remaining illustrations come from the following sources:

93 Cross-written letter from Rassam to Layard: British Library Add. Mss. 38,978, folio 269, courtesy of the British Library.

99 Rassam in European and Eastern dress: from Mogens Trolle Larsen, *The Conquest of Assyria: Excavations in an Antique Land 1840–1860* (Routledge, 1994), 328.

111 Ashurbanipal hunting: from Hormuzd Rassam, *Asshur and the Land of Nimrod*, 30.

115 Chapter 4 vignette: from *Illustrated London News*, 12 January 1853.

119 King Theodore's fortress at Magdala: from Henry Morton Stanley, *Coomassie and Magdala: The Story of Two British Campaigns in Africa* (Harper and Brothers, 1874), 458.

127 Major General Staveley: from Henry Morton Stanley, *Coomassie and Magdala*, 342.

135 Rassam and his fellow captives: frontispiece to Henry Stern, *The Captive Missionary: Being an Account of the Country and People of Abyssinia, Embracing a Narrative of King Theodore's Life, and his Treatment of Political and Religious Missions* (Cassell, Petter, and Galpin, 1869).

147 Photograph of Hormuzd Rassam: frontispiece to Hormuzd Rassam, *Asshur and the Land of Nimrod*.

152–53 Ashurbanipal's "Garden Party": Courtesy of the British Museum.

173 Assyrian siege engine: from Layard, *Nineveh and Its Remains*, 369.

195 Ashurbanipal defaced, detail from the "Garden Party": Courtesy of the British Museum.

198 Chapter 6 vignette: from George Smith, *The Chaldean Account of Genesis*, 237.

207 Humbaba: Courtesy of the British Museum.

216 Gilgamesh slaying the Bull of Heaven: Schøyen Collection, Oslo; photograph courtesy of Andrew George.

231 Ashurbanipal as a day laborer: Courtesy of the British Museum.

239 Cross section of the wall of Uruk: from Raoul Schrott, *Gilgamesch: Epos* (Hanser, 2001), 170.

253 Portrait of Gilgamesh: from Schrott, *Gilgamesch*, 275; the original statue is now in the Louvre, Paris.

260 Jacket cover of Saddam Hussein, *Zabibah wal-Malik* (al-Ja'ireh, 2000).

261 Jacket cover of Saddam Hussein, *Zabibah und der König*, trans. Dorris Kilias (Thomas Bauer Verlag, 2004).

The ornament used between sections in the text is the cuneiform symbol for a star, used as the syllable *an* or the word *shamû*, "sky, heaven."

INDEX

Entries in *italics* refer to captions and illustrations.

ABOUT THE AUTHOR

DAVID DAMROSCH is a professor of English and comparative literature at Columbia University. He is the author of several scholarly studies and the general editor of *The Longman Anthology of World Literature*, and is a past president of the American Comparative Literature Association. He lives in New York City with his wife and children.